STUDIES IN
INTERNATIONAL RELATIONS

Edited by
Charles MacDonald
Florida International University

A ROUTLEDGE SERIES

Studies in International Relations

Charles MacDonald, *General Editor*

INTERVENTION, ETHNIC CONFLICT AND STATE-BUILDING IN IRAQ
A Paradigm for the Post-Colonial State

Michael Rear

Routledge
Taylor & Francis Group
New York   London

First published 2008
by Routledge
270 Madison Ave, New York, NY 10016

Simultaneously published in the UK
by Routledge
2 Park Square, Milton Park, Abingdon, Oxon OX14 4RN

Routledge is an imprint of the Taylor & Francis Group, an informa business

Typeset in Sabon by IBT Global.
Printed and bound in the United States of America on acid-free paper by IBT Global.

Library of Congress Cataloging-in-Publication Data
Rear, Michael, 1960–
    Intervention, ethnic conflict and state-building in Iraq : a paradigm for the post-colonial state / by Michael Rear.
        p. cm. — (Studies in international relations)
    Includes bibliographical references and index.
    ISBN 978-0-415-96466-1
    1. Peace-building—Iraq.   2. Nation-building—Iraq.   3. Ethnic conflict—Iraq.
I. Title.
    JZ5584.I72R43 2008
    956.704—dc22
    2007049636

ISBN10: 0-415-96466-0 (hbk)
ISBN10: 0-203-89547-9 (ebk)

ISBN13: 978-0-415-96466-1 (hbk)
ISBN13: 978-0-203-89547-4 (ebk)

Contents

Preface

The origins of this study can be traced back to a book known as *The Third World Security Predicament* by Mohammed Ayoob. Writing shortly after the end of the Cold War (1995), Ayoob attempted to redefine the issue of security in international relations by shifting the focus from the concerns of the major powers to the issues confronting the considerably newer post-colonial states in the aftermath of the Cold War. In this context, he noted that whereas the more developed states tend to view issues of security in terms of challenges posed by *external* threats, a central theme for newer states in what used to be called the "Third World" are threats to their security emanating from *within* the states themselves. This difference can be explained by the fact that by historical standards, post-colonial states are at a relatively early stage in the state-building process. Consequently, nominal state leaders are consumed by the question of how to consolidate their authority in the face of challenges to either that authority, or perhaps to the state itself, coming from rival leaders of other groups located within the state. From this perspective, the proliferation in the number of internal (frequently ethnic) conflicts witnessed in the post-Cold War era can be linked to a larger theory of the state and the state-building process, which emphasizes the essentially violent nature of the process of constructing a viable state capable of exercising authority within its own territory. As discussed at some length in Chapter Two of this study, Ayoob's observation regarding the violent nature of state-building is interesting but hardly original. Variations on this same theme can be found in earlier works by Barrington Moore, Charles Tilly, and Brian R. Brown, Youssef Cohen, and A.F.K. Organski, among others.

The provocative element in the Ayoob book, however, is his contention that after the Cold War, post-colonial states face obstacles to the state-building process which were never encountered by older, more developed states. These obstacles are a result of the changed nature of the international context within which newer states are forced to operate. This change in context is associated with the phenomenon of globalization and with the increasing willingness of other states and international organizations to intervene in the internal affairs of post-colonial states. The external obstacles cited by Ayoob produce a dilemma for would-be state makers in the Third World: on the one hand, post-colonial states are expected to assume the responsibilities associated with membership in the international system, e.g., democratic governance and respect for human rights, as a condition of sovereignty while, on the other hand, they lack the wherewithal to implement these international norms because they have yet to achieve the sine qua non of statehood—a central government capable of exercising effective control over the population within the boundaries of the country. Compounding this dilemma is the suggestion that the only way to satisfy this fundamental requirement may be through the use of force to either suppress or expel those groups who resist the authority of the state. This use of force, however, runs directly counter to the international norms discussed above. To put the matter succinctly, the conundrum is that the only way for the state to have a chance to develop the capacity necessary in order to *satisfy* the expectations of what some have called the international community would be for it to first *violate* those expectations.

It is this conclusion by Ayoob which serves as the point of departure for my own study. My concern is to understand the consequences of imposing these norms upon states still struggling to resolve fundamental issues of statehood. Although Ayoob's focus is considerably broader and touches upon the impact of a variety of phenomena (he, for example, is interested in the impact of global telecommunications, transportation, etc.) upon state-building, my own interest encompasses the somewhat narrower question of the impact upon the state-building process of various forms of external military intervention in internal ethnic conflicts. These forms range from traditional notions of consensual peacekeeping to such newer and generally more muscular concepts as humanitarian intervention and peace enforcement, which frequently occur without the consent of the belligerents. The theoretical issue raised in the body of this text, and explored with special reference to the case of Iraq, is, therefore, whether the oftentimes single-minded pursuit on the part of outside actors of stopping the violence and saving lives has produced states capable of implementing the norms cited above or whether, paradoxically, a hands-off approach would be a more effective way to reach that desired goal—albeit at a terrible price in terms of human lives. Implicit in this issue is the question as to whether, ironically and perhaps less visibly, the price of intervention may turn out to be even greater in terms of violence and lives lost as a consequence of the failure to develop functioning state institutions.

Since presumably the purpose of intervention is to save lives, the notion that there may be even greater cost in lives to the host society as a result of intervention would seem to be counterintuitive. This notion is also difficult to establish empirically. The simple fact is that there is no way to go back and replay the events without the intervention so as to compare outcomes in terms of the loss of life. Such an assertion, therefore, relies upon the use of what is sometimes referred to as counterfactual analysis. It asks the question: what *would have happened if* there had been no intervention by outside forces in a given ethnic conflict?

Of course, the use of counterfactual analysis inevitably entails an element of risk. The difficulty is that one can posit any number of possible alternative scenarios and outcomes but can never be certain as to what would have happened if events had taken a different course as the result of the presence or absence of a particular factor. Acknowledging that such a risk exists does not mean, however, that it is not worth taking. The countervailing benefit is that the use of this approach makes it possible to develop certain theoretical statements. These rely upon logical inference and can be tested by applying the comparative method to *similar* situations which differ with regard to that critical factor. Thus, for example, this study compares the uprisings in northern and southern Iraq in March/April 1992, which differ as to the use of external intervention, as a way to determine *what would have happened* in northern Iraq had there been no intervention. Such comparisons, while necessarily imperfect since there is no way to guarantee that all other factors in the two situations were identical and, therefore, can be held constant, offer the best available means for testing a theory of this nature given the fact that in politics events can never be completely replicated. Furthermore, the inferential process is not significantly different from that employed when developing a theory using the comparative method involving actual cases. The only difference is that counterfactual analysis relies upon multiple scenarios in a single case study as opposed to multiple case studies. Counterfactual analysis, therefore, offers a way to test whether the presence or absence of intervention may be treated as a decisive variable with regard to the question of state-building and its consequences for the population living within the state.

Utilizing this technique of counterfactual analysis as a way to conceptualize alternative scenarios with differing outcomes, my theory argues that the harmful effects of outside intervention in ethnic conflicts are at least as great, if not greater, than would be the effects of nonintervention. The underlying basis for this claim is my agreement with Ayoob that in those instances in which there is violent ethnic conflict between rival groups within post-colonial states a linkage exists between this type of conflict and the early stages of the process of building a viable state. Central to this thesis is the notion that ethnic conflict serves a dual purpose in the state-building process. In a world in which the territorial boundaries of states are frequently contested either by neighboring states or by secessionist movements within states, the use of force provides an alternative mechanism to the juridical principle of uti possidetis[1] for the determination of the territorial boundaries of the state. This conflict model suggests that the boundaries of the state are those which can be defended militarily against the claims of rival state makers. In addition, ethnic violence also serves the function of consolidating control within these boundaries in the hands of a single victorious state maker through the elimination of rival claimants regardless of whether that elimination takes the form of subordination, expulsion or, in the worst case, genocide. Victory in this bloody and brutal contest represents the first step on the path to what has been described as "empirical statehood," which refers to the capacity for effective governance. Empirical statehood or sovereignty stands in contrast to the more legalistic notion of juridical sovereignty or statehood, which involves formal authority without necessarily effective control.

Given the horrific nature of genocide and the *possibility* (one needs to emphasize that it is not inevitable) that such may come to pass if one adheres to the logic of this theory, one cannot simply address this question from an empirical perspective free from all normative considerations of an ethical or moral nature. Indeed, the implications of this theory are so profound that there are actually a number of different issues woven together.

The first of these is an empirical question as to whether, in fact, the theory is correct in suggesting that ethnic violence is part of the state-building process in post-colonial states. This suggestion takes place against the backdrop of a scholarly debate between those who view the sort of internal violence witnessed in the aftermath of the Cold War as evidence of state collapse and those who see it in historical context as evidence of the first chaotic steps toward the building of viable states.

The next set of issues are normative questions involving moral and ethical considerations. In this case, the question is not whether ethnic violence contributes to the state-building process, but whether such violence, and the terrible loss of life associated with it, can be justified in terms of contemporary ethical standards *even if it does contribute to the state-building process*. In other words, is this an acceptable path to the building of states? Closely related to this issue is the question of how to develop a moral calculus which can weigh the *actual* cost in lives lost building states against the *potential* cost in lives lost if the state-building process does not proceed due to outside intervention. If, for example, the use of counterfactual analysis indicated that more lives would be lost through intervention and interruption of the state-building process than likely would be the case through nonintervention, would there then be a moral imperative *not* to intervene and to allow the violence to unfold until one side achieved a decisive military victory?

A third set of issues involve matters of policy. It is here that the rubber meets the road. If the empirical evidence suggests that ethnic conflict is part of the state-building process in a state-centric world and the normative argument is that the massive loss of life associated with this sort of conflict is morally unacceptable, what should external actors do: intervene or not intervene? Also included in this decision making process are other considerations such as the relative importance of regional stability and the possible threats to that stability from unchecked violence within a state.

Finally, there are political issues as well. These center around the question of who gets to decide whether or not to intervene: Should it be left to individual states, which may have a vested interest in the outcome? Should it be left to regional organizations, which are closest to the situation and perhaps would have the best understanding of events on the ground and the greatest interest in dealing with the situation at hand? Should it be left to the UN, which can claim a greater degree of moral authority as an instrument of global governance by virtue of its nearly universal membership? Should the belligerents themselves (any or all) have any say in the matter of whether others intervene?

Although these issues can be separated for analytical purposes, the reality is that they often form a seamless web. In actual situations, it is frequently all but impossible to treat them separately because the answer to one set of questions will influence the way in which the other questions are answered as well. Thus, for example, if one were inclined to give priority to normative considerations regarding the saving of lives over empirical considerations regarding the building of states, one also would be likely to favor the policy option of intervention over nonintervention on the assumption that it would save lives. Conversely, if the empirical evidence suggested that, in the long run, the state-building process were less costly in lives lost than the perpetuation of failed states and that intervention made state failure more likely, presumably one would be more inclined to favor nonintervention.

In attempting to provide answers to these many questions, my own inclination is to give priority to the empirical issues surrounding the state-building process over normative considerations as to morally acceptable paths to state-building. Based upon this preference, I am extremely wary of policy proposals involving intervention and, consequently, have a general predisposition in favor of allowing the violence associated with ethnic conflict in post-colonial states to proceed uninterrupted.

Appearances to the contrary notwithstanding, this position is not the result of any sort of veneration for the state or belief that human beings are merely a means to the end of creating a state and, therefore, are somehow expendable. It is rather the product of my own understanding of the way states are created combined with my belief that the ethical considerations surrounding this process are more complex than generally is realized. For many, the temptation is to focus on the greater likelihood (by no means a certainty) that outside military intervention of the peacekeeping or peace enforcement variety will stop the warring parties from killing each other along with a sizeable number of civilians. This leads to a tendency to equate intervention with saving lives. Based upon this mental equation, it would seem to be only natural to view intervention as preferable to nonintervention. Some might even go so far as to equate support for nonintervention with condoning genocide. Part of the task of this study, however, is to point out that in a world governed by the law of unintended consequences, such mental equations oversimplify a very complex reality—the nature of which is oftentimes difficult to predict because it involves more than one time frame. The difficulty of the moral calculus under these circumstances is that it pits the *short-term* consequences of nonintervention against the *potentially* more severe *long-term* consequences of intervention. In the absence of certain knowledge of the future, the only guides we have in deciding whether or not to intervene are theory and the evidence of past experience.

Relying upon both theory and past experience, I reject what I regard to be the oversimplified equation between intervention and saving lives and argue instead that the various forms of external intervention discussed above, which are designed to interfere with the violence associated with internal (frequently ethnic) conflict, have the unintended, but very costly, effect of interrupting the primordial stages of the state-building process. If outside military intervention succeeds in stopping the violence, the most likely result will be the absence of a decisive resolution to the underlying conflict. This conflict may be thought of as a neo-Darwinian struggle for power or what Milica Bookman refers to as a "demographic struggle for power." Viewed in this manner, the notion of unresolved conflict is simply another way of saying that none of the warring factions is able to consolidate its authority within the boundaries of the state. Hence, the conflict is frozen in place. A direct consequence of this inability to consolidate power within the hands of a single leader is the failure to establish effective governance over the population of the territory in question. Consequently, the state-building process has been interrupted.

Since the establishment of a government capable of exerting control over the population within the territory of the state is logically prior to any other aspect of the state-building process, e.g. institution-building, democratization, economic development, etc., the failure to resolve this crisis of state authority means that the state will exist as a legal fiction or "juridical state." A plausible inference from this state of affairs is that this so-called "state" would be incapable of making further progress in developing the necessary means to provide for the basic needs of its population. These would include: personal security against domestic threats of the criminal variety through the development of legislative, law enforcement, and judicial institutions; state security against external threats through the development of military forces; and economic well-being through the development and maintenance of a physical infrastructure and perhaps the re-distributive mechanisms of a welfare state.

Thus, a fundamental aspect of my thesis is that the result of external interference in an ethnic conflict for the purpose of stopping the killing will be to leave the fundamental issues of state-building unresolved. This, in turn, will lead to what is typically referred to as a "failed" or "collapsed" state. Such a "state" will, in all likelihood, descend into chaos the moment outside forces withdraw. Although it is difficult to calculate, it would seem to be a reasonable conclusion that the costs to the population in the form of hunger, disease, lawlessness, and the potential for external aggression in the absence of a government capable of exercising sovereignty within its borders may be less visible than those associated with ethnic conflict. This does not mean, however, that these costs are necessarily any less great. Indeed, they may turn out to be even greater!

If, then, the harmful consequences of state failure are to be avoided, the alternative would seem to be the continued presence of outside forces for an indefinite period of time, which may end up stretching into perpetuity. While this alternative may, at first glance, seem preferable from an ethical point of view to the prospect of either slaughter or massive population dislocation, it must be remembered that such an option poses its own ethical, as well as political, dilemmas. These involve the possibility of a return to a form of colonialism from which these newer states only recently have emerged. One can only wonder how long such an outside presence can remain before it comes to be viewed as an occupying force. At such a point, this presence will likely become the target of violent resistance from the population. Thus, in what can only be described as the ultimate irony, the presence of outsiders for the purpose of bringing an end to violence becomes instead a casus belli. At such a point, the death toll among outside forces (and perhaps civilian humanitarian workers) will continue to escalate for as long as this outside presence remains. Alternatively, the external intervention will come to an end as the death toll rises to unacceptable levels, and the situation on the ground will revert to the status quo ante of ethnic conflict. Either way, there will be a continuing loss of life. The ethical question for those who favor such intervention is, therefore: how does one weigh the value of the lives of external forces and civilian humanitarian workers against the lives of the various ethnic communities within the host society? Clearly, the moral calculus is anything but self-evident.

From what has been said here, it should be painfully obvious that there are no simple or morally satisfying solutions. Indeed, the moral calculus which may lead to calls for intervention as a way to save lives is by no means clear-cut. Since my contention is that an interruption of the state-building process will likely lead to human misery and loss of life at least as great as that coming from ethnic conflict, the empirical question surrounding intervention is whether in the final analysis it ends up saving lives or costing more of them. Hanging in the balance is the morality of intervention and the policy question of whether to stand back and permit ethnic violence to occur within states knowing that, in its most extreme form, this may include practices defined as genocide.

My own thesis is that while there would be no justification for such genocidal practices on the part of more developed states (for example, there was no justification for the practice of genocide by the Nazis towards Jews, Gypsies, and Slavs because the policies of this murderous regime bore no discernible relation to the state-building process in Germany), the same cannot be said in the case of similar actions undertaken by ethnic entrepreneurs in newer post-colonial states. At first glance, this may appear to be an ethical double standard. In point of fact, however, precisely the opposite is the case. It is the use of intervention by more developed states (whose own early histories of violent state-building were allowed to occur without interference) in the affairs of less developed states, which constitutes the real double standard. The point is that *context* is all-important, and that one should only apply the same normative standard to *similarly situated* parties. Thus, for example, there is nothing hypocritical in allowing those over the age of eighteen to vote while denying the same right to those below this age as the premise for making this distinction is the determination that the parties are not similarly situated in terms of their ability to make informed decisions. Likewise, my argument is that since post-colonial states and more developed states are not similarly situated in terms of the developmental process known as state-building, it is reasonable to apply different normative standards to each.

From a policy standpoint, the implication of this argument is that in the case of newer states, the normative constraints associated with the application of international law should be either suspended or greatly modified until such time as these newer states have been able to achieve a level of political development in which those in authority are capable of governing effectively without outside assistance. While this sort of dual standard may at first appear to be unreasonable, there is precedent in the area of domestic law. It is no more unreasonable than the existence of a separate criminal justice system for juveniles (even those who commit the most heinous of acts) alongside a parallel system for adults. In both instances, the rationale is the same: *developmentally dissimilar parties should not be held to the same standard.*

In order to address the many theoretical issues raised in this discussion, the text is divided into four sections: *Part I* offers a review of the current state of three discrete bodies of literature dealing with ethnicity/ethnic conflict, state-building, and UN peacekeeping/intervention as a way to both lay the foundations for the development of a more integrated theoretical approach by providing the raw materials from which a synthesis can occur as well as demonstrate the need for a theory which transcends the compartmentalization of the past; *Part II* is devoted to filling the gap in the literature through the development of a theory of state-building in the post-Cold War era designed to integrate the three separate bodies of literature discussed in *Part I*; *Part III* engages in an in-depth case study of the quintessentially post-colonial state of Iraq designed to test the theory developed in *Part II*; finally, *Part IV* offers some final thoughts on the extent to which the case study supports or refutes my theory.

Recognizing that the subject matter dealt with in these pages stands at the nexus of three discrete bodies of literature, the first part surveys the intellectual terrain through a review of the major issues and points of contention within each of these fields of study. *Chapter One* examines several theoretical attempts to come to grips with the nature of ethnicity and ethnic conflict. *Chapter Two* takes an in-depth look at the issue of state-building with a particular focus upon scholarly efforts to deal with the role that violence plays in the state-building process. *Chapter Three* offers a discussion of some of the issues addressed in the literature dealing with UN peacekeeping. This discussion spans the period of the Cold War and the post-Cold War era and offers some understanding of how the literature dealing with peacekeeping has changed as a consequence of changes in the international system corresponding to the end of bipolarity.

One of the central premises of this study is that these formerly distinct subjects dealt with in discrete bodies of literature can no longer (if ever they really could) be treated as unrelated phenomena. The process of integrating these three areas into a single theory is a complex one. The first step is to identify that which is to be explained. While any of the three phenomena discussed in the literature review could be the focus of this discussion, my contention is that a study of the state is critical at this point in time.

In support of this decision to focus on the state, *Chapter Four* discusses the state-centric model of international relations and argues that this model most closely approximates the nature of global politics at the present time. This is not to suggest that the state is the only actor on the world stage. Consistent with the thinking of Kenneth Waltz articulated in his classic work, *Theory of International Politics*, the argument here is rather that, as a general proposition, the state is the most powerful, and, therefore, the most important actor.

Waltz' thesis does not consider, however, the possibility of failing or collapsed states. The existence of such phenomena in an ostensibly state-centric world poses a challenge for theorists and policy makers alike. The fundamental problem is to determine what is necessary in order to develop viable states. To ignore this issue would reduce the state-centric model to a contradiction in terms. If states were not capable of effective governance, it is impossible to see how they could be the most powerful actors on the world stage.

Part of this challenge is also to identify potential obstacles to the process of developing viable states. Accordingly, *Chapter Five* lays out in broad outline the theoretical relationship between ethnic conflict and state-building while *Chapter Six* looks at this issue in somewhat greater depth. The reasons for the collapse of post-colonial states are linked to the wider phenomena of both globalization and the end of the Cold War. The role of ethnicity and ethnic conflict in the transformation of the state from the failing post-colonial state to what is referred to here as the "ethnic state"[2] is discussed as part of the state-building process. It is suggested that the dualistic notion of a dichotomy between state failure and state-building be replaced by the notion of a continuum in which state failure or collapse becomes instead a transition to another *form* of the state—specifically, the transition from ethnically heterogeneous, post-colonial states to ethnically homogeneous, ethnic states.

Chapter Seven moves the discussion to its logical conclusion by completing the process of integrating ethnicity, state-building, and peacekeeping/

external intervention into a single theory for the post-Cold War era. Focusing on the various forms which external intervention in ethnic conflicts has assumed, it suggests how these types of intervention are likely to impact the state-building process.

Simply put, the theoretical framework developed in this study suggests that global politics is primarily interstate politics. Since the premise behind the notion that politics is state-centered is that states are the most powerful units in the world, it makes no sense to speak of a state-centric political system unless the members of that system are viable political entities. Furthermore, since the viability of states is frequently connected to the use of violence (oftentimes against ethnic rivals) for the purpose of consolidating authority within a given territorial area, it is reasonable to infer that outside efforts to interfere with this violence, and, therefore, with the consolidation of authority, will likely result in state weakness or failure. Given this context, the question raised by the theory developed in *Part II* is whether it makes sense in a state-centric world to pursue a policy of intervention in the internal state-building processes of newer states which, if it were to achieve its stated goal of interfering with the violent nature of that process, would also have the effect of undermining the embodiment of the state-centric model, i.e. the states system itself.

Up to this point, the study is largely a theoretical exercise. The most important question, however, has yet to be answered: Does this theory possess explanatory power when confronted with actual situations or case studies? In order to try to answer this question, *Part III* moves the discussion from the theoretical to the empirical. Since cases are inevitably more complex than theories (given the potentially limitless variety of factual permutations), the hope is that at least some aspects of the theory will survive contact with the facts of a given case study. Obviously, the more facts a theory can explain the stronger the theory.

Having chosen to look at the case of Iraq, *Chapter Eight* offers some context for the study of Iraqi state-building by comparing and contrasting general patterns of state formation in the overall region of the Middle East with those found in the prototypical model of Western Europe. This discussion sets the stage for the more in-depth study of Iraqi state formation. The discussion of the state-building process in Iraq in *Chapter Nine* demonstrates that both the state-building process and the obstacles to it more closely resemble the situation one finds in other Middle Eastern states (as well as other post-colonial states more generally) as opposed to that which one finds in Western Europe. In particular, the role of colonial intervention as a contributing factor to both state making and state weakness or failure and the related problem of artificial or arbitrary boundaries are recurring phenomena throughout much of what might be described as the post-colonial world.

This is not to suggest, however, that a study of Iraqi state-building necessitates discarding the Western European model. Quite the contrary. Acting as a kind of ideal type of the path to successful state formation, the absence of intervention in the Western European model provides a useful counterpart to the experience of Iraq, a country which has been identified as a quintessential example of a post-colonial state. By contrasting this ideal type with the case of Iraq, it is possible to see the role that intervention has played in both generating ethnic/sectarian conflicts in post-colonial states and also in preventing those conflicts from being resolved.

Finally, *Chapter Ten* draws certain conclusions regarding the theory developed in the preceding chapters. It identifies both those areas in which Iraq seems to be compatible with this theory as well as those aspects of the Iraqi situation which are not accounted for by the theory. These would include such things as the *intra-ethnic* violence among rival Kurdish factions and the issue of ensuring regional security as a potentially competing imperative to that of pursuing state-building. While this study concludes that the Iraqi situation is fundamentally consistent with the theory articulated in the preceding chapters, it also suggests that those areas not accounted for by the theory point to the need for both further research in the form of additional case studies as well as an ongoing process of theoretical refinement.

Part I
Literature Review

Chapter One

Theories of Ethnic Identification and Conflict

INTRODUCTION

As indicated in the Preface, the aim of this study is to develop and test a theory which seeks to integrate the phenomena of ethnicity/ethnic conflict, state-building, and external intervention in the post-Cold War era. The first step in this process is to survey the ways in which these phenomena have been addressed in the scholarly literature in the past. Accordingly, this first part is devoted to a review of three discrete bodies of literature which have developed over the years. Since it is my contention that previously these three phenomena were addressed largely independently of one another, the first three chapters will each take up a different area of study. This will facilitate the process of theory-building in *Part II*.

The development of a theory is a complex and contradictory process. On the one hand, no theory emerges full-blown ex nihilo. Every theory draws upon previous scholarly works. In this sense, every theorist stands upon the shoulders of those who came before. On the other hand, every theory seeks to distinguish itself from what has come before by identifying some issue or phenomenon which the literature has not adequately addressed and to offer some solution or explanation. Consequently, the purpose of conducting this survey is twofold. One is to identify some of the key issues and themes in each body of literature as well as some of the leading theories which have been developed thus far. From this, it will be possible to discern the role that previous scholarship has played in the development of my own theory. The other purpose is to critically evaluate these theories in terms of certain questions which are left unanswered thereby highlighting the need for a new theory.

Although there are individual contributions made by this or that aspect of my theory, by far the most important contribution from a theoretical standpoint is the suggestion that one of the things which separates the post-Cold War era from its predecessor is that the subjects of ethnicity/ethnic conflict, state-building, and external intervention need to be re-conceptualized in an integrated manner. *Part II* will be devoted to precisely this task.

As a prelude to this endeavor, this chapter will look at the question of ethnicity and ethnic conflict. The emphasis will be on the questions which have preoccupied theorists up to this point. Foremost among these have been the attempt to explain the reasons for ethnic identification and the reasons why conflict develops between various ethnic groups. This discussion will make it possible to distinguish my own work from what has come before. The key difference lies in the fact that I am less concerned with the *causes* of ethnic identification or conflict than I am with their *effects* upon other developments—specifically, the process of (re)building states.

In the next chapter, the focus will shift to the issue of state-building. Although a number of issues will be addressed, the primary concern will be to understand the role that violence has played (and perhaps still plays) in the building of states. Without this discussion, it would be impossible to understand the ways in which my own theory seeks to connect the interruption of violent ethnic conflict in the post-Cold War era to the interruption of the state-building process in post-colonial states.

Finally, the third chapter will look at the evolution of UN peacekeeping. Beginning with the original concept of peacekeeping as an interposition force or group of unarmed observers placed between belligerents with the consent of the parties, this chapter will explore some of the newer issues raised by the end of bipolarity. Of particular concern are comparatively recent attempts to develop more muscular and intrusive forms of external intervention in the absence of consent by the belligerents. Such efforts are based upon a looser construction of the provision in the Preamble of the UN Charter calling for the preservation of international peace and security. This newer interpretation calls for UN action in situations, such as internal conflict, which were previously thought to be within the domestic jurisdiction of states and, therefore, beyond the scope of the UN as articulated in Article 2 Section 7.

The principal purpose in discussing this literature is to identify what I would regard as a failure on the part of theorists in this area to consider the issue which is at the heart of this study: the violent nature of the state-building process. This failure has resulted in a tendency to either reduce issues of peacekeeping to narrow legal questions concerning the definition of the concept of the domestic affairs of states and the right of the UN to intervene in these so-called affairs or to questions of whether the success of peacekeeping missions should be defined in terms of ending the violence or resolving the underlying conflict (whatever this phrase might mean). Absent from the scholarly literature is any discussion of whether intervention is *preferable* to nonintervention in terms of the question of its positive or negative impact upon the state-building process in host states. This study aims to fill this gap in the literature.

It is to the literature dealing with the matter of ethnicity and ethnic conflict that this discussion now turns.

MAJOR TRENDS: PRIMORDIALISM VERSUS INSTRUMENTALISM

Over the years, a vast literature has developed dealing with ethnicity and ethnic conflict. Theories abound as to the causal antecedents for ethnic identification: "Ethnic attachments are variously seen as ways to preserve a precious cultural heritage; to soften class lines; to protect or to win economic and political advantages for disadvantaged groups; to furnish a more intimate and flavorful connection with large, impersonal societies; and to retard the shift of overwhelming power to the state."[1]

Given the multifaceted nature of human behavior and the difficulty often encountered by social scientists seeking to isolate causal variables in the real world, where the experimental controls often present in a laboratory generally do not exist, it is perhaps not surprising that these theories of ethnicity oftentimes are additive rather than cumulative. In other words, theories tend to proliferate but without building upon one another. Although there is considerable overlap, these attempts to explain ethnic consciousness generally can be grouped into one or more of the following categories: biological, cultural, economic, and/or political depending upon those factors which a particular scholar regards as salient in producing this sense of group awareness.

Although the approaches to ethnicity may vary widely, there are at least a couple of common questions shared by most, if not all, members of the scholarly community who have studied this subject. These questions have tended to focus upon two fundamental issues: Why do individuals attach significance to membership in ethnic groups as an organizing and mobilizing principle? Why does ethnic identification sometimes result in conflict between groups? Some scholars would add a third question: What, if anything, can be done to manage these conflicts when they do occur? This last question will be dealt with separately as it touches upon the other issues of state-building and UN intervention.

The ambiguous nature of ethnicity has given rise to two very different approaches to the study of this phenomenon among social scientists:

primordialism and instrumentalism.[2] Broadly speaking, primordialists see ethnicity as a fixed quality which provides for continuity across generations; instrumentalists, on the other hand, see ethnicity as contextually based and forever in flux depending upon the particular characteristics assigned importance by a given society.[3] Thus, for example, an instrumentalist would argue that while a Mexican and a Colombian more than likely would be seen, and would see themselves, as members of two distinct communities throughout Latin America, these same two individuals would more than likely both be viewed as members of the "Hispanic/Latino" community by the wider population of the United States and, consequently, would likely come to view themselves this way within this particular social context. As a place to begin a discussion of ethnicity, it is useful to start with a further explication of these two fundamentally different approaches to the subject.

Perhaps the closest thing to a biological theory of ethnicity would be the primordialist approach. According to Milton J. Esman, primordialists believe that " . . . ethnicity as a collective identity is so deeply rooted in historical experience that it should properly be treated as a given in human relations."[4] This approach represents a minority viewpoint within the scholarly community. Whether this means that the assumptions underlying primordialism are flawed or whether it merely reflects a bias within the social science community against the idea that ethnicity represents a distinct phenomenon independent of other social antecedents is, of course, an open question.

Adding to the complexity of this subject is the fact that even some members of the primordialist school do not see biology as the driving force behind ethnicity. Primordialists can be subdivided into those who see ethnicity as a biological phenomenon rooted in the need to transmit certain genetic qualities to the next generation through the maintenance of ethnic solidarity in order to ensure ethnic purity and those who focus on the *cultural* rather than the alleged *biological* aspects of ethnicity. While not necessarily denying that ethnicity is inherited, the latter group understand inheritance more in terms of cultural legacies rather than the transmission of genetic material. They tend to emphasize the role of socialization processes in the formation of ethnic identity. For them, the focus is on the transmission of shared cultural experiences and historical memories, whose unique character forever ties the youngest members of the ethnic community to those who came before them and forever separates them from those outside the group.

Whether emphasizing culture or biology, the common feature which distinguishes all primordialists from instrumentalists is the belief by the former that ethnicity as a social phenomenon has an independent existence that is not rooted in any particular social context. Consequently, people do not *define* their ethnic identity; *they are defined by it.* This is in marked contrast to the instrumentalist belief that ethnicity represents a social construct that is a function of a particular social context.[5]

TYPES OF INSTRUMENTALISM

As with primordialism, instrumentalism takes a variety of forms. Within the instrumentalist category, opportunistic theories conceptualize ethnicity as a resource to be used by individuals in pursuit of some other end which may in turn be discarded if some alternative method better serves those same ends.[6]

A variation on this theme is the rational choice approach, which attempts to explain behavior in general (and ethnicity in particular) by borrowing from economics the notion of rationality and applying it to ethnicity. From this perspective, ethnicity becomes a rational choice which is made by an individual in an effort to acquire individual, mainly economic, values.[7]

While reserving final judgment, J. Milton Yinger argues that this theory appears to suffer from the same fallacy of reductionism as does the sociobiological approach to ethnicity advocated by scholars such as Pierre Van den Berghe. In a similar fashion, rational choice theories downplay the importance of structural conditions and assume that ethnicity is primarily, or perhaps exclusively, a function of individual choice or decision making.[8]

A subcategory of this rational choice approach is known as constructivism. The notion that ethnic affiliation represents some sort of calculated decision by individuals or groups is popular with those constructivists who seek to explain ethnic mobilization and ethnic conflict in terms of manipulation by ambitious ethnic entrepreneurs. Constructivists are less concerned with the role of economics than that of politics. In particular, they focus upon appeals by ethnic entrepreneurs to ethnic identity as a means of acquiring and/or maintaining power and influence within what is seen as essentially a socially constructed community.[9] Thus, for example, constructivist theorists would explain ethnic conflict in places such as the former Yugoslavia as the result of efforts by ethnic entrepreneurs, including the Serbian Slobodan Milosevic and the Croatian Franjo Tudjman, to cynically utilize ethnicity as a way to secure for themselves a power base through the manipulation of whole populations in the aftermath of the collapse of communism. In this case, the prospect of losing economic and personal security to members of other ethnic communities is especially potent as a tool to be manipulated by skillful politicians interested in rallying other individuals to identify with the ethnic group and the agenda of its leader.

Such contrived appeals are particularly effective when accompanied by violent conflict between groups because, as Chaim Kaufmann points out, ethnic violence tends to generate a security dilemma.[10] The symbiotic nature of these security dilemmas and the appeals of ethnic entrepreneurs can be seen in the spiraling effect of increased conflict and ever-hardening ethnic identification as the two together provide a rationale for the self-perpetuation of ethnic identity.[11]

Milica Zarkovic Bookman offers a somewhat different approach to this idea of ethnic manipulation. Instead of focusing on the efforts of entrepreneurs to create insecurity through the artificial manufacturing of ethnic differences leading to security dilemmas and the hardening of ethnic identification, the emphasis is placed instead upon what is termed the "demographic struggle for power." While accepting the general notion that ethnicity is itself a manufactured phenomenon, the key to this concept is not the manipulation of ethnic *symbols* but the manipulation of ethnic *numbers* within the population of a given multi-ethnic state.[12]

There is much to recommend in the Bookman thesis, and elements of it are incorporated into the present study. In particular, the notion that ethnic conflict is tied to the territorial state and that the goal of the "demographic struggle for power" is the creation of ethnically homogeneous states. In this sense, ethnic conflict may be seen as a mechanism for the building of states, whose boundaries more accurately reflect the cultural characteristics of the populations living within those territorial parameters. This view stands in marked contrast to the notion advanced by I. William Zartman that ethnic conflict represents not the building of states but rather their collapse.

While the Bookman thesis is useful in certain respects, this is not to suggest that it is without its weaknesses. As a theory of ethnic conflict, it is perhaps quite useful, but as a theory of ethnic identification, it suffers from many of the same problems faced by other constructivists.

A major difficulty for proponents of the constructivist school is the classic problem associated with so-called "Great Man of History" theories. While cynical opportunism may explain the *motives* behind the actions of ethnic entrepreneurs, it provides little assistance in the effort to understand the apparent connection between leaders and followers. If ethnicity is nothing more than an artificially constructed reality (and presumably, therefore, the differences between people are not based on anything real but instead are manufactured), how does one choose a target population?

Perhaps even more importantly, what explains the willingness of that population to accept the categories developed by the power-seeker?

Recognizing this difficulty, Chaim Kaufmann points out that ethnic identities are, to some degree at least, determined by the immutable fact of one's ancestry: "Competition to sway individual loyalties does not play an important role in ethnic civil wars, because ethnic identities *are fixed by birth* [italics added]. While not everyone may be mobilized as an active fighter for his or her group, hardly anyone ever fights for the opposing ethnic group."[13]

Of course, this is not to say that manipulation plays no role. Clearly, a figure such as Hitler was able to exclude persons of Jewish ancestry born in Germany from the category of "ethnically German" through the creation of a separate classification for Jews despite the fact that many of these people had deep ancestral roots in, and strong allegiance to, their country of origin. It was, however, precisely through this sort of skillful manipulation that he was able, in effect, to narrow the meaning of the term "German" so as to define it in terms of some alleged racial or blood connection rather than geographical contiguity.

From this discussion, it is possible to conclude that while there is some room for manipulation of ethnic symbols, it would seem that the possibilities for the construction of ethnicity are not unlimited. Thus, any theory which focuses solely upon the ethnic entrepreneur while ignoring other factors such as the biological or cultural characteristics and/or the motives of the target population as well as the social and economic conditions at the time is at best only a partial explanation for ethnic identification and conflict. Such a theory overlooks the fact that both ethnic identification and conflict require the prior existence of an underlying foundation or common bond between those seeking to exploit ethnicity and those in the target audience.

Indeed, the example of Nazi Germany and the Jews illustrates several further complications for the constructivist approach and, more broadly, instrumentalist theories in general. Most important among these is the lack of attention by theorists of this persuasion to the distinction between self-identification and ascription. This results in a levels of analysis problem. While instrumentalist theories make the case for the fluid nature of ethnic categories, they do not address the question of whether it is the individual, the ethnic group, or the larger host society which decides whether someone is or is not a member of a particular ethnic group.

If identity is ascriptive, which is to say that the larger host society decides, then what happens if either the so-called ethnic group or individuals assigned membership within that group reject the criteria upon which the larger society makes such decisions? This sets up the peculiar situation in which someone could be a member of the group and not a member of the group simultaneously. Thus, for example, the Nazi classification of "Jewish" based upon so-called racial criteria included individuals who either would not meet the halachic (Jewish law) criteria for membership within the community because of the absence of a Jewish mother or who would not consider themselves members of that community because of religious conversion or lack of affiliation.

This ascriptive notion of assignment of an ethnic identity shares with the primordialist approach the notion that ethnicity is an inherited, rather than a selected, set of characteristics of an individual. At the same time, however, it differs from primordialist theories in that the host society determines the precise nature of these characteristics and who possesses them whereas primordialists would argue that these characteristics by their very nature adhere to the individual through biological (as in the case of race) or cultural (as in such cases as religion or language) transmission. As a result, ethnic membership is not assigned by the larger community to any individual or group within it but is rather an *a priori* category much as hair color or skin color would be.

The issue of ascription also raises the question as to why the host society finds it necessary to assign ethnic classifications to those living within its boundaries. Such classifications are rarely, if ever, value neutral and generally relate to issues of super- and subordination involving one's status within the society. Some examples of this phenomenon would include not only Jews in Nazi Germany but also so-called "blacks" and "coloreds" in apartheid South Africa (designations which, in the case of the former, ignored tribal distinctions among native peoples of this region), "whites" and "blacks" in those parts of the United States in which segregation was the norm, as well as "Jews" and "Arabs"[14] in Israel. While the specific reasons for ascription may vary from society to society, it does appear that there is some relation to the issue of social stratification within the society and an attempt by either those already in power or those seeking power to utilize these classifications as a way to acquire or maintain a dominant position for themselves and those they define as members of their own group.

As an alternative to the host society, it is possible for the decision as to whether someone is a member of an ethnic group to be left to the members of the ethnic group themselves. In that case, the question arises as to how such decisions are made. Which members, for example, within the group are deemed competent to make such a determination? Who confers this authority upon them?

As has been seen, the constructivist answer to the question of competence is that the decision is made by power-seeking ethnic entrepreneurs. This, however, only begs the question: why are their determinations accepted by the group, and how is it possible for such authority to be conferred in the first place without the *a priori* existence of an ethnic group capable of deferring to the judgment of some of its members? Unfortunately for instrumentalists and constructivists alike, the latter question only leads one to the intellectual equivalent of a cul-de-sac: *once the prior existence of an ethnic group independent of the efforts of those seeking to manipulate symbols so as to manufacture such a group is conceded, it is no longer possible to maintain the core argument that the group is manufactured or constructed by an ethnic entrepreneur. In the absence of this central thesis, both instrumentalist and constructivist theories lose their validity.*

The challenge for instrumentalists is further complicated by their argument that the boundaries of the group itself are constantly in flux due to their artificially constructed nature. This leaves open the possibility that an individual will reject the classification assigned by other members of the ethnic group. Returning to the example of the Jewish community, what if, for example, the Jewish community determines that an individual meets its criteria for being Jewish but that individual feels no attachment to the community? In what sense would that classification be meaningful in terms of its impact upon the behavior of those who reject their inclusion within the social category?

A third possibility would be to leave the decision up to the individual. This, too, however, poses certain problems. If the individual is the one to decide, then what are the criteria upon which this decision is made? What are the common bonds which connect a collection of individuals each using his or her own (not necessarily the same) criteria for claiming membership in the common ethnic group? Thus, for example, what if some individuals claim membership in the Jewish community based solely upon patrilineal descent while others say that membership requires matrilineal descent? What if someone not born to a Jewish parent feels an affinity for Jews and Judaism while others insist that a conversion ritual is necessary for membership in the community? In other words, does the whole notion of ethnicity, now emptied of any specific content, become a meaningless classification?

Unfortunately, primordialists are no more able to explain the complex phenomenon of ethnicity than instrumentalists. If instrumentalists are unable to account for the underlying foundation(s) of ethnicity, e.g. the meaning of "Germanness" linking the people of Germany with Adolf

Hitler (who ironically was actually Austrian), the primordialist approach is unable to explain the fact that some Germans did not respond to Hitler's appeals despite a supposedly shared ethnic "essence." Indeed, primordialists would no doubt be hard-pressed to explain the exclusion of Jews from the category of ethnic Germans inasmuch as this particular community of Jews was arguably more thoroughly assimilated into the culture of the host society than was the case with Jews in many, or perhaps most, other countries in Europe. It would seem, then, that this discussion highlights the complexity of the problem of explaining ethnicity but brings us no closer to a solution.

Perhaps a way out of this conundrum would be to focus on the issue of ethnic security dilemmas raised by Kaufmann. The attempt to understand why such security dilemmas occur in the first place opens the door to a shift in the theoretical focus away from "Great Man" theories and toward explanations which consider the role of social, economic, and/or political contexts. Just as security dilemmas arise in international relations because of the anarchic structure of the international system (which is really just another way of describing the insecurity which results when states are responsible for their own security in a self-help system lacking a central government), perhaps ethnic identification and conflict are the result of a domestic security dilemma between groups, which arises when the governing authority collapses and leaves a power vacuum structurally analogous to international anarchy. Consistent with this thesis is the argument that ethnic identification and violent conflict often coincide with the collapse of empires (such as the Austro-Hungarian empire after the First World War and the British and French empires after the Second World War) or states.[15]

This discussion would seem to suggest that a more plausible explanation for both ethnic identification and conflict than primordialist or constructivist theories may be found in the combination of the collapse of central authority and the spiral of intensifying ethnic identification and conflict, which follow from the existence of a power vacuum and the emergence of a security dilemma.

Unfortunately, while perhaps plausible on the surface, this argument does pose certain problems. One of the difficulties is that in the absence of some discussion of the manipulation of ethnic symbols by ethnic entrepreneurs, it provides no explanation as to why the collapse of central authority should result in a tendency for individual identities to coalesce around ethnicity as opposed to some other social category such as class or ideology. Indeed, during the Industrial Revolution, the social fault lines in most industrializing societies were centered primarily around the issue of class while during the Cold War, the fundamental social cleavage was arguably ideology rather than ethnicity.

Furthermore, the pairing of state or empire collapse and ethnic conflict only serves to beg the question as to the direction in which the causal arrow should point. Joshua Bernard Forrest suggests that the question of whether state collapse *produces* substate fragmentation or is merely a *reflection* of it is a complex one with no single answer. In his view, one possibility is that suggested by those such as Chaim Kaufmann and Adam Roberts. According to this scenario, ethnic identification and conflict may be a top down process in which state collapse occurs and this, in turn, stimulates ethnic conflict as various substate groups are confronted with a security dilemma. Another alternative is that the causal arrow may point the other way. In some cases the relationship between ethnic identification and conflict and state/empire collapse may be a bottom up process in which increasingly mobilized substate regional and/or ethnic actors (although regionalism and ethnicity are not necessarily synonymous, the two frequently overlap, and when they do, this increases the likelihood of either secession or irredentism) challenge state leaders bringing on the collapse of existing states.[16]

Clearly, the effort to associate ethnic identification and conflict with the collapse of political systems is problematic. Indeed, the problem may be even greater than Forrest suggests. Esman, for example, points out that some scholars contend that ethnic mobilization and conflict may actually be a function of the *strength* of a state rather than its weakness or collapse. According to this argument, as the state becomes stronger and penetrates more areas of society, it follows that it will assume a greater role in people's lives. Under these conditions of increasing state penetration of society, ethnic groups begin to resemble interest groups. As such, they increasingly find it necessary to compete in the political arena for access to those in power in order to obtain influence over governmental policies affecting the allocation of scarce resources. This competition produces a heightened sense of ethnic awareness leading to a greater degree of mobilization. As these different groups are becoming mobilized to compete over the distribution of resources, the result will be conflict between groups, which may assume either a political or a military form depending upon the nature of the political system.[17]

In a sense, this discussion represents a microcosm of the difficulty with the entire literature dealing with ethnicity and ethnic conflict. Those theories which focus upon the attempt to explain ethnic identification (whether relying upon ideas about the manipulation of symbols or primordial ties) do not explain the connection between the mere fact of the existence of such ties, however real or contrived they may be, and the fact that oftentimes violent conflict erupts between different groups as a result of the emphasis upon ethnic identification. In other words, why does ethnic difference lead to ethnic conflict?

Likewise, those theories which start at the other end of the spectrum and attempt to explain the phenomenon of conflict between ethnic groups in terms of such factors as political collapse, state penetration, security dilemmas, or "demographic struggles for power" not only disagree with one another about the reasons for ethnic conflict but offer no explanation as to why intergroup conflicts should assume a specifically ethnic character. In other words, they offer no explanation either for ethnic identification or for the reasons why conflict in society coalesces around ethnic categories as opposed to some other socially constructed categories.

A tacit acknowledgment of the distinction between intergroup conflict per se and its specifically ethnic variant can be found in Bookman's opening statement: "Throughout history there have been struggles for territory and control of its resources. Only sometimes have these struggles been based on ethnicity."[18] No further attempt is made by the author to explain why such conflicts sometimes focus on ethnicity while at other times they do not. It is simply assumed that since ethnicity is a manufactured reality, sometimes it plays a central role while at other times it does not. While this may or may not be an apt description of reality, it is unsatisfactory from a theoretical standpoint. The reader is left to wonder whether the presence or absence of ethnicity from conflict is purely random. If so, then we are no closer to understanding the appeal of ethnicity and its ability to move large numbers of people to actions up to and including genocidal behavior.

One effort to address this problem might be seen as a variation on the constructivist approach. Instead of focusing on manipulation of symbols by ethnic entrepreneurs interested in enhancing their own power within an artificially constructed community, this approach looks at the efforts by imperial powers to manufacture ethnicity as part of an imperial strategy of divide and rule. Building upon the work of noted scholar Jeffrey Herbst, who suggests that seemingly ancient ethnic affiliations were oftentimes manufactured instead by colonial powers interested in serving their own interests,[19] Mohammed Ayoob makes the following claim: "Even in India, where religious-communal identities (but not antagonisms) at the local level had crystallized before the advent of the British Raj, it was during the colonial period that these identities were augmented, consolidated, and pitted against each other—often as a result of a deliberate policy of 'divide and rule'—at the 'national' level, finally leading to the partition of the country in 1947."[20]

Karen Barkey and Sunita Parikh concur in this view of the role of British colonial policy in India but take it one step further to argue that states as well as empires have manipulated ethnicity to serve their own interests.[21]

Interestingly, this sort of neo-constructivist attempt to explain both the emergence of ethnicity and the existence of ethnic conflict seems to fly in the face of another scholarly approach more closely related to the primordialist position, which suggests that rather than manufacturing ethnicity, the colonial powers instead ignored *pre-existing* ethnic groups in their rush to carve up Africa and Asia. Inexplicably, the same Mohammed Ayoob who championed the notion of colonially manufactured ethnic identities also argues for the existence of pre-colonial ethnic ties and the disregard shown for these affiliations by European imperial powers.[22] Indeed, Ayoob is not alone in his attention to the disruptive impact of colonial boundaries. For many scholars, this line of reasoning regarding the arbitrary nature of colonial boundaries as well as its destabilizing effect upon post-colonial states has assumed the status of conventional wisdom, especially in the African context. [23]

Of course, one might attempt to reconcile the apparent inconsistency between these two views of the relationship between ethnicity and colonial policy by suggesting that in some cases, ethnicity was manufactured while in others it was not. This would be a neat solution, which may even have the added benefit of historical evidence to support it. The problem is that while it might seem to settle the matter, it really brings us no closer to an understanding of what *causes* people to coalesce around ethnic labels. Merely stating that on the one hand, we have A and, on the other hand, we have B fails to explain why we have these two hands. In the end, therefore, from a theoretical perspective, we are left empty-handed.

Another possible solution would be to suggest that perhaps it is not *either* A or B but rather *both* A and B. Leaving aside for the moment any questions as to the historical accuracy of the following, there is nothing inconsistent between the assertion that colonial authorities destroyed some older ethnic communities by the manner in which they divided up colonial territories and the assertion that they simultaneously manufactured newer ethnic identities as part of a deliberate colonial strategy intended to divide native peoples and perpetuate colonial domination. While not logically inconsistent, these assertions unfortunately do not offer a coherent theory of the reasons for ethnic identification other than to suggest implicitly that the explanation of the phenomenon is too complex to be reduced to any single factor. This may, in fact, be correct, but it would also seem to be tautological in that it is essentially making the claim that sometimes ethnicity is manufactured while at other times it is the result of pre-existing ties.

In addition to problems of logical consistency and coherence, theories of ethnic identification and/or conflict based on colonial policies and legacies also face an empirical problem. The issue of the role of colonial policy in the creation of ethnicity and the exacerbation of ethnic tensions is further complicated by the claim that the evidence for this assertion is lacking. Walker Connor suggests that it is possible to test the claim that ethnicity is a function of colonialism and the deliberate efforts of colonial powers to manufacture and/or promote ethnic awareness and conflict. Based upon his research, he finds no support for this claim.[24]

Clearly, the position taken by Walker Connor and that offered by those who agree with Mohammed Ayoob cannot both be correct. Indeed, while certainly not definitive, the internal inconsistency of Ayoob's argument identified above would seem to lend greater credence to Connor's assertion.

THE IMPACT OF MODERNIZATION AND GLOBALIZATION UPON ETHNICITY

Introducing another element into the equation, Connor suggests that the phenomenon of ethnic identification should be understood in the context of modernization. His explanation focuses upon the increasing ability of central authorities to *penetrate* areas left previously untouched. This state penetration in the form of improvements in transportation and communications results in increasing levels of *contact* between formerly isolated communities. In his view, increased contact with the outside world creates a desire within the previously isolated community to defend its own culture, which, in turn, serves to heighten the consciousness among members of the community as to their own distinct ethnic identity.[25]

Thus, whereas Esman sees state penetration as fostering ethnic mobilization to advance the economic or political interests of the community, Connor sees it as generating a desire for cultural preservation on the part of the members of a community. This cultural approach has the added advantage of being able to explain the reason for the focus upon ethnicity whereas economic or political theories of interest group behavior do not explain why the rallying point is ethnicity rather than class, region, gender, etc.

At the same time, however, Connor's contact thesis still assumes the existence of a prior community. Otherwise, what is it that is endangered and needs to be preserved? In other words, he does not seem to be attempting to explain why ethnic groups form per se. He sees the development of ethnic consciousness not as something sui generis in the sense of the creation of some new form of identification and association wholly other than forms of identification based on criteria such as socioeconomic status or ideology. Instead, this emerging consciousness represents a defensive attempt to preserve something old by transforming it. Thus, the group ties which existed when the community was isolated pre-date the modernization process. The only thing which changes is that members of the community become more aware of those ties as a result of contact with the outside world. The fundamental problem of explaining why these ties develop in the first place, however, remains unanswered.

While containing many worthwhile features, Connor's contact thesis must also be seen as the intellectual equivalent of "throwing down the gauntlet." It represents a direct challenge to one of the dominant approaches within the social sciences to the study of ethnicity: modernization theory and its more recent variant dealing with the concept of globalization.

Supporters of modernization theory have traditionally rejected the primordialist view that ethnicity is some sort of historical given and have preferred instead to view ethnicity as representing an outmoded, vestige of pre-modern society. The conventional wisdom was that ethnicity will ultimately be replaced by integration into a wider national community as societies themselves undergo the many processes of transformation collectively referred to as modernization. These include: urbanization, improvements in the means of transportation and communication, and increased penetration of society by government. According to classical modernization theorists, each of these changes associated with the transition to modernity results in the development of closer linkages between distinct communities within the state who had previously existed in relative isolation from one another. As this process intensifies, old social bonds are replaced by a wider sense of community coterminous with the idea of the modern nation.[26]

Classical modernization theory can be subdivided into liberal and Marxist theoretical traditions. For liberalism, the emphasis on the individual rather than the group and the belief that one's social and economic status are a function of individual achievement causes adherents of this school to view ethnicity as an outmoded and dysfunctional social phenomenon which attempts to link social and perhaps economic status to assigned membership in a particular group. It is assumed that in the modern world, such attachments will gradually attenuate themselves until they either disappear or become nostalgic social categories emptied of any meaningful content.[27]

From the Marxian perspective, modernization is viewed in terms of the class struggle between the bourgeoisie and the proletariat. Ethnic groups or nations are categorized as either "progressive" or "reaction-ary." In this way, ethnicity is incorporated into the class struggle such that support for "progressive" nations is seen as furthering the class struggle. Alternatively, some Marxists see the issue of ethnicity in terms of appeals to be used by the capitalist bourgeoisie in an effort to divide the working class by creating a vertical allegiance between the national proletariat and its corresponding bourgeoisie thereby retarding class consciousness on the part of the workers of the world.[28] Marxists assume that the overthrow of the capitalist system will eventually result in the proletariat becoming aware of its "true" interests and consequently will lead to the discarding of such examples of false consciousness as ethnic identification.

The fact that neither of these theories of modernization can account for the continuation or re-emergence of ethnicity, despite their shared expectation of its imminent disappearance (indeed, in the case of Marx-ist theories, adherents of this school must confront the additional annoy-ance that it would seem that Marxism itself is disappearing only to be replaced by the rise of ethnicity across the former Soviet Union and East-ern Europe!), is reminiscent of Mark Twain's old dictum that reports of his demise were greatly exaggerated. In the case of modernization theories, this failure has caused some scholars to go so far as to question the rela-tionship between modernization and ethnicity.

While liberalism has not suffered the historical fate of Marxism, it may be too soon to proclaim, as did Francis Fukuyama at the end of the Cold War, the triumph of liberalism and "the end of history." In terms of the liberal emphasis upon individualism rather than group identity, the experience of post-communist transitional societies, such as the for-mer Yugoslavia or even the former Soviet Union, suggests that the future direction of such societies is still very much an open question. Following in the tradition of Walker Connor, Anthony D. Smith challenges the lib-eral assumptions underlying what had been the prevailing view among modernization theorists, going back to Karl Deutsch, which held that the modernization process would inevitably lead to the attenuation of ethnic identity.[29] Although writing before the end of the Cold War, Smith's argu-ment is equally, if not more, relevant in its aftermath.

As the fortunes of modernization theories dating back to the 1950s and 1960s have waned, they have reappeared in an updated form during the 1990s. This variation on the theme of the relationship between mod-ernization and ethnic identification can be found in the literature dealing with globalization. Former UN Secretary-General Boutros Boutros-Ghali captured the essence of this argument in his observation that the paradox of globalization particularly in the post-Cold War era would seem to be that barriers between people appear to be both falling and rising simultaneously.[30]

John Lewis Gaddis sees this paradox of simultaneous integration (which he defines in terms of the "freedom from want") and disintegration (which he defines in terms of the "freedom from fear") as both a fundamental feature of modern history and perhaps the defining characteristic of the post-Cold War era.[31]

In an effort to explain how this integrative phenomenon of globalization is related to the disintegrative phenomenon of the rise of ethnic consciousness, the scholarly heirs to Walker Connor's contact thesis, such as Benjamin R. Barber, believe that both ethnic awareness and the resulting conflict between groups in the post-Cold War era are a function of the development of a truly globalized economy and the globalization of culture brought on by commercial penetration and advances in telecommunications. For Barber, globalization exacerbates ethnic conflict as local cultures struggle to preserve their cultural identities against the homogenizing tendencies of a global tide of commerce and media—a phenomenon which he calls "Jihad vs. McWorld."[32] This formulation reflects his understanding of the paradox of a world that is simultaneously experiencing a higher degree of economic and cultural integration than ever before with the collapse of Cold War barriers while at the same time witnessing an increasing tendency toward political disintegration and fragmentation as ethnic conflicts proliferate and tear apart what were once assumed to be viable states at a price of intolerable human suffering.

Thus, globalization theory can be thought of as an extension of that body of literature within modernization theory which holds that the forces of the modern world *stimulate* rather than retard ethnic consciousness. Just as earlier writers such as Walker Connor believed that exposure to outside groups within the state and penetration of remote areas by the government made possible by improvements in transportation and communication can produce a kind of defensive ethnic awareness, Barber suggests that this same process is now being acted out on a world stage. Barber, however, takes it one step further. It is not merely the *contact* between different global cultures which produces "Jihad" but the *dominance* of what for much of the world is an alien Western culture labeled "McWorld" which produces this ethnic sentiment particularly in its most militant forms.

Anthony D. Smith, on the other hand, takes a somewhat more nuanced view of this relationship. On the one hand, as indicated above, he argues that this literature represents a useful corrective to the earlier modernization literature, which had taken for granted the disappearance of ethnicity. On the other hand, he maintains that, ironically, those theories which see ethnicity as a function of modernization or globalization rather than as an independent phenomenon in its own right are in their own way prisoners of the same liberal assumptions about the transient nature of ethnicity as the theories they seek to criticize.[33]

J. Milton Yinger offers a third alternative between the view that modernization and/or globalization undermines traditional attachments and the view that these forces strengthen these attachments. He suggests that the disagreement here may be more apparent than real. As he sees it, modernization does not *eradicate* ethnicity, but it does *transform* it. The appearance of a heightened sense of ethnic consciousness conceals the fact that this transformed ethnicity has been emptied of much of its content.[34]

CONCLUSION

In the end, this discussion has come full circle. Theories of ethnicity and ethnic conflict appear to have an additive rather than a cumulative effect. Instead of building upon one another, they oftentimes appear to be talking past one another. Perhaps due to the multifaceted nature of the phenomenon of ethnicity or perhaps due to a lack of intellectual rigor on the part of theorists, there is a tendency for theories to proliferate but without the development of some consensus within the discipline, which makes it possible to build upon one another.

Another fundamental problem is that none of the theoretical schools identified in this review of the literature is able to account for *both* ethnic identification *and* ethnic conflict. In order to understand ethnic identification, a theory must do more than simply establish that there are unscrupulous individuals looking to exploit ethnic difference. It must go further back in the causal chain and explain why it is that specifically ethnic appeals resonate with some significant segment of the population: "Seldom is ethnicity invented or constructed from whole cloth: a cultural and experiential core must validate identity and make solidarity credible to potential constituents."[35]

Perhaps the closest thing in the literature on ethnicity to an explanation of the appeal of ethnic categories are those theories which explore the psychological reasons why modernization promotes ethnicity by focusing on its calming and reassuring functions in a world characterized by anxiety, upheaval, and cultural threats from the outside.

At the same time, however, these theories generally fail to make a crucial distinction between the notion of *manufacturing* ethnic identity and of *activating* a latent ethnic identity. The former involves the attempt to identify root causes in the creation of something new while the latter is simply concerned with identifying the antecedents which will stimulate a pre-existing, albeit latent or dormant, characteristic. It would seem that in order for ethnicity to both calm and reassure people confronting the anxieties associated with modernization in the manner suggested by the critics of what Smith calls the "liberal assumptions" of modernization theory, it would have to build upon some prior form of association. Smith refers to these earlier associations at the core of the modern "ethnic revival" as "ethnies." The theoretical dilemma is that in order to explain ethnicity, one must either start with the larger social context (in which case, there is no explanation as to why the appeal should assume a specifically ethnic form) or treat ethnicity or some core form of the ethnic group as a given to be activated under certain social conditions (in which case, the theory loses its ability to explain why that form of association comes into existence in the first place).

The problem is further complicated by the issue of ethnic conflict. Once ethnic identification is explained, the next challenge for a theorist is to explain why this tendency on the part of large numbers of people to think in terms of ethnic categories should lead to conflict with others who identify with a different group. Logically, there is no necessary nexus between self-identification with the members of a particular group and the existence of conflict with other groups. Such a connection must be established.

Kaufmann's focus on the idea of a security dilemma does establish this connection but fails to explain why ethnicity arises as a social category. Furthermore, his argument that ethnicity leads to insecurity and conflict once exploited by ethnic entrepreneurs is at variance with the argument mentioned above that ethnic identification in the modern world provides psychological *security* rather than insecurity for the individual.

What, then, explains this collective insecurity and the resulting security dilemma which is exploited by self-seeking entrepreneurs? Presumably, the satisfaction of security needs for the individual should lead to a reduction of ethnic conflict by reducing the problem of security dilemmas rather than heightening ethnic tensions. Yet, the evidence is strongly on the side of increased ethnic conflict.

Thus, we are left with the conundrum that in order to explain ethnic conflict in terms of insecurity, we must first negate those modernization and/or globalization theories which seem to offer the best hope for explaining the appeal of ethnic identification in the first place—namely those which address the issue of the sense of psychological security. The approach suggested by Bookman would offer a welcome solution to this dilemma were it not for the fact that it too makes no attempt to explain why ethnic identification occurs or, for that matter, why the struggle for power should assume an ethnic character.

Clearly, this discussion has not resolved the questions of why ethnic identification arises or leads to conflict. This is not to suggest, however, that it is without merit. Its value lies instead in the appreciation of the state of the discipline as it relates to the explanation of ethnic identification and conflict. Without such a discussion, it would be impossible to understand the relationship between the current study and the existing body of literature. In particular, the ways in which this study seeks to make a contribution to the understanding of the wider subject matter by utilizing that literature in the development of its own theoretical insights and empirical research. That contribution, however, need not, and is not intended to, resolve all of the outstanding questions raised above. The purpose is rather to address one particular area within the vast subject of ethnicity and ethnic conflict.

Since the focus of this analysis is on the *interaction* between ethnicity, state-building, and UN peacekeeping/peace enforcement, the fact that ethnic identification plays such a dominant role in the post-Cold War era and that it frequently results in conflict within states can be treated for the present purposes as a given. This is not meant to imply a preference for or against the primordialist position. Nor is it intended to suggest that the question of how to explain ethnic identification is somehow unimportant. Rather, it is intended to suggest that those are questions which are beyond the scope of the current study and that whatever the nature or the causes of ethnicity, one would be hard-pressed to deny the existence of conflicts around the world which are at a minimum framed in the idiom of ethnicity.

Having described several of the theoretical approaches addressed in the literature, this study will address this matter of ethnicity from a different direction. As indicated in the introduction, another way to look at this issue is to focus less on the *causes* of ethnicity or ethnic conflict and more on the *consequences* or *effects* of these in the modern era. The challenge is then transformed from explaining the *reasons* for the emergence of ethnicity or ethnic conflict in a given era or a given society into explaining the *significance* of these phenomena once they do emerge.

This challenge leads directly to the role of ethnic conflict in the state-building process. Just as the literature in the field of ethnicity offers some perspective and some of the raw materials for the theory which will be developed later in this study, the same is true for the state-building literature. Of particular interest is that part of the literature which deals with the relationship between violence and the early stages of state formation (determining territorial limits or boundaries) and regime consolidation (establishing effective control over the population within those limits), which is the subject of the next chapter. This discussion will serve as a prelude to understanding the general theoretical relationship between ethnic conflict and state-building. It will also make it possible to understand the impact that peacekeeping has upon that relationship both as an abstract matter and as an empirical matter once the study turns to the issue of state formation in Iraq.

Chapter Two
Approaches to the State-Building Process

INTRODUCTION

Part of the thesis which will be tested in this study suggests that the ethnic violence observed in places sharing a post-colonial past is actually part of the empirical process of state-building reminiscent in certain important respects of the earliest stages of state formation in Western Europe. According to this thesis, the eruption of internal conflicts throughout much of the post-colonial world, especially in the period following the end of the Cold War, represents an effort by would-be state makers to reverse those aspects of juridical statehood which resulted in the creation and preservation of artificial states containing unstable political communities. It is suggested that there is a direct relationship between the unstable nature of these political communities and the arbitrary way in which post-colonial state boundaries were drawn.

While it is true that the chronological order in which juridical and empirical statehood occurred is the opposite of that found among the oldest states in Europe (where empirical statehood preceded the juridical norms which enshrined the state as sacrosanct), there is no necessary connection between chronological order and relative importance as an explanatory variable. It simply may be that post-colonial states are today replicating the earlier Western European experience of developing empirical statehood albeit by means of a different path: instead of first developing the empirical attributes of statehood and then codifying them juridically, they are moving from the juridical norms of statehood to the development of the empirical attributes of state viability. If so, then the ethnic conflicts witnessed in the post-Cold War era may actually be seen as part of an empirical process of state-building.

24

My argument represents an extension of theories developed over the years concerning the relationship between violence and the development of states. Among the issues explored in previous works have been the role of violence in: the consolidation of state power, the consolidation of the number of states in the states system through territorial conquest, and the path to democratization. In order to understand the contribution which the theory developed in this work makes to the literature, this chapter will be devoted to a discussion of this rather extensive literature dealing with the larger issue of state-building and especially the role that violence has played in the development of states. Of particular interest is the importance of violence to the territorial formation of states and the concentration of power within those states. These processes have occurred through the elimination of obstacles to the state-building process in the form of rival state makers. It is to the literature that this chapter now turns.

STATE-SOCIETY RELATIONS: STRONG VERSUS WEAK STATES

One approach to the study of state-building focuses upon the issue of state-society relations. It is not primarily concerned with questions of how the state comes into being but rather with the viability of the state after it comes into existence. Along these lines, a number of scholars have raised the issue of so-called "strong" versus "weak" states.

This literature raises an interesting and important question that is rooted in the differing intellectual traditions of Thomas Hobbes and John Locke regarding the relationship between the state and civil society. For Hobbes, the state is an institution which exists apart from civil society. As such, the strength of the state is determined by its institutional *coercive* capacity to dominate society. In his view, this is a necessary precondition for the ultimate purpose of the state: the establishment and preservation of order. Locke, on the other hand, argues that the state is not separate from, and above, society but is instead a creation of it, and, therefore, is dependent upon the support of society. Consequently, his argument is that the strength of the state is determined not by its capacity to dominate civil society but by its capacity to rely upon the *consent* of the members of society so as to provide *both* order and liberty. Locke's position stems from a somewhat more benign view of the state of nature, which causes him to reject the Hobbesian belief that the preservation of order is a higher value than the protection of liberty.

The question for scholars interested in this particular aspect of the state and the issue of state-building is the following: should the strength of the state be understood in terms of the development of *institutional struc-tures* associated with the coercive apparatus of the state (police, military, etc.) or in terms of *limitations* upon those coercive capabilities designed to allow for the existence of legitimate, albeit limited, government based upon popular consent alongside a thriving civil society (non-governmental organizations and forms of association) operating beyond the purview of the government?

In a view which harkened back to Locke's emphasis upon the impor-tance of civil society and the notion that effective governance requires legit-imacy, which can only come from the consent of the governed, Alexis de Tocqueville argued in *The Old Regime and the French Revolution* against the widely held notion that French monarchical absolutism represented a strong state because of its capacity for coercion while British constitutional monarchism represented a weak state because of its relative lack of coer-cive instruments available to the state thereby causing it to place a much greater reliance upon consent in order to achieve its objectives.[1]

In its contemporary form, this issue of state-society relations and the question of strong versus weak states can also be approached from a some-what different angle: the problem of state collapse. Based upon the experi-ence of several post-colonial African states, I. William Zartman comes to a conclusion similar to that of Tocqueville. Building upon the idea that government requires legitimacy in the form of consent in order to be effec-tive and that an excessive reliance upon force or coercion is a sign of state *weakness* rather than strength, Zartman sees the reliance upon state coer-cion in many post-colonial African states as both a cause and an effect of state collapse.

His argument is that state collapse occurs as the leaders of a state are forced to rely upon increasing levels of repression in order to maintain con-trol in a period during which they have lost the ability to satisfy the demands of various segments within society. According to Zartman, this results in the loss of legitimacy for the government as those whose demands remain unmet withdraw their support for the regime and perhaps the state itself. In this atmosphere, the state contracts and begins to rely increasingly upon a core of (oftentimes ethnic) supporters and the spiral of repression escalates. In the end, the government is no longer able to maintain control without the support of the population causing the regime to implode. At the same time, its sustained use of repression against the population either destroys or prevents the emergence of a civil society, which Zartman maintains is neces-sary as the foundation for legitimate authority and effective governance.[2]

Whereas both Tocqueville and Zartman as well as many other schol-ars maintain that societal support is crucial to state strength, some scholars have come to a very different conclusion—one which emphasizes coercion over consent in a manner reminiscent of Thomas Hobbes. Among these, one finds such scholars as Charles Tilly and Gabriel Ardant. As Karen Barkey and Sunita Parikh explain, this opposing view maintains that state strength is not a function of the state's ability to acquire the consent of society but is rather a function of the degree to which the state is able to separate itself from society and dominate it. The focus is upon the coercive capabilities of the state and maintains that in order for the state to extract the resources necessary to engage in state-building, it must first exist apart from society. Only then can the state utilize its coercive instruments in order to dominate society so as to compel it to serve the interests of would-be state-builders.[3]

As this discussion illustrates, a major problem with the entire concept of strong and weak states is the confusion which results from the existence of competing definitions. Without a common frame of reference, the appearance of scholarly disagreement turns out, upon closer examination, to be nothing more than an argument about semantics. Using the works of three contemporary scholars who have all at one time or another addressed the issue of strong and weak states, Brian L. Job discusses the difficulties that emerge under these conditions, which bring into question the utility of this approach to the study of state-building: "In the course of their works, Caroline Thomas, Barry Buzan, and Joel Migdal regard the 'weak state' as a central explanatory theme. Beneath the surface similarity of their use of the 'weak state' phrase are quite differing assumptions and understandings about the nature of the Third World and its security problems."[4]

One possible solution to this problem would be to de-construct the notion of the state. Rather than thinking of the state as an undifferentiated unit, it might be useful instead to think of it as a work in progress. This, after all, is what the whole notion of state-building is all about. By converting the idea of the state from a noun (the state as a static entity or unit) into a verb (the state as evolving process), it might be argued that the discrepancy between those in what I have termed the "Lockean" consensual/civil society tradition and those in the "Hobbesian" coercive/institutional tradition is more apparent than real.

In order to reconcile these seemingly incompatible traditions, it is necessary to identify different phases of the state-building enterprise. It is then possible to compare and contrast them in terms of the relative importance which should be attached to the development of coercive institutions or to the development of a civil society capable of operating outside of government while still consenting to the authority of governmental institutions. In this view, the earliest stages of the state-building process are consumed with the issues of establishing territorial boundaries and consolidating power in the hands of a single individual or institution. At a later stage in the state-building process, however, as Ian Lustick points out in his book *Unsettled States, Disputed Lands*, the boundaries of the state have been established and institutionalized to such a degree as to enjoy widespread legitimacy and to be largely beyond contention. In this later stage, would-be rival state makers have been effectively neutralized or eliminated such that *leadership* of the state may be contested but the *legitimacy* of the state itself is beyond question.

Based upon this discussion, it can be argued that the strength of a state in the earlier period is primarily dependent upon coercion as a way to establish the territorial parameters of the state and to forge a consensus regarding the identity of the state within which a diversity of political ideas can effectively develop. At a later point in the state-building process, however, the strength of the state depends primarily upon the sort of societal consent associated with such democratic ideas as political mobilization and popular participation.

The question then becomes one of trying to understand how this transition to democracy takes place. In other words, how does the strength of the state come to be associated with consent rather than coercion? This issue, discussed below in greater detail, is central to the works of Barrington Moore and Bruce D. Porter. For the moment, however, the important point is that the intellectual confusion concerning the issue of strong versus weak states may not be over the meaning of "strong" or "weak" states but rather a result of the failure to distinguish between different *developmental stages* of the state-building process—each of which contains its own particular requirements for governing.

STATE VIABILITY: NORMATIVE AND EMPIRICAL CONSIDERATIONS

Yet another point of departure for those interested in the issue of state-building concerns the existential question of stateness itself. At issue here is nothing less than the question: when and how does a state become a state? This question involves a rather lively debate concerning the relative importance of normative and empirical considerations in the development of statehood. At issue in this debate are two sets of questions: Can empirical phenomena related to state-building be discussed apart from their normative implications? If the empirical and the normative can be separated, what is the role that international norms and values play in the creation and preservation of states as distinct from internal developmental processes such as the building of political institutions and the creation of an economic infrastructure—both of which are associated with the functioning of a viable state?

In his discussion of the state-building process, Mark Kesselman touches upon a very old dilemma in social science research: the debate between normativists and positivists over the question of whether it is possible and/or desirable to separate the "is" from the "ought" so as to engage in value-free social science. In his critique of *Political Order in Changing Societies* by Samuel Huntington and *Crises and Sequences in Political Development* by Leonard Binder, Kesselman chastises these authors for concealing a normative bias in favor of those in power under the guise of value-free social science research into the state-building process. Reserving his strongest criticism for Huntington's emphasis upon political order and political decay, Kesselman argues that it is misleading to talk about political order as if it were an objective, neutral concept. Instead, he suggests that a discussion of order or decay within the state cannot take place in the abstract. It also must take into consideration the *type* of state for this is a crucial variable in understanding both different types of order or decay as well as whether the sources are to be found in the rulers or the governed.[5]

Whereas Kesselman argues that the "is" and the "ought" cannot be separated in politics, Robert H. Jackson and Carl G. Rosberg expressly deal with the normative aspects of state-building by drawing a rather sharp distinction between what they have described as the "juridical" and "empirical" aspects of statehood.[6] Of particular interest to them is the importance for the preservation and/or breakup of existing states of *de jure* normative factors (including external norms of state sovereignty, territorial integrity, and nonintervention in domestic affairs) generated by international society as opposed to *de facto* empirical factors, which include economic development, the presence of an integrated and stable community, and the development of effective institutions.

To be sure, this is not exactly the same issue that concerns Kesselman. Whereas he is focused upon the issue of regime type, they are interested in the role that international norms play in the preservation of otherwise nonviable states. Nevertheless, Jackson and Rosberg do make it quite clear that values or norms can be (indeed in their view ought to be!) separated from empirical processes as a way to understand the continued existence of these states. While interested in the impact of the juridical upon the empirical, the fact that they distinguish between the two indicates that they believe that it is possible to discuss them separately.

Jackson and Rosberg argue that the juridical aspects of statehood are indispensable to an understanding of the preservation of post-colonial states particularly in Africa. Rejecting what they see as a bias in favor of empirical statehood on the part of scholars such as Max Weber and David Easton because it represents too narrow a definition of statehood, Jackson and Rosberg argue for an appreciation of the importance of international norms to an understanding of the preservation of states which lack the internal capabilities necessary to be self-sustaining.[7]

From their perspective, the introduction of the issue of international norms is not merely a supplement to a discussion of the internal requirements for building effective states. Rather, they argue that since the path to state formation was different in Africa from that of Western Europe, priority should be given to the juridical over the empirical in the study of post-colonial state-building.[8]

One of the ironies identified by Jackson and Rosberg is that the concept of juridical statehood is not only essential to an explanation of the *preservation* of so-called weak states, which would otherwise disappear, but also has played a crucial role in the *perpetuation* of state weakness. International guarantees of the continued existence of weak states, which thereby prevents their disappearance, has made it unnecessary for these states to develop the empirical attributes of statehood normally associated with strong states. As a consequence of this process, Jackson and Rosberg argue that these states continue to exist but without ever developing the internal capacity to govern or the external capacity to defend themselves.

Mohammed Ayoob explores some of the implications of this distinction between juridical and empirical statehood as it relates to post-colonial states. Whereas Jackson and Rosberg utilize this distinction between empirical and juridical statehood primarily in order to understand the preservation of *weak states*, Ayoob picks up the argument and focuses upon the perpetuation of *state weakness*. The problems faced by would-be state makers in post-colonial states as they attempt to develop strong states while confronting an international environment whose norms tend to perpetuate state weakness by undermining the efforts to acquire the empirical attributes of statehood are the essence of what he terms the "Third World security predicament."[9]

A similar pattern to that described by Ayoob also can be observed in the post-Cold War collapse of formerly communist federal states, in which the oftentimes arbitrary nature of internal boundaries was the functional equivalent of the earlier colonial experience with boundaries. As was true of the colonial possessions of the former imperial powers, these internal administrative boundaries generally did not follow demographic patterns. Indeed, in some cases, notably Titoist Yugoslavia, there was a deliberate effort to draw federal boundaries in such a manner as to prevent the emergence of ethnic homogeneity within the republics. While this strategy may have made sense in the context of the federal union by weakening centrifugal forces within the polyglot state, it proved to be disastrous once the federal republic dissolved into its component republics. As was true of post-colonial states following independence, the formerly federal communist states of Yugoslavia and the Soviet Union experienced ethnic conflicts when heretofore *internal* administrative boundaries were converted into *international* boundaries despite the quite different functions these two types of boundaries serve.[10]

From this discussion, it is possible to extrapolate that ethnic conflict up to, and including, genocide in a post-Cold War era in which, as Ayoob points out, the norms of juridical sovereignty have begun to weaken are producing ethnically compact and homogeneous states in place of the previously unstable multi-ethnic, post-colonial or post-communist states.

Milica Bookman offers qualified support for this notion of the role of ethnic conflict in the creation of more stable homogeneous states. While recognizing the potential for future instability if the expelled population continues to harbor dreams of returning home, there are cases in which expulsion has resulted in greater stability thereby enhancing the empirical aspects of statehood.[11]

Bookman's approach to state-building stands in marked contrast to that adopted by Jackson and Rosberg. Whereas they place a greater emphasis upon the issue of juridical statehood than its empirical counterpart in the case of post-colonial states due to the fact that for these states juridical norms concerning statehood preceded the empirical basis of statehood and have served to maintain otherwise non-viable states, Bookman's argument would appear to be that in the case of both post-colonial states and certain heterogeneous post-communist states, the internal dynamics of empirical statehood may be overtaking juridical statehood in the post-Cold War era. In this regard, my own thesis is closer to that offered by Bookman.

Since the juridical states created during the decolonization process lacked the empirical requirements associated with state capacity, the notion of moving from the juridical to the empirical also contains within it the possibility that, in the process, the superstructure of juridical norms associated with statehood will undergo a transformation causing the underlying basis of statehood to be changed. As such, the normative basis of statehood will change from that of an earlier era.

J. Samuel Barkin and Bruce Cronin tend to view the relationship between international norms and statehood in this fashion. Whereas Jackson and Rosberg focus on the issue of juridical sovereignty in terms of continuity and the preservative effects of international norms on otherwise non-viable states, Barkin and Cronin conceptualize the international norm of sovereignty differently. As they see it, sovereignty is best understood as a *variable*. According to this view, the international community vacillates between two different sets of norms concerning the issue of sovereignty. One set favors the *state* and the other gives priority to the *nation*. Consequently, rather than looking at state-building as a continuous process beginning in Europe and extending to the rest of the globe the way Jackson and Rosberg do, Barkin and Cronin inquire into the nature of this process. They find significant discontinuities concerning the specific form or nature of the state-building process which reflect the prevailing set of norms during a given historical period. In other words, the notion of "sovereignty as a variable" means that states will look very different during periods which view legitimacy in terms of the norm of *state* sovereignty than they will during periods which favor the norm of *national* sovereignty.[12]

This notion of sovereignty as a variable serves as an interesting extension to the work done by Jackson and Rosberg. In contrast to the view that the role of international norms is to preserve states, particularly those states which would otherwise collapse, Barkin and Cronin appear to suggest that if sovereignty is viewed as a variable, it might just as well *undermine* as preserve existing states. Indeed, if one accepts the premise that the norm of *national* sovereignty has replaced the norm of *state* sovereignty in the post-Cold War era, it might be argued that this normative shift has removed the juridical supports which helped to preserve otherwise nonviable states. In accordance with the argument by Cronin and Barkin concerning the preference given to *national* independence over territorial integrity, one would expect that weak states will either develop the empirical capacity to maintain their existence in the face of both internal and external challenges or they will go the way of so many other failed states throughout history. Either these heterogeneous states will breakup into smaller entities based upon national identity or they will disappear through absorption into other more powerful states.

One problem with the thesis of Cronin and Barkin, however, is their failure to develop a clear and consistent theory which can account for the changes which occur in international norms. On the one hand, their work seems to resemble those in the field of international relations theory known as power transition theorists. One such scholar, Robert Gilpin, argues in *War and Change*, for example, that world order undergoes transformations as a direct result of systemic wars. In some respects, there are also similarities to regime theorists, who argue that international regimes are the institutionalization of the values of the most powerful, hegemonic state(s).[13]

On the other hand, Cronin and Barkin point to concessions being made to the demands of ethnic minorities in countries which were part of the winning coalition during the Cold War, e.g. Belgium, Canada, and Spain, in order to specifically reject the notion that changes in international norms can be explained using the power politics model.[14]

The notion of sovereignty as a variable opens up other possible issues as well. Instead of thinking of sovereignty in terms of such qualifiers as territorial or national sovereignty, it also can be thought of in terms of the expansion or contraction of the legitimate sphere of activity. During periods of expansion, state sovereignty would preclude outside intervention in a state's domestic affairs. At such moments, issues such as ethnic conflict or human rights violations, perhaps even up to and including genocide, would come under the heading of the norm of noninterference in the domestic affairs of states. During other periods, however, in which the notion of state sovereignty undergoes contraction, this concept would not be understood as a shield against external intervention in domestic affairs. Another way of putting this is that the scope of domestic affairs would be narrowed during periods of contraction.

Along these same lines, Thomas G. Weiss, David P. Forsythe, and Roger A. Coate address the issue of the changing nature of sovereignty as it relates to this point concerning outside intervention in the internal affairs of states. In so doing, they implicitly build upon the argument by Cronin and Barkin that sovereignty is a variable and suggest that in more recent times, the scope of state sovereignty has undergone contraction. This argument forms the basis for their support for a more assertive role by institutions such as the UN, as well as other unspecified forms of multilateral intervention, in areas which previously would have been considered to be violations of state sovereignty and, therefore, beyond the scope of international action.[15] This issue of intervention will be dealt with in greater detail in the next chapter.

POWER POLITICS: THE ROLE OF VIOLENCE IN STATE-BUILDING

In contrast to those scholars who place a greater emphasis upon the role that normative issues play both domestically (democratic, authoritarian, totalitarian, etc. regimes) and internationally (juridical concepts such as sovereignty) as it relates to the issue of state-building, other scholars emphasize the role of power politics in the development of states. These scholars are very much in the tradition of political theorists such as Hobbes and Machiavelli.

Within this area of the state-building literature, two distinct scholarly approaches can be identified. One treats the state as an abstract, undifferentiated entity and focuses upon the existential issues of how a state comes into existence and how would-be state-makers use violence to accumulate or centralize power. Among those who adopt this approach are Youssef Cohen, Brian R. Young, and A.F.K. Organski as well as Charles Tilly, Barry Buzan, and, to some extent, Mohammed Ayoob.

A second scholarly approach to the relationship between violence and state-building regards the state not as an entity but, to paraphrase Cronin's and Barkin's description of sovereignty, as a variable. Here the concern is not with existential questions of how a state is created or how the central government goes about accumulating power from those at the periphery but with the factors responsible for political development along a trajectory leading to any of a variety of different forms of government. Of particular interest is the role that violence plays in the process commonly referred to as democratization. Among those who have focused their attention upon this aspect of state-building are Barrington Moore and Bruce D. Porter.

While some scholars, such as I. William Zartman, view the violence associated with contemporary civil wars in Africa as evidence of state contraction and ultimately collapse, others sound a note of caution. In contrast to Zartman, Cohen, Young, and Organski argue for taking a longer view of history. They point out that while the violence in Europe during the sixteenth- and seventeenth centuries was doubtless seen by some at the time as evidence of political decay and collapse, as in the case of the Holy Roman Empire following the Thirty Years' War, it needs to be remembered that the terrible violence associated with this war and the destruction of the Holy Roman Empire also ushered in the modern states system through the Peace of Westphalia in 1648.[16]

Bruce D. Porter takes the argument a step further. He argues that the experience of medieval Europe points to the fact that both external and civil wars had an integral role to play in the building of states. In order for governments to mobilize the resources necessary to wage either aggressive or defensive wars, it was necessary to centralize political power. Such efforts, however, inevitably produced resistance from either regional power centers or from certain social classes, such as the peasantry and the bourgeoisie, resulting in civil wars.[17] In his view, these civil wars were actually part of the process of state formation rather than state collapse as they served to overcome the fragmentation of medieval European feudal societies: " . . . civil wars played an equally crucial role in shaping states. By triumphing in civil wars, central governments established their authority and asserted the all-critical monopoly on violent force that Max Weber identified as the essence of the modern state."[18]

In contrast, then, to those who view civil wars as evidence of state collapse, Porter's argument raises an interesting question, which goes to the very heart of the present study: if civil wars play a crucial role in the state-building process, as they did in Europe, then does external intervention in the form of peacekeeping or peace enforcement in contemporary ethnic civil wars interfere with the creation of viable states?

In this regard, the case of the American Civil War may be instructive as it offers an actual historical example of just this sort of cruel, but very real, dilemma. As Porter argues persuasively, the Civil War was a pivotal event in the development of the United States, which settled by force an issue which had long threatened the continued existence of the country in terms of its territorial integrity.[19]

Given the humanitarian imperative to put an end to a war which already had become tremendously costly in the number of lives lost as well as the economic incentive for manufacturing countries such as Great Britain to intervene on the side of the agrarian Confederacy, (or, at the very least, to interpose themselves between the belligerents in a manner analogous to contemporary peacekeeping forces) and the fact that this very nearly did occur, one can only ponder what such a hypothetical action would have meant for the future development of the United States.[20]

In all likelihood, the preservation of the Confederacy through an imposed cessation of the fighting would have meant that the issues which gave rise to the conflict in the first place, including the question of states' rights and the moral issue of slavery, would have remained unresolved. In addition, the United States would have been a very different, and in all probability far less powerful or wealthy, country from that which exists today. It also seems likely that slavery would not have ended when it did, if at all. Thus, untold numbers of individuals would have continued to suffer miserably from this egregious institution.

Such a provocative hypothetical gives one reason to pause for a moment before assessing the moral calculus by which humanitarian considerations are weighed against considerations of state-building. It is just this sort of attempt to weigh these considerations which will occupy a sizeable portion of the theoretical and empirical parts of this study.

Further complicating this issue is the fact that not all humanitarian considerations point to the same conclusion. For example, how does one weigh the moral imperative to save lives against the moral imperative to end slavery if the only way to end slavery is at the cost of continued bloodshed? In other words, should a war which serves a humanitarian purpose be allowed to proceed uninterrupted even though it will undoubtedly cost additional lives? Conversely, somewhat reminiscent of the notion of a just war theory, are all wars, by definition, inhumane because of the loss of life regardless of the purposes for which those lives are lost? If so, is intervention to stop the fighting before a military resolution of the conflict can occur a humanitarian imperative no matter the consequences in terms of the peace? By what standard is this decision made? Who gets to make such a decision and under what authority?

Likewise, the notion that humanitarian considerations represent categorical imperatives or moral absolutes is a further complication which fails to consider the contextual nature of most issues. To understand this, one can look at the issue of so-called "ethnic cleansing." While the UN condemned as a violation of humanitarian norms and international human rights law the practice of forcibly removing individuals from territory merely because the identity and loyalties of those individuals might pose a threat to the establishment of territorial control over areas in the former Yugoslavia, it also has called for the dismantling of Israeli settlements in areas beyond the so-called "Green Line" claimed by the Palestinians on the grounds that such settlements are "illegal" and constitute an impediment to the development of a future Palestinian state. Assuming, given the emotional nature of this issue, such settlers refused to leave voluntarily, their removal would require the use of force.[21] Since these settlers would be removed from the disputed territories because of their identity as "Jews" or "Israelis" and because of the notion that the presence of such individuals, whose loyalty would undoubtedly be to Israel rather than Palestine, is incompatible with Palestinian state-building, the forcible removal of these individuals would appear to fit the definition of "ethnic cleansing." Clearly, it would be a case of removing individuals because of their ethnic/national identity in order to facilitate the creation of an ethnically homogeneous (in this case, Palestinian Arab) state. Yet, at least in this instance, the members of the so-called international community have shown a decided preference for the issue of state-building by the Palestinians even if it comes at the expense of the so-called humanitarian imperative of preventing "ethnic cleansing."

Thus, this discussion illustrates two important points. First, humanitarian considerations are complex and rarely unidirectional. Second, regardless of where one's sympathies may lie in either the Yugoslav or Israeli/Palestinian cases, it certainly would appear that the notion that humanitarian considerations always do, or even always should, take precedence over other considerations including the building of states is far less clear than many advocates of intervention in the name of humanitarian principles perhaps would care to admit.

Returning to the issue of the relationship between violence and state-building, many of the theories of violent state formation discussed in this chapter are built largely upon Charles Tilly's seminal work on the subject of early Western European state-building, *The Formation of National States in Western Europe*. Tilly lays out a theory of the relationship between war and the building of states which emphasizes the role of coercion in the extraction of resources from a reluctant population. As he sees it, the state-building enterprise consists of a cyclical process of coercion leading to extraction of resources from the population which, in turn, fuels the expansion of the coercive apparatus (the military). The ability to finance this military capability enables state-makers to use it to wage wars of territorial conquest and expansion. These wars, in turn, make available even more economic resources, which are extracted from an even larger population of unwilling subjects. In this fashion, the process feeds upon itself. The only limitations are the inability of state-makers to extract resources from the population due to insufficient coercive capacity or their inability to continue territorial expansion through conquest due to the presence of other would-be state-makers capable of defending their own territorial possessions. Thus, state-building has both an internal and an external dimension to it: externally, it concerns the expansion of territory through conquest; internally, it involves the ability to control the population so as to facilitate the extraction of economic resources. Frequently, this entailed the forcible suppression of oftentimes stiff resistance. The conclusion to be drawn from this historical experience is summarized in the following phrase: "War made the state and the state made war."[22]

Unlike Tilly, Porter focuses *primarily* upon the *external* dimension as it related to the European experience with violent state-building. In the process, he demonstrates that an important part of this endeavor was the forcible consolidation of numerous territories into an ever-smaller number of larger states. He points out that between the fourteenth and the twentieth centuries, the number of "political entities"[23] in Europe went from approximately one thousand to a mere twenty five.[24] Citing no less an authority than Ernest Renan, Porter makes clear that this process of consolidation was accomplished largely by force: "Unity is always realized by brute force."[25]

Conspicuous by its absence from this scholarly approach to state-building is any discussion of values or norms. Thus, there is no discussion of either the type of state created or the principles of international law governing the behavior of states. This sort of "Hobbesian" war of each against all (or perhaps "Spencerian" Social Darwinist survival of the fittest approach to state-building would be a more apt description) free from any normative constraints governing either internal or external conduct is a function of the fact that the Western European experience was without precedent and, therefore, there were no models to guide behavior. Tilly, for example, argues that unlike the situation confronting later state-builders in Central or Eastern Europe or elsewhere around the world, the rules of international society developed *simultaneously* with the building of states in Western Europe. This, for him, is a critical difference between the earlier and later state-building experiences and raises questions about the relevance of the earlier experience as a guide to more recent efforts to construct states.

THE RELEVANCE OF CONTEMPORARY CONFLICTS

While there is widespread agreement among scholars within what have been described here as the "Hobbesian" state-building tradition that the emphasis should be upon conflict and power politics as the arbiter of competing efforts by would-be state makers, Cohen, Brown, and Organski take the argument a step further. In so doing, they enter an area which is far more controversial. They go on to suggest that while the circumstances are not exactly the same in the modern era as those which existed in medieval Europe, there are enough similarities between the two situations to warrant a comparison. In their view, the violence associated with monarchs seeking to centralize power at the expense of the nobility and the violence used by modern state governments seeking to concentrate power at the expense of ethnic, tribal, or religious groups on the periphery in newer states both speak to the same *underlying logic* related to the process of building states through the accumulation of power at the center.[26]

It needs to be acknowledged that one difficulty which this type of argument (as well as the one I will be making in *Part II*) faces is the problem of reasoning ex post facto. Since we can only see the transition to some form of political order *after the fact*, the usefulness of the theory is problematic when dealing with contemporary cases of disorder, which may or may not lead to the same result as that which occurred in Europe.

To say that a difficulty exists with this type of argument is not, however, to suggest that the problem is necessarily insurmountable. It merely means that one must rely upon the use of analogous reasoning. The challenge is that all analogies are imperfect and contain both points of similarity and difference. The critical question is whether the points of similarity are more significant than the areas in which differences exist.

As has been alluded to already in the discussion of Tilly's approach to state-building, this question of whether historical parallels can and should be drawn between the violent upheavals in medieval Europe and the ethnic violence experienced by contemporary post-colonial or post-communist states in terms of the issue of state-building is a crucial one. At issue is the question of whether a study of some past set of circumstances represents little more than an exercise in intellectual curiosity aimed at understanding some unique event or, conversely, represents an attempt to build a more general theory which can be applied to a wider set of phenomena including a wider range of contemporary fact situations.

In terms of the particular question at hand, there appears to be disagreement within the literature as to the applicability for the rest of the world of state-building models based upon the experience of Western Europe. Some scholars maintain that the two situations, while not identical, are sufficiently analogous to warrant the conclusion that the violence experienced in the contemporary era is an integral part of the process of the formation of states in general just as it was during the earlier period of European state formation. For others, the political and economic contexts at the various points in time at which various states enter the international system are so vastly different from each other that it would be both a gross oversimplification and completely misleading to suggest that the violence experienced by newer states is an example of the same historical process which the earliest states experienced.

Similar to the argument by Cohen, Brown and Organski, Barry Buzan claims that the violence occurring in Third World states resembles the violence which took place in the early stages of European state formation: "Because they are still in the early stages of the attempt to consolidate themselves as state-nations, domestic violence is endemic in such states. Under these circumstances, *violence is as likely to be a sign of the accumulation of central state power as it is to be a symptom of political decay* [italics added]."[27]

On the other hand, Charles Tilly appears to equivocate on this crucial point. At times, he clearly states that the European experience was unique: "The European state-building experiences will not repeat themselves in new states. The connections of the new states to the rest of the world have changed too much."[28] In particular, he suggests, in a manner reminiscent of Jackson's and Rosberg's notion of "juridical statehood," that military conquest no longer plays a major role in the state-building process.[29]

Based on such remarks, Peter H. Merkl concludes: "Charles Tilly emphatically contends that the European situation was unique and has little relevance for the developing countries of today. The various current theories of political development from A.F.K. Organski to Samuel P. Huntington come in for some penetrating criticisms as 'unhistorical,' unsequential, retrospective, prescriptive, and rarely aware enough of European history prior to the 19th century."[30]

At the same time, however, Tilly provides evidence that would suggest that he did not intend to take so emphatic a position on this issue. It is true that he does claim that the Western European experience was unique. Yet, in what appears to be a curious reversal from his previously stated position, he then suggests that a study of the earlier European experience is useful for understanding contemporary state-building in newer states. Even more curious is the reason offered. He suggests certain historical parallels in their respective state-building experiences including the role of the military in this process. This despite the fact that he had just rejected the notion that the military plays the same role in the state-building process for the newer states as in the earlier epoch: "The profundity of all these changes might make worthless any inference whatsoever from European experience to today's world. The authors of this volume take a slightly more sanguine view of the matter . . . There appears, for example, to be a strong and general connection between the ultimate bulk of national governments and the extent of their reliance on land armies in their formative periods."[31]

Although at times seeming to contradict himself, it appears that Tilly's ambivalence is an attempt to salvage something from the past which may be useable in the present. He suggests that there are three possible ways in which the early Western European experience may be relevant: the first is that contemporary theories build upon the experience of this earlier epoch; the second is the fact that Europeans are largely responsible for creating the international system, which serves as the context within which contemporary state-building occurs; and finally, the third concerns the way(s) in which certain variables, such as the costs of maintaining the armed forces and the extent of the apparatus or means for extracting resources from the population, are related to one another.[32]

While still not prepared to rule out entirely any relationship between the past and the present, Tilly's colleague, Stein Rokkan, takes a more emphatic position against the idea that contemporary state-building reflects the same patterns as those experienced in Western Europe. Focusing upon the related issues of state- and nation-building instead of the role of coercion, extraction, and conquest, he detects significant differences between earlier and later state-building experiences: "We shall then proceed to compare the typical Western European configurations with those of other regions of the world and try to pin down the *decisive contrasts between the early conditions for state- and nation-building and the conditions for the late-comers of the postcolonial era*."[33] In order to accomplish this, he conceptualizes state- and nation-building in four distinct phases: *Phase I* consists of political, economic, and cultural unification; *Phase II* involves the inclusion of larger sectors of the masses through such devices as conscription and compulsory education; *Phase III* refers to mass participation in the political system; and finally, *Phase IV* involves the growth and expansion of administrative agencies whose purpose is the redistribution of economic resources.[34]

Rokkan argues that whereas in Western Europe these four phases more closely approximate a sequential order, the tendency for these phases to occur closer together or perhaps even concurrently has increased with each successive wave of state formation[35] resulting in what he terms a "cumulation of critical challenges"[36] faced by newer states that was not faced by those in Western Europe. Based upon his analysis of these variations as well as other variables, Rokkan concludes that while contemporary state- and nation-builders may be able to utilize the experience of those who came before, the challenges they face are fundamentally different.[37] Of course, to the extent that one accepts Rokkan's thesis that the experiences are fundamentally different, it remains unclear how these earlier experiences may be utilized by contemporary state- and nation-builders.

Mohammed Ayoob offers a synthesis of many of the views expressed thus far and relates it to the experience of post-colonial states in the Third World. Similar to Buzan, Ayoob views the principal issue confronting these states to be the search for security. He suggests, however, the need for a reformulation of the notion of security beyond the traditional preoccupation of developed Western states with security from external threats. From Ayoob's perspective, the Western approach represents an inadequate description of the security challenges confronting newer states and should be expanded to include the concerns found within these developing states, which involve the need for security against *internal* threats.[38] This issue of internal security is seen as being rooted in the need to build stable states.[39]

Ayoob also agrees with both Tilly and Rokkan that the historical pattern which led to the development of stable states in Western Europe cannot be repeated in newer states because of the existence of the juridical norms identified by Jackson and Rosberg, which did not exist at the time of Western European state formation. In the case of Third World states, however, these norms act to preserve otherwise non-viable states rather than allowing for the sort of exit from the international system which Tilly suggests happened in Western Europe between the 1500s and the 1900s.[40]

He then goes on to combine this difference with Rokkan's notion of a "cumulation of challenges" as it relates to the state- and nation-building processes in the Third World. As Ayoob sees it, the conflation of the state- and nation-building processes forces state-builders in the Third World to confront issues of mass politics not faced by their Western European counterparts at a similar point in their historical development. The critical difference, then, becomes the fact that state makers in the Third World must address the same issues as those faced by state makers in the Western world but without the all-important luxury of time to address them free from outside intervention.[41]

Thus, whereas Tilly and Rokkan both believed that the past could be used as a guide by contemporary state-builders in navigating the challenges confronting them despite the differences between the earlier and later situations, Ayoob sees the lessons of the past as pointing to a seemingly insoluble "security predicament" for Third World states attempting to emulate the West. *At the root of this predicament is the fact that a series of international norms have developed over time alongside the creation and expansion of the European states system. These include such principles as juridical sovereignty and respect for the human rights of the individual. The problem is that these norms both require newer, less developed states to behave the same as fully developed states and, at the same time, deny them the means necessary to accomplish this.*[42]

Further complicating this problem is Ayoob's contention that, in the present international context (which includes the idea that states be democratic and respect human rights as well as various other issues related to the strategic interests of other states), the same sort of coercion which he argues is required as part of the logic of state making is not merely in conflict with other values and considerations but is actually counterproductive to the state-building enterprise itself.[43]

While somewhat less concerned with the specific question of whether past cases of state-building are relevant to the present, Bruce D. Porter and Barrington Moore share Stein Rokkan's interest in the issues of social and political development. Unlike Rokkan, however, they do not explicitly schematize this development in terms of sequential stages. Nevertheless, attention is paid to those aspects of state- and nation-building which, for Rokkan, come under the heading of *Phases II, III,* and *IV.*

Despite this shared interest, however, a major difference from Rokkan's approach is that each in his own way places a much greater emphasis on the issue of violence or warfare in these processes of social and political transformation. As Bruce D. Porter explains, this approach to state formation and political development focuses on " . . . the impact of war on the rise and development of modern states. It is concerned not with what causes war, but with what war causes—with how it affects the internal dynamics, structure, and power of the political systems that wage it."[44]

At the same time, Moore and Porter also differ with each other. The main difference between them is that Moore tends to see the impact of violence as an agent of social change in terms of the removal of social, and primarily economic, obstacles to development. This, in turn, lays the foundation for the eventual creation of one or another type of political system. Porter, on the other hand, tends to be more concerned with the ways in which societies undergo changes internally in response to the military and economic requirements of waging wars. In other words, Moore's neo-Marxian approach to the relationship between social (class) structure and political system tends to be linear and in some ways deterministic such that a given constellation of class relations (which itself is partly a function of the presence or absence of revolutionary violence at the pivotal moment during which society enters the modern world) will almost certainly yield a particular political outcome from among the available options of democracy, fascism, or communism. The point, however, should not be overstated. While particular sets of social arrangements among classes tend to yield particular outcomes, this is not to say that the social class alignments themselves are in any sense pre-determined.

Porter's approach to this issue differs from Moore's in that it is interactive rather than linear. Instead of the state being a product of society the way it is for Moore, both the social structure and the political system are in some sense products of each other. Thus, for example, authoritarian or totalitarian states can have an impact upon society by attempting to dominate civil society through coercion and repression while society can have an impact on at least authoritarian states in the form of demands for representation and political participation during periods of war.

This difference stems in large part from the types of violence which they look at. Moore tends to focus on the impact of internal, revolutionary violence upon the class structure of society as a prerequisite to political change whereas Porter is more interested in the role that the preparation for, and/or actual waging of, external wars plays in restructuring the political system and the relationships between groups within society.

Interestingly, both similarities and differences can be seen here between each of these authors and Charles Tilly. Similar to Tilly, Porter also is concerned with the issue of acquiring the resources necessary to wage war. There is, however, an important difference. Whereas Tilly is interested in the *capacity* of rulers to extract resources from the population as part of the early process of territorial expansion, Porter is more interested in understanding the impact that the *method* of extracting resources has upon society and the political system.

Likewise, Moore also shares certain features with Tilly in that both are interested in the issue of the removal of obstacles or impediments to political development within society. The key difference between them, however, is that Tilly tends to conceptualize these obstacles in terms of resistance by classes or regions to the coercive efforts by would-be state makers to centralize power through the extraction of resources necessary to build an army and engage in conquest; Moore, on the other hand, views these obstacles in class terms as remnants from a feudal past which must be eliminated in order for society to develop along the lines of capitalism and democracy. Failure to do so will result in the rise of either fascism or communism depending upon the particular arrangement of classes in a given society. Thus, for Moore, it is the continuation of obstacles to capitalism which results in some form of centralized dictatorship whereas for Tilly, it is the continuation of obstacles to state makers which impedes centralization.

As indicated in this review of the state-building literature, a central question raised by both Porter and Moore concerns the relationship between violence and the development of democratic political systems. For his part, Porter sees a paradox in the potential for wars of conquest designed to promote territorial coalescence and the accumulation of power at the center at the expense of the periphery (the same sort of state-building process described by several of the authors discussed above) to result instead in decentralization or democratization of political power.

On this point, Porter picks up the discussion where scholars such as Tilly or Cohen, Brown, and Organski leave off in their respective discussions of the centralizing effects of warfare upon the state. Whereas they tend to look at violence simply as part of the natural process of early state formation, he identifies this centralization of political power with specifically authoritarian forms of the state.[45]

He points out, however, that the historical evidence does not always support this conclusion. In fact, as stated above, a key feature of his argument is that, ironically, wars designed to promote territorial coalescence and/or the accumulation of power at the center can, and sometimes do, result in the democratization of the political system. In large measure, this is a function of the need to gain the support of those people whom the rulers depend upon in order to wage these wars.[46] Over time as more limited forms of warfare involving only military combatants have gradually given way to total war involving entire populations, it has become increasingly difficult for rulers of authoritarian societies to continue to deny the very people whom they depend upon for waging war a voice in government.[47]

This discussion recalls Rokkan's description of *Phases II* and *III* of the nation-building process. It will be remembered that for Rokkan, *Phase*

II consisted in part of conscription and *Phase III* of mass politics. Here, Porter is explicitly linking the two processes in a manner which not only treats them as sequences of development but also explains the nature of the connection between them. Mass politics is a direct result of the expanded role of the population as a whole in both the preparation for, and the waging of, modern wars.

Another aspect of this transformation of society, which coincides with the opening up of the political process during periods of war, is the tendency for wars to result in social integration through the breakdown of social barriers between members of different classes. The cooperation from various segments of society necessary in order to wage modern wars makes it increasingly difficult to maintain such class distinctions while people are interacting regularly across such lines.[48]

Finally, again in a manner reminiscent of Rokkan's fourth phase of political development, Porter identifies the role of war as an impetus to the development of social welfare policies.[49]

Whereas Porter equates democratization with the cooperation necessary to wage modern warfare and the resulting political mobilization of the masses in support of greater participation in the decision making processes, Moore takes a different view of the relationship between war and democratization. Focusing upon the underlying class structure of society rather than the need of the rulers for popular support in their pursuit of external wars of conquest, he looks instead at the role played by revolutions and civil wars in the development of democratic societies.[50] The significance of the Puritan Revolution, the French Revolution, and the American Civil War in his view lies in the removal of those classes which act as impediments to the emergence of democratic capitalism.[51]

On one point, however, Moore and Porter appear to be in at least partial agreement. The transformation of society that takes place as part of the movement towards democratization involves the integration of society through the removal of certain social barriers. As indicated above, the precise nature of this transformation and/or its impetus are matters of considerably less agreement.

For Moore, the barriers to be removed are the continued existence of those feudal classes (the aristocracy and the peasantry) which serve as obstacles to the development of the early stages of capitalism. These early stages involve the commercialization of agriculture. So long as these classes effectively resist modernization and persist in their authoritarian social and political patterns, democratization either will not occur or will be very unstable at best. It is only by means of a bourgeois revolution or its equivalent, which either incorporates or destroys the remnants of these feudal classes, that a feudal society can be transformed into a bourgeois society as a prerequisite for the development of a liberal democracy. In other words, in order for capitalism and democracy to develop, the necessary hegemony of the bourgeoisie must entail a leveling of society. This may occur relatively peacefully, as in the case of England, or it may take the form of sudden violent convulsions or "bourgeois revolutions" as in the cases of the French Revolution and the American Civil War.

Even in the case of England, however, Moore suggests that the commonly held belief that the English transition to democracy was a gradual process is misleading in that it overlooks the violent upheavals which preceded this gradual transformation. These consisted of the English Civil War (which broke the power of the king thereby severing his connection with the peasantry as their protector against the continuing encroachments of the market economy into the realm of agriculture) and an alliance between the nobility and the bourgeoisie (in which the nobility essentially joined the bourgeoisie by transforming itself from a landed aristocracy concerned only with produce for consumption into a commercial class interested in the commercial use of agriculture as a market commodity). The result of these two developments was the system of land enclosures, which effectively destroyed the remnants of the peasant base of society by either forcing the peasants off the land or forcing them to adopt bourgeois values by becoming commercial farmers producing for the marketplace rather than for their own and their lord's consumption. In other words, these developments had the cumulative effect of a bourgeois revolution in England in many ways analogous to the more violent and sudden upheavals experienced in France in 1789 or the American Confederacy in the 1860s.

Moore also argues that unless the peasantry is effectively destroyed as a social class, the outcome of a society's political development likely will take the form of either fascism or communism.[52] As evidence, he cites the examples of Germany, Japan, China, and Russia. He goes on to say that if it nevertheless should adopt democratic institutions, such as occurred in India, these likely will be unstable because of the lack of a firm societal foundation for the political system.

Before leaving this discussion of the literature dealing with the violent nature of state-building, one final point that is worth mentioning concerns Moore's rather interesting approach to the issue of violence as it relates to political development and social transformation. Rather than simply describe the violent nature of the transition to democracy and capitalism, he offers what at times seems quite clearly to be an affirmative defense of violence. Reminiscent of Mark Kesselman's critique of Samuel

Huntington, Moore argues that not all violence is the same. One must distinguish between *revolutionary* violence and *repressive* violence by the state. He suggests that too often those who criticize revolutionary violence do so out of either ignorance or a concealed bias in favor of the equal or greater violence perpetrated by those supporting the status quo.

CONCLUSION

As the discussion of the possible beneficial effects of (ethnic) violence in the current study is likely to face similar criticism, it is worth remembering Moore's defense of the role of violence as an agent of change, which includes a discussion of the possible harmful effects which can occur in the absence of such a period of violent upheaval.[53]

One need not agree with everything Moore has argued concerning violence to appreciate his larger point. While, for example, his argument concerning the role of revolutionary violence in communist systems is dubious at best given the repressive nature of the systems created, his larger point concerning violence is worthy of some consideration. This is particularly important given the ongoing policy debates in the post-Cold War era concerning the question of whether to intervene in violent conflicts within states in order to stop the violence. If one reads Moore in a narrow sense, it could be argued that he was talking specifically about revolutionary violence by the oppressed and that this has little to do with the sort of ethnic violence occurring in much of the world. If, however, one understands his reference to violence and social transformation through the removal of obstacles to social and political development in a broader sense, then one must stop to consider whether non-violent changes in society may not actually produce some unintended and disastrous consequences.

Furthermore, as Moore's discussion of violence reminds us, it should be remembered that many of those who criticize the violence occurring in countries around the world today and call for international efforts to prevent these atrocities do so undoubtedly with the best of intentions but also do so from the relative comfort of countries which have already passed through one or more periods of terrible bloodshed on the way to state and national consolidation. Moore's caveat concerning the role of violence in the historical development and transformation of societies and the potential for even greater long-term misery when it is absent is on one level at least a reminder to the reader that to somehow assume that newer countries can simply bypass this terrible phase and instantly set up stable democratic societies which respect human rights may prove to be as ill-advised as it is well-intentioned.

Before moving on to a discussion of the third and final body of literature dealing with the issue of peacekeeping as it relates to internal conflicts, it is worthwhile to take a moment to locate my own thesis within the context of the issues discussed in this chapter.

My own argument that ethnic violence is part of the state-building process in post-colonial states, which serves both to determine the boundaries of the state and to consolidate control within those boundaries represents a synthesis of many of the views expressed in the scholarly literature. In anticipation of the criticism that a theory which addresses the *constructive* role that ethnic violence plays in the state-building process somehow represents a defense of genocide, the first point worth mentioning is that there is nothing new or unusual about a theory which links violence with state-building. Indeed, as this discussion has demonstrated, there is a long tradition in the literature of attempts to do precisely this. Although each author gives to the subject of violence a different nuance, the common theme is this idea that violence is an integral part of the state-building process.

My own theory is concerned with a particular kind of violence—specifically, violence between ethnic groups in post-colonial states. To understand the influence that the literature has had upon my theory, it is helpful to think of the theoretical part of this study as a composite of several related, but distinct, strands of thought. Tilly's idea that war defined the boundaries of the most successful states and Jackson's and Rosberg's idea that juridical norms regarding territorial integrity contributed to the preservation of weak states appear in my theory as the idea that in the post-Cold War era, rival ethnic entrepreneurs struggle to break free of the constraints imposed by post-colonial boundaries, which do not reflect existing demographic patterns of settlement. Ethnic conflict supplants juridical norms as the mechanism by which boundaries are determined and is linked to the idea that boundaries reflect the military capacity to hold and defend territory. Moore's idea that violence can be used as a way to remove obstacles in the path of political development (for him, the remnants of feudal society) merges with the arguments by Tilly, Porter, Ayoob, and Cohen, Brown, and Organski that civil war represents the mechanism by which power is consolidated at the center by repressing resistance at the periphery during state making. Out of this synthesis comes my contention that the creation of viable states requires the removal of impediments to the state-building process. These impediments are rival state makers who resist efforts to centralize power in the much the same way that feudal lords resisted the centralizing efforts of the monarchy in parts of Europe.

Added to this synthesis is the element of ethnicity. In this, I was persuaded by the arguments of those such as Ayoob and Cohen, Brown, and Organski, who saw in contemporary ethnic conflicts in post-colonial states echoes of past struggles to consolidate power within the state. It bears mentioning as well that when this notion of ethnicity is linked with Moore's idea of removing obstacles to political development, the argument which emerges in this study is that so-called "ethnic cleansing" should be understood in terms of the political development of the state.

Finally, as the discussion moves to the issue of peacekeeping, it is worth keeping in mind that my contention that interference with ethnic violence interrupts the state-building process and may produce even worse consequences is adapted from Moore's argument that the absence of a bourgeois revolution can have more serious *long-term*, albeit perhaps less visible, consequences for society than if such a revolution were not to occur. The specific long-term consequences may be different from those identified by Moore; the thrust of the argument, however, is the same.

Chapter Three

The Role of UN Peacekeeping
in Ethnic Conflicts

INTRODUCTION

The idea of peacekeeping as a way to deal with conflict in international politics was an innovation of the UN Security Council rather than a formal instrument of the Charter. Sometimes informally referred to as Chapter Six and a Half so as to indicate that these operations fall somewhere between the peaceful resolution of disputes described in Chapter Six and the more muscular collective security-type enforcement operations envisioned by Chapter Seven, the notion of peacekeeping as conflict containment and management performed an important function in a limited number of hot spots during the Cold War. In an era of often heightened tensions between the superpowers, each of which possessed vast arsenals of nuclear weapons, the possibility that conflicts within states or between states might escalate into a catastrophic global thermonuclear war necessitated some mechanism capable of reducing the likelihood that this would occur. In this poisonous environment, the lack of unity among the Permanent Members of the Security Council all but precluded the possibility of achieving the consensus needed in order to implement the provisions of Chapter Seven. At the time, it was virtually axiomatic that any attempt to put Chapter Seven into effect would likely serve the interests of one but not the other superpower. Consequently, any such resolution by the Security Council would almost certainly be vetoed.

Of course, the one notable exception to this scenario during the Cold War was the Korean War. Approval of a UN operation was made possible, however, only because the Soviet Union was temporarily boycotting the Security Council and the People's Republic of China was not a member of the United Nations at the time.

It should also be remembered that the absence of the Soviet Union and the failure to include the Communist government in Beijing in the decision making process leading up to creation of this enforcement operation virtually guaranteed a bloody and protracted conflict with no clear victor. During the Korean War, Chinese forces battled "UN" (primarily US) forces in a conflict which raised the specter of a possible invasion of China as well as the possibility of intervention by the Soviet Union on the side of the Chinese and the North Koreans. The potential for a nuclear confrontation demonstrated the wisdom of the inclusion by the framers of the Charter of a Security Council veto and the danger of engaging in legalistic maneuvers to take advantage of the Soviet absence in order to approve an enforcement operation.

It is no accident that Chapter Seven was not invoked by the Security Council again until the Iraqi invasion of Kuwait in 1990. It is worth noting that this time both the Soviet Union and the People's Republic of China were present during the decision making and, in the very different atmosphere of the post-Cold War era, gave their consent to the operation against Iraq.

Ironically, the same lack of consensus between the major powers which paralyzed the Security Council also necessitated that it take some sort of action to prevent local or regional proxy wars from spiraling out of control. It is in this context that the idea of peacekeeping was developed as an ad hoc response to specific conflict situations such as those in Palestine, India, the Congo, and Cyprus.

Since peacekeeping operations were designed on a case by case basis in response to local circumstances, the concept itself often defies clarity and precise definition. Under the broad umbrella of "peacekeeping," various operations have been undertaken. These range from unarmed or lightly armed observer missions intended to monitor agreements between belligerents to lightly armed interposition forces designed to separate, and act as a buffer between, warring parties to more heavily armed missions with more robust rules of engagement. This last category approaches what has come to be known as the "peace enforcement" end of the spectrum and is designed to impose a solution on the parties to a conflict.

Despite this wide range of approaches, it would be untrue to say that the notion of peacekeeping lacks any sense of coherence. The underlying logic has always been to end bloodshed and save lives. The divisions of the Cold War ironically created a kind of negative unity of purpose in the mutually perceived need to contain conflicts.

Ironically, the end of these Cold War divisions and the prospect that for the first time in its history a united Security Council would be capable of *asserting* itself and *inserting* itself in conflict situations around the world in ways that were heretofore not possible because of the Cold War exposed instead a lack of clarity as to when, where, and how to respond to the proliferating number of hot spots around the world. The end of bipolarity, and with it the risk that local conflicts might escalate into a global nuclear war, reduced considerably the pressure on the members of the Security Council to intervene in conflict situations. Areas of the world once thought to be of vital strategic importance in a bipolar, zero-sum world, such as the Horn of Africa (or for that matter the entire continent of Africa!), have come to be viewed quite differently by the major powers.

This is not to suggest that there has been a decline in the number of UN operations around the world. On the contrary, they have actually increased since the end of the Cold War along with the rising number of mostly internal conflicts. While the reduced fear of a wider global war has not resulted in a reduction of peacekeeping engagements, it has resulted in a reduced sense of urgency about the necessity to intervene. One consequence of this perceived lack of urgency has been a fundamental re-thinking of the purposes of such engagements for the first time in the history of the organization: Should the enhanced capabilities of a now more unified Security Council be used merely to stop bloodshed by separating belligerents in a manner more akin to traditional peacekeeping operations such as UNFICYP (UN Force in Cyprus)? Should it go beyond this to include securing the provision of humanitarian relief to affected civilian populations even if this is against the wishes of one or more of the belligerents, as in the case of UNOSOM (UN Operation in Somalia)? Should it be used to provide safe havens for targeted civilian populations within a state against the wishes of the host government as in the case of Operation Provide Comfort in northern Iraq? Should it be used to impose solutions on belligerents, by force if necessary, the way that NATO forces did in Kosovo? Should it be used to engage in the longer-term processes of building states and nations by re-building the infrastructure of countries torn apart by war and/or assisting in the development of political institutions and the monitoring of democratic elections such as was done by UNTAC (UN Transitional Authority in Cambodia)? Finally, can the sort of expanded role for UN forces contemplated here be reconciled with such fundamental UN principles as the sovereign equality of states and the provision in Article 2 (7) of the Charter dealing with nonintervention in the domestic affairs of states?

These issues confronting decision makers are reflected in the scholarly literature as well. Although not limited to the post-Cold War period, the literature during this new era has been largely preoccupied with the sorts of questions raised above. This literature reflects a wide range of opinions. At one end of the spectrum are those who argue that the UN can, indeed must, intervene in contemporary conflict situations in ways never before contemplated in order to save lives and uphold basic humanitarian standards. At the other end are those who argue that such intervention, even if well-intentioned (a point which cannot necessarily be assumed according to some critics of intervention), would be counterproductive and, therefore, the UN should allow countries to work out their own problems.

Unlike those who favor non-intervention, those who support intervention have the burden of clarifying the criteria for measuring success: Is a mission successful if it merely manages the conflict and stops the killing even if this means that peacekeeping troops will remain on the ground for an indefinite period or does the success of a mission depend upon its ability to resolve the underlying issues in dispute? Without answers to such questions, the argument for intervention would lapse into incoherence.

Since most of the literature in the post-Cold War era has tended to support the idea of intervention by the UN, it is appropriate to begin with a discussion of the issues raised by these authors before turning to a discussion of dissenting viewpoints.

THE DEFINITION OF SUCCESS IN PEACEKEEPING

At first glance, the issue of defining what constitutes a successful peace-keeping mission would seem to be a rather simple and straightforward one. This deceptively simple question, however, conceals a much more complex issue about the nature of peace itself: Exactly what is the nature of the peace to be kept? On this question, opinions tend to diverge.

Some scholars define peace in purely negative terms as consisting of the *absence of violence*. Peter R. Baehr and Leon Gordenker, for example, suggest that all that is required for a peacekeeping mission to be successful is that it stop the killing: "If the fundamental conflicts remain, perhaps the time gained by peacekeeping and other methods of pacific settlement could ultimately resolve more conflicts. *If not, as* (sic) *least in the short run, human lives have been spared and even more misery avoided* [italics added]."[1] A similar point is made by Joseph R. Rudolph: "Likewise, as Alan James has cautioned, peacekeeping operations should not be assessed solely on the basis of whether the conflict is resolved but also on the degree to which they forestall escalation and otherwise contribute to the preservation of life and property."[2]

Other scholars, however, find this approach less than satisfactory. They define peace in positive or affirmative terms to mean something more than the mere absence of violence. According to this view, true peace also requires a *resolution of the underlying conflict which led to violence in the first place*. These scholars tend to be concerned that the sort of negative peace defended by Baehr and Gordenker among others will result in what Nathan Pelcovits has described as "chronic invalidism."[3] This term refers to the tendency for conflicts to become frozen in place without a resolution once the fighting stops. The assumption is that in the absence of what Zartman has described as a "hurting stalemate," there is no incentive for the parties to address the underlying issues which initially were responsible for the violence.

Consistent with this line of reasoning, William J. Durch raises the question: "Is a mission that keeps foes apart indefinitely a success for having spared them new bloodshed, or a failure for having made them dependent on its presence, for having removed the need to settle old grievances?"[4] A similar concern is expressed by Sally Morphet: " . . . where there has been no fundamental agreement, peacekeeping is more likely to become part of the problem inasmuch as it can provide an excuse not to tackle actual peacemaking."[5]

It is important to point out, however, that this discussion is not intended to suggest that these scholars are against the idea of interposition as a way to manage disputes until a resolution can be found. They are instead pointing out what might be seen as a potential danger inherent in this enterprise.

In an attempt to reconcile the differing views outlined above as to the nature of peace and the role of peacekeeping in conflict situations, Paul F. Diehl offers a third alternative. Instead of viewing conflict management and conflict resolution as antithetical objectives for UN peacekeeping missions, he sees them as representing a continuum. The advantage of his approach is that it avoids the trap of either/or thinking by appreciating the many nuances of this issue. As a result, it allows for the possibility that a mission may be deemed to be *partially* successful: " . . . the first criterion for the success of a given peacekeeping operation is its ability to limit armed conflict between the protagonists. The second is the peacekeeping operation's role in the resolution of the underlying dispute. . . . The *ideal* [italics added] peacekeeping operation is one that is able to prevent or deter fighting during its brief deployment, in the course of which the disputants reach an agreement and no longer need an interposition force."[6] Thus, whereas Durch or Morphet would presumably regard a mission that meets only the first criterion as a failure, Diehl would most likely consider it to be a partial success.

Interestingly, Diehl's approach appears to reject the assumption made by those such as Pelcovits or Zartman that in the absence of sufficient pain, the parties are unlikely to address the sources of the conflict. He seems to suggest instead that a peacekeeping operation may provide the parties to a conflict with a much needed respite from the fighting so that they may settle the outstanding issues between them. If so, then a cessation of hostilities would *promote* rather than hinder a resolution of the conflict.

In addition to the discussion of the purposes for which intervention takes place, there is also an ongoing attempt by scholars to study the experiences of past operations for the purpose of making generalizations about peacekeeping. These generalizations or lessons learned are designed to identify the elements which played a crucial role in the success or failure of previous missions in order to improve the prospects for the success of operations undertaken in the future.

Such an endeavor is not without its own set of difficulties, however. One of these is the rather limited number of peacekeeping operations to date even including those initiated during the post-Cold War era. With such a small sample size, the development of generalizations is extremely hazardous.

Another difficulty is the ad hoc nature of these operations and the range of circumstances they have been designed to address. The danger is that lessons "learned" from one operation may not be applicable to a different situation because they are operating under an entirely different set of circumstances. This problem is similar in certain respects to that which was discussed in the previous chapter concerning the lessons learned from the Western European experience with state-building. Since the conditions of the modern world are radically different from those which existed in the early period of Western European state formation, it is possible to argue that it is not clear that any lessons gleaned from that experience are relevant to the challenges facing post-colonial state makers operating in the post-Cold War era.

Despite these difficulties, however, various scholars have sought to rise to the challenge. One of these is William J. Durch. He argues that past experience suggests that the success of a peacekeeping mission depends upon a variety of factors including, but not limited to, the consent of the parties, the clarity of the mandate, the support of the major powers, and the level of funding for the mission.[7] Implicit in this discussion is his belief that the success or failure of a mission is largely within the control of those who organize and implement the peacekeeping operation itself.

On the other hand, John Mackinlay differs with Durch on this last point. He offers a more pessimistic assessment of the capability of peacekeepers to affect the outcome of their mission. Whereas Durch believes that peacekeepers can influence the chances for success through proper preparation and planning, Mackinlay believes that the role of UN peacekeeping is basically limited to the *avoidance of failure*, which is not quite the same thing as ensuring success. In his view, the success of a mission depends upon the conditions on the ground, which are beyond the control of peacekeepers. If the situation is ripe for a resolution, then the UN can be effective as a facilitator. If not, then there is little the UN can do to affect the outcome.

Mackinlay, however, does not take the position that peacekeepers are completely at the mercy of circumstances. He does believe that peacekeepers can affect the outcome but only in a negative sense. In his view, ineptitude on the part of peacekeepers on the ground can undermine a mission even though the conditions for success are present.[8] Thus, he seems to take the rather strange position that peacekeepers cannot make things better, but they can make them worse.

The problem with this argument is that it represents a kind of semantic sleight of hand. To say that peacekeepers cannot contribute to success but can avoid failure is logically inconsistent. It assumes that a distinction exists between actively contributing to the success of a mission and the more passive form of avoiding mistakes, which might cause the mission to fail. Since the peacekeepers could have made mistakes which would have caused the mission to fail (such as not taking advantage of opportunities presented to them by the belligerents on the ground), it is reasonable to argue that the decision to avoid these mistakes by opting instead to seize the opportunities offered means that they instead have contributed to the success of the mission. Thus, the line between contributing to success and avoiding failure is a semantic distinction without a difference.

Just as there is disagreement between Mackinlay and Durch as to the importance of the role performed by peacekeepers, the question of whether the consent of the belligerents is needed in order for a peacekeeping mission to be successful is another issue which divides scholars. Thomas Weiss, David Forsythe, and Roger Coate challenge the conventional view held by Durch and others that the consent of the parties is a necessary, albeit insufficient, condition for success: "In its newest and most dangerous operations the United Nations needs in some cases to move beyond the consent of the warring parties and to resort to military capabilities that were not available to UN soldiers in the past."[9]

HUMANITARIAN INTERVENTION VERSUS STATE SOVEREIGNTY

Weiss, Forsythe, and Coate raise important questions about the traditional understanding of the idea of state sovereignty. In an effort to elevate the importance of humanitarian concerns, they suggest that the notion that consent is a prerequisite to success is an outgrowth of the traditional Westphalian concept of sovereignty. This concept assumed that one should not intervene in the internal affairs of a state. While this idea may have made sense during the Cold War, when most conflicts were *inter*state and state boundaries were considered to be sacrosanct, they point out that in the post-Cold War era, conflicts are increasingly *intra*state. In these situations, the consent of the parties for such things as humanitarian intervention oftentimes has been difficult to achieve as demonstrated by examples such as Somalia and Bosnia. In cases such as these, the problem is that either there is no government at all capable of consenting or perhaps the extent of the government's control over actual territory is so limited as to render its consent useless. Alternatively, the government itself may be the perpetrator of humanitarian crimes of genocidal proportions against its own population thereby making it extremely unlikely that the government would give its consent to intervention designed to prevent this assault on the population.[10]

Max Boot makes a similar argument, but he takes it even a step further by challenging not only the *practicality* of the Westphalian system of state sovereignty in situations in which there is no effective government but also the *legitimacy* of the underlying assumptions about sovereignty of the Westphalian states system. Interestingly, the crux of his argument is not so much an attack on the idea of sovereignty as it is an argument as to why respect for state sovereignty should not be applied to the artificial boundaries of post-colonial states. Consequently, he suggests that Western powers should have no compunction about violating boundaries which they created in the first place.[11]

This challenge to the concept of sovereignty poses its own set of problems. One of these is the classic issue which was confronted by the OAU (Organization of African Unity now known as the African Union) during decolonization, when it was decided that, however flawed they might be, a challenge to the boundaries inherited from colonialism would unleash a Pandora's box of secessionist claims and internal violence further destabilizing the region.

Critics of the sort of argument made by Boot can point to the potential that this rationale for so-called humanitarian intervention provides for outside mischief. His argument that Western states should not respect "artificially created" boundaries assumes that some boundaries are "natural" while others are "artificial"—a dubious distinction at best. The implication would seem to be that intervention is permissible provided the boundaries of the state are artificial. Given the prior history of colonialism and its various beneficent rationales, this would seem to be a virtual invitation to Western states to return to an unsavory colonial past.

Thomas M. Franck and Nigel S. Rodley illustrate the complexity of the question of whether humanitarian intervention is morally justified by pointing to the discrepancy between the ideal and the reality of historical practice. In their view, the idea of intervention to protect human rights sounds good in theory. Despite the high-minded rhetoric of humanitarian intervention employed ostensibly for the purpose of saving lives and/or securing human rights, however, the problem is that the historical record suggests that such interventions have generally been motivated at least as much, if not more so, by a desire to protect foreign property or to strengthen a social, political, and economic status quo, which favors the external party.[12]

Seemingly anticipating the arguments made by those in favor of humanitarian intervention even if it violates the traditional Westphalian understanding of state sovereignty, Franck and Rodley counter by issuing what amounts to a challenge to supporters of so-called humanitarian intervention to devise some standard by which legitimate interventions can be distinguished from old-fashioned imperialism. In their view, this cannot be done.[13] The point of the challenge, however, is to provide a cautionary reminder of the underlying rationale for the principle of state sovereignty.

While Franck and Rodley believe that such a standard is impossible to create, Jerome Slater and Terry Nardin take up the challenge and seek to do develop just such a standard. They argue that there is a tension between the principle of nonintervention associated with state sovereignty and the need to protect human rights. The former protects national independence, cultural diversity and ensures a level of international restraint, which are all necessary to the maintenance of international order. The latter is designed to protect people against the repressive behavior of their own governments by sanctioning intervention in the most egregious cases while refusing to allow such regimes to hide behind the mantle of territorial sovereignty.[14]

In order to resolve the tension between the logic of preserving sovereignty through nonintervention and the logic of protecting human rights through intervention, Slater and Nardin suggest that certain distinctions must be made. They argue that it is possible to distinguish between a *right* to intervene, which is a moral issue, and a *decision* to intervene, which is a prudential issue. Thus, it is possible to argue that merely because one has the *right* to intervene does not compel one to make that *decision*.

Furthermore, they maintain that another distinction which is important and goes to the issue of the right to intervene concerns the locus of sovereignty. Slater and Nardin contend that sovereignty resides not in some abstraction called the state nor in the rulers but in the people. In effect, rulers exercise sovereign rights *in trust for the people.* Here, we see echoes of John Locke or perhaps Thomas Jefferson. Reminiscent of Locke's social contract theory or perhaps the American Declaration of Independence, they argue that if this trust is abused, the ruler forfeits the legitimacy necessary to continue ruling thereby making intervention legitimate.[15]

Francis M. Deng, Sadikiel Kimaro, Terrence Lyons, Donald Rothchild, and I. William Zartman concur. In *Sovereignty as Responsibility,* they suggest that to treat sovereignty as some sort of absolute principle which insulates the state from all outside intervention rather than as a kind of fiduciary responsibility exercised by governments in trust for their people is a perversion of the original purposes of sovereignty. These purposes were to provide stability and to meet human needs in a way that no other form of organization could. They contend that to understand sovereignty as elevating the state or its leaders above the people confuses the means (the state) with the ends (the satisfaction of human needs as the primary objective of political activity). In their view, this confusion results in the state becoming an end in itself.[16]

They further suggest that those who would claim the rights of sovereignty within the state must do so not only within the context of responsibility for their own people but also within the context of a set of responsibilities to the international community as codified in such instruments of international law as the Universal Declaration of Human Rights. These authors maintain that, for the most part, states do fulfill these obligations on their own or else voluntarily seek assistance from outside sources in those instances in which they have been unable to execute their responsibilities unilaterally.

While this represents the norm, there are, however, exceptions. The argument is that in those comparatively rare instances (many of which involve ethnic conflicts) in which state leaders both fail to meet their responsibilities to their own people and also seek to use what the authors regard as a spurious concept of state sovereignty as a justification for refusing outside assistance, these leaders forfeit their right to legitimacy. As a result, the international community is entitled to intervene by force if necessary.[17]

While Deng and his colleagues appear to offer a set of criteria for humanitarian intervention, which suggests that intervention is not at odds with sovereignty but is designed to promote the purposes for which sovereignty was intended, there are certain problems with their argument and with that of all of those in the interventionist tradition. One of these is that it fails to meet the challenge laid out by Franck and Rodley.

The problem is not merely an abstract matter of moral philosophy involving the question of identifying those circumstances under which humanitarian intervention is justified. Equally, if not more, important is the political question of identifying *who* gets to decide when a breach of human rights has not only occurred but has become so egregious as to warrant outside intervention. The notion that there exists a sovereign responsibility to "the international community" is a clever device which *seems* to identify a locus of decision making in such matters but, in fact, does not do so.

Upon closer examination, this so-called "international community" is arguably nothing more than an abstraction consisting of those acting on behalf of various individual *states*. The problem is, however, that abstractions do not make decisions; actors do. Consequently, the notion that "the international community" has a right to intervene brings us no closer to an understanding of the combination of individual motives and social forces which will influence the decisions of specific actors in the direction of either intervention or non-intervention.

Undoubtedly, one could find cases in which intervention would be warranted. Without an understanding of the factors driving the decision makers, however, the argument by Franck and Rodley that it is impossible to make a useful distinction between genuine humanitarian intervention and colonial domination, which can stand up to empirical scrutiny, deserves serious consideration. Thus, even if it were possible to develop a consensus as to the criteria for intervention (something which even its supporters concede has not yet occurred), there remains the difficult problem of ensuring that those who claim to be acting on behalf of such a consensus are not merely using such claims as an ideological smokescreen designed to conceal foreign policies rooted in expansionist ambitions or other self-interested objectives.

In addition to the difficulty of distinguishing between genuine humanitarian intervention and colonialism (one is reminded of such seemingly high-minded slogans as "the white man's burden" or the "mission civilisatrice" for example), another problem with the arguments in favor of intervention is that of identifying the criteria for determining success or failure. In contrast to Deng and his colleagues or Nardin and Slater, it will be suggested in succeeding chapters of this study that the measure of success should not be the degree to which intervention upholds human rights but rather the degree to which it either contributes to, or interferes with, the creation of stable states capable of self-government.

In making this argument, I am mindful of the criticism by these authors that focusing upon *the state* rather than *the people* confuses the means with the ends. This is a serious argument, and it deserves to be taken seriously. To be sure, the mid-twentieth century experience with fascism demonstrates that there is indeed a danger that focusing upon the state and its interests may result in the elevation of the state into an object of veneration—with all of the potential consequences that this has for state repression and the denial of human rights.

At the same time, however, if one is to avoid the slippery-slope argument, it should be pointed out that to say that such a danger exists is not the same as suggesting that attention to the needs of the state inevitably results in fascism. Indeed, these same authors clearly understand the importance of the state when they suggest that it has a vital role to play as an instrument for the promotion of human rights.

If states are to assume this heavy responsibility identified by the advocates of "sovereignty as responsibility," it follows that they must possess the *capability* to carry out the responsibilities entrusted to them.What happens, however, if a state is still at a relatively early stage in the state-building process, as is often the case with post-colonial states? How can such a state assume the responsibilities entrusted to it?

A rather benign interpretation of the "sovereignty as responsibility" argument would be that it represents a well-intentioned but unreasonable set of demands upon the leaders of nascent states by those whose own states are much further along in the state-building process and who lack an appreciation for the difficulties faced by the leaders of these newer states. A less generous interpretation would see in these rather burdensome expectations the deliberate creation of an impossible set of demands upon newly independent states. These demands can then serve as a pretext for a new form of colonial domination in the guise of forcible "humanitarian intervention."

In addition to the questions raised above, there is one final consideration: what if the sort of intervention without the consent of the host state contemplated by those such as Deng ends up retarding the development of the state's governing capacity by interfering with the internal violence which, as was seen in Chapter Two, is frequently associated with the initial accumulation of state power?

It is at this point that I perceive a difference between my own position and that of those such as Francis Deng. Whereas the authors of *Sovereignty as Responsibility* place relatively little importance on the issue of state-building because of their belief that to do otherwise is to confuse the means with the ends, my own contention is that this omission may end up undermining the argument they have so carefully crafted. In this regard, it should be stated at the outset that there is no disagreement that the state should be understood as a means rather than an end. *The question, however, is how to enable the state to act as a means to the end of what might be described as the general welfare.* On this point, my suspicion is that the argument in favor of allowing members of the international community to *bypass* the state through external intervention without the consent of the host government will prove to be counterproductive. By short-circuiting the violence, which is an essential component of the state-building process, the result will be to further weaken already weak, post-colonial states. In the absence of the capacity for self-governance, states will be unable to fulfill the responsibilities which the advocates of this idea of "sovereignty as responsibility" suggest is the very purpose of the state.

If my thesis is correct, then a decision to intervene will likely result in a different kind of slippery-slope. Intervention designed to promote human rights in states which are trying to consolidate central authority (oftentimes by denying those same human rights) would interfere with the ability of the state to develop the sort of governing capacity generally taken for granted in more developed states. This, in turn, would require continued intervention in order to do for the people of the state what their own crippled government lacks the capacity to do. In short, a vicious cycle is created: *the longer the state remains weak the longer intervention is required in order both to provide services which the central government lacks the capacity to offer and to protect the people from the efforts of their own government to consolidate its authority through the repressive denial of human rights. At the same time, however, the longer the intervention continues the longer the state continues to remain weak.* Thus, the cycle continues to spiral out of control without an end in sight.

CONCLUSION

This brings the discussion back to the "Third World security predicament" identified by Mohammed Ayoob. The essence of this dilemma comes down to the question of whether it is preferable to allow human rights violations in the near-term so as to facilitate the creation of states capable of protecting human rights in the long-term or whether it is preferable to intervene in the immediate situation and perhaps jeopardize the future development of states capable of carrying out their responsibilities to their citizens and to the wider "international community," if such can be said to exist. This fundamental question will be the focus of subsequent chapters and is the reason why it was necessary to engage in such an extensive review of what may be seen as three potentially incompatible bodies of literature. It is hoped that this discussion will offer some scholarly context for the issues to be addressed in this study in greater detail and will assist the reader in locating both the points which this study shares with that literature as well as those points at which it departs from it.

Part II
Theory-Building

Chapter Four
The State-Centric Model and its Critics

INTRODUCTION

The issues raised in *Part I* were designed to serve as a prelude to the development of an integrated theory of the state-building process in the post-Cold War era. In a similar vein, this chapter helps to lay the foundation for the development of my theory by addressing a fundamental issue, which is central to the entire endeavor: in an era of globalization, when many scholars have questioned the continued relevance of the state as the central actor in world politics and others have gone even further to question whether the sovereign states system even has a future, why focus upon the state as the object of study and construct a theory of the state-building process?

Unless it is possible to articulate the reasons for the continued relevance of what is often referred to by International Relations specialists as the state-centric model, the critics of this model would be correct that there is little reason to proceed with the development of a theory of state-building. Conversely, a defense of the state-centric model justifies an inquiry into the factors which influence the building of states and provides a powerful rationale for the need to be attentive to the state-building process even if doing so conflicts with other important values, such as human rights, which may interfere with the creation of states capable of effective self-governance. To act otherwise would be to undermine the fundamental rationale of the state-centric model by weakening the building blocks of that model: sovereign territorial states. Accordingly, this chapter serves as a necessary bridge between the review of the literature and the development of a theory of the state-building process in the post-Cold War world.

To put the matter another way, I take no position on the question of whether the state *should be* the central actor in world politics. To do so would be to enter into the realm of political philosophy rather than political science. As a political scientist, my objective in this chapter (and throughout the entire study) is to carry on in the tradition of Realists, such as John Herz, by identifying what I perceive to be the *what is* rather than the *what ought to be* of politics.[1]

In pursuit of this goal, it is my contention that for the foreseeable future the sovereign state will remain the most important political actor on the world stage. As Kenneth Waltz has argued in *Theory of International Politics*, this is not to suggest that the state is the only actor in global politics but rather that it occupies a central position because it is the most powerful actor. Consequently, it deserves to be treated as the unit of analysis in this study.

As a first step towards the development of a theory of the role that ethnic conflict and peacekeeping/peace enforcement play in the state-building process, this chapter will address the scholarly debate surrounding this very issue of the continuing relevance of the state. During this discussion, I will also make clear my own reasons for supporting the state-centric view.

Building upon this foundation, the next two chapters will explore the impact that various phenomena, most notably ethnic conflict, have had upon the viability of the state. This will lead to the development of a theory of the role that ethnicity and ethnic conflict play in the building of state capacity. The underlying premise for all of this is that a state-centric model presupposes the existence of states capable of effective self-governance, which tends to be at variance with the experience of numerous weak post-colonial states formed as the product of juridical norms. In a world largely consisting of such weak states, there is reason to doubt the notion that the state remains the primary political actor.

Finally, the last chapter in *Part II* relates various types of external intervention in internal (frequently ethnic) conflicts to the broader issue of building viable states. My thesis is that the linkage between ethnic violence and the state-building process suggests that interference with that violence also interferes with the state-building process. In so doing, it not only perpetuates state weakness or possibly state failure and collapse, it also poses a fundamental challenge to the continuity of the states system and its state-centric premise.

It is, therefore, to the issue surrounding the relevance of the state and the Westphalian states system that the discussion now turns.

THE SOVEREIGN STATE: CENTRAL POLITICAL REALITY OR OBSOLETE, ARTIFICIAL ENTITY?

In order for social science to address the matter of the state in a manner which seeks to separate the study of *what is* from the study of *what ought to be,* the first question which must be addressed is whether the state should be understood as a reality with an independent existence from that of the observer or as an abstraction which merely conceals some more fundamental social reality, which is itself a more appropriate subject for study. Only then can one address the issue of whether the state-centric model is correct in treating the state as the central political reality in world politics.

Clearly, the state, or any social phenomenon for that matter, is not real in the same way that one might describe a natural phenomenon as real. One cannot, for example, see or touch a state. If this were to be the measure of reality, then the state is little more than an abstraction manufactured in the minds of individuals. Yet, such a definition of reality would be wholly unsatisfactory. If the state were nothing more than a product of the minds of individuals, one would have only to purge one's mind of any thoughts of the state in order for it to disappear.

Experience suggests that this simply will not do. It is, for example, impossible to transact business or travel across state boundaries without being brought into direct contact with some aspect(s) of this thing called "the state" whether it be in the form of tax collectors, government regulators, or border checkpoints. In this sense, the state is not merely a subjective experience or a reflection of the values or thoughts of any particular individual but is rather a social entity the experience of which is shared by all who encounter it. As such, "the state" becomes a shorthand term for a social organization which exercises ultimate control over a defined territory and population.

In the sense that the state consists of a set of social arrangements or institutions rather than naturally occurring phenomena, it is perhaps to be expected that there would be those who would look at "the state" and question either the validity and/or the continued viability of these institutions especially when confronted with changing circumstances in the global arena. If, therefore, one is to offer an explanation as to why the state as an institution (and more specifically the processes by which it comes into being) remains a legitimate focus of study in the post-Cold War world along with an argument to the effect that these processes are ignored at one's own peril, a good place to begin such a discussion would be with those theories of the state which view it as either obsolete or as some sort of artificial, transient phenomenon. Such theories suggest that the state will be replaced at some future point by an alternative set of social arrangements, which better reflect contemporary conditions.

The issue in this discussion is the proper focus or unit of analysis for the study of world politics. The consequences for political conduct are enormous as the different approaches to the unit of analysis problem operate off of fundamentally different sets of assumptions. Those for whom the state is some sort of ephemeral abstraction, which either conceals or perhaps obstructs the unity of the human race, look instead to the so-called "international (or perhaps *global* would be a more appropriate term) community" as an entity distinct from its component parts. These scholars argue that the international community has both the capacity and the right to act directly upon individuals even if doing so means bypassing the state. It is this capacity and this right of intervention which serve as the basis for viewing states as artificial barriers dividing a wider community and for believing that this wider human community is instead the appropriate unit of analysis.

On the other hand, those, such as this particular author, who view the state as a viable social reality consider the so-called "international community" and its institutions, such as the UN and the IMF, to have no independent existence because the conduct of such institutions actually consists of the actions of individual states acting in concert while retaining their individual prerogatives. Consequently, this so-called community is derived instead from a more fundamental unit—the sovereign state. As a derivative of the state, it, therefore, lacks the capacity or the right to act directly upon individuals. It follows from this that the state would be considered the appropriate unit of analysis for the study and the conduct of international relations. While I have stated my own view on this issue, it is clear that this question remains one in which there is a quite lively scholarly debate especially, although by no means exclusively, in the post-Cold War era. It is to these arguments that the discussion now turns.

THEORETICAL CRITIQUES OF THE STATE-CENTRIC APPROACH TO INTERNATIONAL RELATIONS

For more than a century, scholars representing a wide range of perspectives have wrestled with the existence and persistence of the anarchical, Westphalian states system, in which the principal units are sovereign, territorial states. While the reasons may vary depending upon the particular orientation in question, a point of convergence in many scholarly writings is the belief that the state is an artificial construct. Viewed in this manner, the fragmentation of the world into territorial states poses a serious challenge to what is understood to be either the cosmopolitan ideal and/or the actual underlying reality of the unity of the human race. At the heart of this challenge is the belief that a world of sovereign states existing in an anarchic, egoistic, self-help system is also a world in which the state is elevated above the wider human community as the highest form of political association. Inevitably, such a system generates divergent and often conflicting interests among states as well as a deeply-rooted fear on the part of state leaders that other states may pursue their own interests by force of arms. The result of these conflicting interests, and the systemic insecurity which they produce in a self-help system, is the classic notion of the so-called "security dilemma" often associated with Realist scholars such as John Herz. In such a system, the potential for war is ever-present and, in fact, erupts with an alarming frequency made all the more disturbing by the destructive capacity of modern weapons to annihilate entire population centers.

The cosmopolitan view of the states system as an artificially created division of the human race into territorial units (which only serve to retard the development of species consciousness by concealing the fundamental unity of all human beings) and the linkage often made between the units of this system and war has led to a steady stream of thinkers from virtually every major theoretical approach to the study of global politics who have hypothesized, prognosticated, and/or advocated the demise of the territorial state and, along with it, the Westphalian states system.

Writing more than a century ago, Karl Marx and Friederich Engels were among the earliest to tackle both the existence and the persistence of the state. While by no means a central part of their efforts to understand the relations of production, especially under capitalism, they nevertheless did make the case that the state is an instrument of organized bourgeois coercion and domination over the proletariat. The state also serves to create a vertical form of national association, which cuts across class lines. This vertical association impedes the development of a horizontal worldwide class consciousness on the part of the proletariat because workers in each country remain tied to their own native bourgeoisie and, at the same time, separated from workers in other countries.[2] From a Marxist perspective, however, this is, at best, a delaying tactic in terms of what is considered to be the inevitable proletarian revolution.

As with many aspects of Marx' writings, including those concerning what he considered to be the inevitability of proletarian revolution and the nature of post-capitalist society, he is somewhat unclear as to whether the proletarian revolution will be a single, global phenomenon occurring everywhere simultaneously and spontaneously (a position closer to that held by Marxists such as Rosa Luxembourg or Leon Trotsky) or will occur in a series of episodes as each proletariat deals with its own national bourgeoisie (a position closer to that of Vladimir Lenin and Joseph Stalin, both of whom, especially Stalin, appeared to believe that revolution could occur one country at a time).

While many factors including personal ambitions and internal political circumstances all contributed to the rivalry between Stalin and Trotsky following the death of Lenin, it is also fair to say that the ambiguities in Marx' writings concerning the role of the state in proletarian revolution were an important reason for the theoretical debate within the Marxian camp over the question of whether it was possible to build socialism in one country or whether one needed to export revolution beyond the national frontiers.

Internecine disputes among Marxists over the modalities of proletarian revolution aside, Stanley Hoffmann points out that Marxists do appear to be quite clear and consistent in their belief that, viewed as "superstructures," social categories such as "the state" and "the nation" are essentially irrelevant to the materialist understanding of the historical process. According to this deterministic approach to history, the state as an instrument of organized class domination and as an artificial form of vertical organization which only serves to divide human beings will "wither away" once the fundamental antagonism between the bourgeoisie and the proletariat is overcome in a classless post-capitalist society.[3] Thus, the Marxian notion of a classless society would also appear to be a stateless society (at least in the sense in which Marx defines the state).

In much the same way that Marx' understanding of "class" in terms of relations of production differs from other definitions which emphasize income or social status, however, an objection may be raised at this point as to whether Marx' understanding of "the state" as organized class domination is, in fact, the same as the way this social category is understood in Westphalian terms. The latter generally defines the state as a sovereign territorial unit in an anarchical self-help system. While Hoffmann appears not to make any distinction, the question is crucial inasmuch as the Marxist notion of the state "withering away" may not mean the same thing for Marxist and non-Marxist alike. It is entirely possible, therefore, that in the arcane language of Marxist political theory, the state may "wither away" in the sense of an end to class domination while at the same time, the Westphalian states system continues to function as a political order operating autonomously from the issue of class altogether. Indeed, Richard Adamiak seems to make this very point concerning the place of the state in Marx' *The Communist Manifesto*.[4]

Perhaps the best that can be said is that the prediction of the disappearance of the state is one which is hampered by the all too frequent problem in Marxist literature of vagueness and the propensity towards linguistic equivocation, in which the same word or phrase means different things to different listeners depending upon whether they are operating from a Marxist or non-Marxist set of premises.

Prognostications of the decline or demise of the state are not limited to those within the Marxian tradition, however. Interestingly, although the Realist tradition in international relations is perhaps best known for its reliance upon a state-centric model of the international system as composed of competing state units engaged in a struggle for power, one of the leading Realist thinkers of the mid-twentieth century, John Herz, appears to have had serious misgivings about the continued viability of the territorial state.

Applying Realist principles of power politics, interstate conflict, and the use of military force to an era characterized by the existence of air power and nuclear weapons, Herz initially appeared to anticipate the collapse of the states system. His argument was based upon the notion that the modern state came into existence as a result of the linkage between territory and security for the population. The advent of weapons of mass destruction and mobile delivery systems such as aircraft had, however, rendered the "hard shell" of territory obsolete as a means of providing security.[5]

Although Herz maintains in his article "Rise and Demise of the Territorial State" that he did not intend to convey the impression that he was anticipating the literal demise of the state, he does acknowledge that nevertheless he did appear to suggest that very thing. Whatever his intentions may have been, it is not surprising that this article left that impression when one considers the following: the use of the term "demise" in reference to the state in the title of the article itself; his argument that modern weaponry had rendered the traditional link between territory and security obsolete such that there were no longer territorial dimensions large enough by which the state could provide this security; his argument that the linkage between territory and security had been the reason for the emergence of the modern territorial state in the first place; his call at the end of the article for an end to the classic Realist dichotomy between the categories of "national security" and "internationalist ideals" in response to the changes of the modern era; and finally his suggestion that it was no longer utopian to believe that the world would move towards what he called "an attitude of universalism." At the very least, these indicate that his earlier work was that of an individual deeply ambivalent about the future prospects for the continuity of the state.

In some respects, Herz' examination of the viability of the modern state was a precursor and a specific case of what later came to be known as the idea of "globalization." As Paul Hirst explains, globalization theories focus on various processes which are allegedly undermining the state. In this regard, there is a particular emphasis upon economic and technological changes and their political consequences as expressed in the development of supranational entities.[6]

Gene M. Lyons and Michael Mastanduno agree with Hirst's characterization of globalization theory suggesting that, for adherents of this school, the increasing role of non-governmental organizations in international relations means that the state is no longer the primary actor in international politics.[7]

In his discussion of the concept of what he calls "turbulence" in world politics, James N. Rosenau takes the argument made by globalists a step further by suggesting that the state is being undermined not only from above but also from below.[8]

Rosenau, however, does stop short of predicting the demise of the state suggesting instead that the most likely scenario for the foreseeable future is one of continued instability in world politics. In this unstable situation, both the state and the forces which challenge it will continue to coexist. It is this uneasy coexistence which he describes as "turbulence."

Similar to globalists in their emphasis upon the increasing importance of actors other than the state are liberal institutionalists such as Thomas G. Weiss and Jarat Chopra. While accepting many of the globalist claims about increasing interdependence arising out of developments above and beyond the control or reach of the state and the corresponding effect of these phenomena upon the state, the focus of the argument tends to be somewhat different. Liberal institutionalists draw certain conclusions from the diminution of the state's centrality in terms of an evolution of international norms in favor of such activities as humanitarian intervention within what had previously been considered to be the inviolable domestic affairs of states. They argue that the emergence of humanitarian norms and the expansion of their application over time, and especially since the end of the Cold War, can be detected in the widening of the role played by both intergovernmental and non-governmental international institutions.

From the perspective of this offshoot of Wilsonian liberalism, the key issue is not so much whether states will continue to exist but whether the state can still claim to be sovereign in the manner described by the Westphalian model or whether the world has effectively moved beyond this model. Chopra and Weiss clearly believe that there is a growing movement toward the development of cosmopolitan norms in which *the individual* replaces *the state* as the object of global concern. They describe these new norms as "a developing global humanitarian space."[9]

This re-conceptualization of human affairs in cosmopolitan rather than statist terms is based upon a perception of the erosion of state sovereignty. It negates the traditional statist argument against interference in the domestic affairs of states by erasing the distinction between the concepts of "internal" and "external" as these have traditionally been applied to the conduct of states. If the terms "internal" and "external" lose their meaning in the new world order, then the term "intervention" also becomes meaningless as a conceptual category since state boundaries no longer serve as barriers against actions directed toward the saving of lives anywhere within this "global humanitarian space." If the world is to be understood as a global commons, then all are inside the same territorial space and there can be no such thing as intervention from the outside.[10]

There would seem to be two major problems with this approach to the issue. If, as Weiss and Chopra suggest, sovereignty is being eroded and the state is being subsumed within the wider category of "global humanitarian space," it is unclear who are the non-state actors that will provide the "assistance" of which they speak. It will not do to suggest the United Nations since, for the foreseeable future at least, it remains an organization composed of independent *sovereign states.* Consequently, unless there is some other actor out there capable of acting with or without the consent of repressive regimes, humanitarian assistance will have to come from other sovereign states. If the provision of humanitarian assistance is dependent upon the willingness of sovereign states to act, however, this would tend to undermine the premise that sovereign statehood is a thing of the past.

The second problem concerns the purposes for which these activities will be undertaken. Since the liberal institutionalist notion of the gradual erosion of state sovereignty suggests that the state is becoming (or perhaps already is) obsolete, then clearly the purpose of "assistance" cannot be to strengthen state capacities. Such an effort would be counter to the direction of history as Weiss and Chopra understand it. At the same time, however, the *duration* of these humanitarian operations remains problematic. In the absence of a rehabilitated state, it is unclear who will assume the responsibility for managing the situation on the ground once those who have undertaken this mission extricate themselves. It would appear, then, that what Weiss and Chopra have suggested would, implicitly at least, require an indefinite presence.

This implicit suggestion raises a number of serious questions concerning the willingness of donors to perform such operations for an indefinite period, the availability of resources for the provision of such assistance as the number of trouble spots proliferates, and the nagging moral and political problem discussed in the previous chapter of how to distinguish such behavior from old-fashioned imperialism. After all, one could easily make the argument that in the heyday of European imperialism during the nineteenth and early twentieth centuries, actions undertaken by European powers within their empires were not really "interventions" nor were they a violation of anyone's sovereignty inasmuch as the colonies were part of the empire and, therefore, events within the empire were really an internal matter. One is left to ponder, therefore, whether, perhaps unintentionally, "global humanitarian space" is really nothing more than a new name for an old enterprise.

Along similar lines, in a seeming reply to those such as Weiss and Chopra, Howard H. Lentner argues that the fundamental weakness of this viewpoint is that it ignores the critical role that the state continues to play in both developing and implementing these new norms of international conduct.[11]

Although the situation has changed somewhat in the direction of more assertive multilateral activity in areas previously regarded as within the sphere of sovereign states, the question of state sovereignty is actually not new. At issue is the meaning of the term "sovereignty" itself. Those operating out of the Wilsonian liberal tradition have always tended to see any constraint upon the behavior of states, whether in the form of treaty obligations or the existence of international law and organizations, as evidence of the erosion of sovereignty in the modern world. The Realist tradition, however, has always tended to dismiss such arguments as a fundamental misunderstanding of the meaning of sovereignty. For those in the Realist tradition, especially neorealists such as Kenneth Waltz, state sovereignty has never meant the absence of constraints upon state behavior but rather the ability of the state to make decisions for itself within the context of whatever constraints may exist.[12]

The difficulty here is that the term sovereignty is subject to multiple meanings. This allows both those who claim that it is eroding and those who maintain that it is intact to hold firm to their respective positions. Those, such as former UN Secretary-General Boutros Boutros-Ghali, for whom sovereignty means the ability to effectively exercise control over a given territory free from *any* external intervention or constraints can point to examples of such intervention or constraints as evidence of the diminution of sovereignty in the post-Cold War era.[13]

On the other hand, those for whom sovereignty refers to the *structure* of an anarchical system characterized by the absence of any higher authority can point to the absence of anything even remotely approaching the existence of a world government as evidence supporting the claim that the state remains sovereign.

As the above discussion demonstrates, the continuity of the sovereign territorial state has been, and remains, an open question. Theories abound suggesting possible alternatives to the Westphalian states system. Some have already written its epitaph while others suggest that it is either in the process of disappearing, or, at the very least, should be. Among the

evidence cited by those predicting the state's demise are cases of state contraction and eventual collapse generally associated with internal ethnic or
clan-based violence. This state contraction/collapse thesis, perhaps most
often associated with I. William Zartman in his book *Collapsed States*,
maintains that as state leaders come increasingly to depend upon members
of their own ethnic community, their sphere of effective territorial control
narrows. Violent conflict between groups ensues until ultimately the state
is no longer able to function and eventually collapses. Such theories, particularly when paired with some of the globalization theories mentioned
earlier, which suggest that the state is being undermined from above and
below simultaneously, anticipate the decline of the sovereign states system
as it has existed since Westphalia.

THEORETICAL CRITIQUES OF THE STATE:
A STATE-CENTRIC RESPONSE

The above discussion is not without merit. There is certainly evidence
for the thesis that globalization is increasing the connections across state
lines between people. It is also impossible to ignore the collapse of central
state administrations in the former Soviet Union and Yugoslavia or the
complete absence of any governing authority in many parts of Africa such
as Somalia.

   These facts are not in dispute. The question, however, is: what
conclusion(s) should one draw from these facts? An answer to this question requires a recognition of certain *other facts* as well, which are often
ignored by critics of the state-centric model. One of these facts is the proliferation in the number of states as the twentieth century has unfolded.
The decolonization process in the 1950s and 1960s and the breakup of
multinational states such as the Soviet Union, Yugoslavia, and Czechoslovakia after the Cold War have resulted in more than a threefold increase
in the number of states in the world just since the end of World War II.
Indeed, somewhat paradoxically given his tendency to perceive the erosion of state sovereignty, former UN Secretary-General Boutros Boutros-
Ghali also has argued that this ongoing development is evidence of the
continuing centrality of the sovereign state: "To the hundreds of millions
who gained their independence in the surge of decolonization following
the creation of the United Nations, have been added millions more who
have recently gained freedom. Once again new states are taking their
seats in the General Assembly. *Their arrival reconfirms the importance
and indispensability of the sovereign State as the fundamental entity of
the international community* [italics added]."[14] Indeed, the states system,

which at the time of the Second World War was largely a European, or perhaps more accurately Western, system is today a truly universal political system. One easily could make the case that, contrary to the notion of a world coming together, the world is more *fragmented* today than it was in the first half of the twentieth century due to the collapse of all the major global empires. For the most part, globalists tend to gloss over this fact.

Another fact frequently overlooked by critics of the state-centric approach is that virtually every ethnic conflict occurring in the world represents either an effort to increase the number of states by seceding from an existing state controlled by a rival ethnic group or an attempt to challenge some other dominant ethnic group for control of the existing state apparatus. *In either case, the challenge is not to the existence of the state system per se but to a particular set of power relations within an existing state which favor some other ethnic group.*[15]

In her discussion of failed states, Susan L. Woodward takes globalization theories to task for their failure to grasp the essential role of the sovereign state in the globalization phenomenon. Similar to Lentner's argument in defense of the continuing relevance of the state, she suggests that, if anything, the problems created as a result of the existence of so-called "failed states" actually demonstrates the continuing importance of the state.[16]

Of course, to say that the state is *necessary* in order for globalization to occur is not to refute the claim that globalization may also be undermining the state as a matter of empirical fact. There is no necessary linkage between the *need* for states and the *fact* of their continued existence. Her point is a prescriptive rather than a descriptive one: *if* globalists were correct that the state is eroding, such a process would be counterproductive given the ongoing necessity for the existence of states. Consequently, she seeks to re-conceptualize the notion of globalization in a way which can be reconciled with the preservation of the states system.

Woodward's argument brings an important insight to the discussion about the role of the state under conditions of globalization, which is often lacking among those who see an inherent contradiction between increasing global interdependence and the continuation of the sovereign territorial state. Even if one were to dispute her claims about the state, one would still be left with the seeming disconnect between theories of globalization and/or state collapse, on the one hand, and the facts described above on the other. If those who argue that the state is in decline are correct, how can both the oftentimes ferocious ethnic struggle for either independent statehood or for control of existing states and the ever-increasing number of new states in the world ushered in through secessionist movements be explained? It would appear that the only way that the argument in support of state decline can be reconciled with these facts would be to either ignore the facts or to make the case that ethnic communities engaged in internal warfare are composed of fundamentally irrational actors, who are engaged in a determined and brutal struggle to gain control of a political institution (the state) which some analyst has declared to be obsolete.

Given these facts, a more plausible explanation would appear to be that, to paraphrase Mark Twain, reports of the state's demise are greatly exaggerated. If such is the case, then what is needed is a theory which can explain the acceleration of the number of ethnic conflicts in the world and the relationship between these conflicts and the state.

Toward that end, the task is to develop a set of theoretical propositions suggesting that while the state itself may not be in decline as a form of social and political organization, a particular *form* of it may be. In other words, the phenomenon underway in the post-Cold War era may not be state *decline* but state *transition*.

The argument is that the evidence of the past several years since the end of the Cold War suggests that the classical model of a civic nation-state consisting of various ethnic or clan or tribal groupings all sharing a common juridical entity called the territorial state to which all owe allegiance is, in those parts of the world in which the state is often described as "post-colonial," in the process of undergoing a fundamental transition or reorganization into a new form of state, which I have labeled "the ethnic state." The defining characteristic of this reformulated state is the use of ethnicity as an organizing principle around which a concerted effort is made to bring about the convergence of ethnicity and territorial boundaries.

Asbjorn Eide explains the essential features of this new form of state: "'Ethno-nations' give rise to a different set of political and legal problems. One version of ethno-nationalist ideology is the following: Nations are to be defined in ethnic terms, referring to a common past history, tradition, preferably also common language. Secondly, ethnic nations should have their own states, so the society composing a state should as far as possible be congruent with the 'nation'. Thirdly, the loyalty of members to their ethnic nation should override all other loyalties."[17]

This notion of the "ethno-nation," which is the foundation for what is referred to here as the ethnic-state, stands in marked contrast to the concept of the *civic* nation. Again, Eide explains the difference between the two concepts: "Ethno-nationalism has been contrasted with civic nationalism, which holds that everybody living within the state should be part of the nation on a basis of equality, irrespective of his or her ethnic background. This notion follows from the evolution of the concept of

'State-nation', via the notion of 'citizen nation' to the 'civic nation. It goes beyond the 'citizen nation' in that it includes the permanent residents as part of the civic nation, even before they obtain citizenship."[18]

It bears mentioning that the transition to the ethnic state posited here is not the first such transformation of the sovereign state to occur since the advent of the modern Westphalian states system. Just as the transformation of the sovereign state from a dynastic state to a nation-state in the period between the French Revolution and the end of the First World War did not signal the collapse of the state per se but rather its transformation from one *form* to another, it would seem to be a more plausible explanation to suggest that that which is being witnessed in the post-Cold War era represents another kind of transition—this time from the ethnically heterogeneous, failed post-colonial state to the more homogeneous idea of the ethnic state.

It is important at this point to offer a caveat. Even if this explanation of events is correct, it is impossible to say with any degree of certainty whether this type of state will be the last to develop. It may well be that what is being witnessed is itself a transient phenomenon, which in time will yield to some other form of state. At present, the most that can be said is that if the state is viewed in historical perspective, what emerges is not a picture of some undifferentiated, eternal entity, but rather a political entity which has evolved or mutated over time.

Having made the case for the continuing centrality of the state, albeit in an altered form, the challenge, then, is to explain why this transformation of the state has occurred at this particular moment in time, and how it is related to the issue of ethnic conflict. That will be the focus of the next two chapters.

Chapter Five

Ethnic Conflict and the State-Building Process

Toward an Integrated Theory for a Global, Post-Cold War Era

INTRODUCTION

As previously stated, the end of the Cold War has made necessary the development of a new paradigm concerning the phenomena of ethnicity/ ethnic conflict, state-building, and peacekeeping/peace enforcement. In addition to viewing these phenomena as having an existence independent of the Cold War bipolar struggle between East and West, this new paradigm must also explain how they are interconnected with each other such that each has an impact upon the others. The preceding chapters show that this is in sharp contrast to the bulk of the work done in each of these fields of study during the Cold War. Reflecting the Cold War emphasis upon the idea of bipolarity, many of the earlier works discussed in *Part I* viewed these three phenomena independently of each other while generally seeing them as either products of, or subordinate to, the larger bipolar struggle between East and West. Thus, for example, peacekeeping was generally discussed in the context of conflict containment designed to prevent an escalation of a local conflict into a superpower confrontation as opposed to any discussion of its impact upon the state-building process in states experiencing ethnic conflict.

This general tendency found in the literature (while arguably understandable in the context of the ever-present threat of nuclear annihilation as a matter of overriding political urgency and given the natural tendency to focus on issues which seem relevant at the time) inevitably resulted in certain theoretical distortions. This can be seen in the case of ethnic conflicts during the Cold War, which were frequently recast as local expressions of the East-West conflict.[1] One or both belligerents were viewed as existing in a patron-client relationship with the superpowers. In this context, the local actors were reduced to little more than proxies, who lacked their own agendas. Their sole function was to serve as pawns in the expansionist designs of the superpowers, who, in their scramble for global hegemony, were perceived to be the primary actors.

This Cold War bipolar paradigm (whose interstate nature fit in nicely with the Realist conceptualization of states as "black boxes" or irreducible units) merged with the prevailing assumption at the time that states were viable entities (an assumption rooted in the international norm of juridical sovereignty) in order to supplant any notion that conflicts in the world might be essentially internal matters possessing their own distinct logic and set of dynamics. To have re-conceptualized conflicts in this way would have required that the designs of the superpowers be seen as frequently subordinate to those of the local parties. In other words, so-called communist-inspired/directed insurgencies would need to have been recast as internal (frequently ethnic) struggles for control of states or perhaps secession from them. At most, the role of outside powers would then have been to exploit these conflicts rather than to create or direct them.

It should be pointed out, however, that this version of reality was not simply a matter of scholarly ignorance or indifference. Frequently, it also represented a deliberate effort on the part of local actors to obscure the internal nature of their conflicts by portraying them in East-West terms. Such portrayals were a calculated attempt to exploit the Cold War competition as part of a strategy to obtain political, economic, and, perhaps most importantly, military support against their rivals. This strategy resulted in a growing number of patron-client relationships between the superpowers and regimes or rebel factions throughout the so-called Third World.

At the same time, such portrayals of local conflicts also served the interests of the superpowers themselves. As actors primarily concerned with the wider global struggle, a shift in emphasis to the question of state capacity or viability could easily undermine their hegemonic designs. The emerging focus upon the internal governance of South Vietnam during the Vietnam war, for example, contributed to the weakening of the domestic consensus within the United States in favor of the war. This, in turn, complicated American efforts to extend its influence into that part of the world and, arguably, helped to bring about American withdrawal from the area. In the zero-sum logic of the Cold War, this withdrawal represented for the Americans an unfavorable shift in the global balance of forces.

Whether scholarly blind spot, calculated manipulation of the facts by belligerents, ideological rationalization for superpower hegemony, or some unfortunate combination of all of these, it nevertheless must be pointed out that the tendency to subsume ethnic conflict, state-building, and UN peacekeeping under the heading of the Cold War by viewing them through the lens of bipolarity had certain consequences for our understanding of these phenomena. These consequences have become more fully apparent since the end of the Cold War. In addition to the theoretical distortions cited above, the bipolar world view also resulted in a failure to develop a paradigm which could relate these phenomena to each other independently of the Cold War. Thus, when the Cold War ended and these phenomena persisted, scholars found themselves in the position of attempting to "reinvent the wheel."

The perceived need for a post-Cold War paradigm is evident in the flurry of attempts by scholars and policymakers alike to come to terms with the issues surrounding the nature of ethnic conflict and the reasons for its resurgence following the collapse of the Soviet Union, the proliferation of failed and collapsed states, and the expanded role of the UN in addressing these phenomena in a world without superpower conflict. This role has included the development of more muscular and intrusive forms of intervention than anything attempted during the Cold War years with the possible exceptions of the Korean operation in the 1950s and the Congo mission in the early 1960s.

These developments suggest that the changes in the wider global context commonly referred to as globalization and the concomitant changes in the international political system associated with the end of the Cold War have so altered global politics as to necessitate a paradigmatic shift within the fields of both International Relations and Comparative Politics. The need for such a shift grows out of the sort of conditons Thomas S. Kuhn identified as requiring a "scientific revolution." This occurs when the existing paradigm (in this case bipolarity) no longer is capable of explaining some set of observable phenomena.

In this case, the challenge is to fashion a new theory which can both explain the impact that the changes in the international system have had upon ethnic conflict, state-building, and UN peacekeeping and re-conceptualize these phenomena through the development of a more integrated model designed to identify the interrelationships that exist in the new era.

It is my contention that, despite an abundance of theories thus far which have tackled one or another of these phenomena, no theory fully captures their interconnectedness. Some theories have attempted to integrate two of the three but not all three. Thus, for example, Mohammed Ayoob discusses the relationship between ethnic conflict and state-building but fails to address the role of UN peacekeeping except as part of the wider Third World security predicament of the post-Cold War world in which globalization and changed international norms have complicated the process of state-building. I. William Zartman sees ethnic conflict as an aspect of state collapse thereby seeing no connection to the issue of state-building. Thomas G. Weiss appears unconcerned with the issue of state-building preferring instead to treat the issue of UN peacekeeping in ethnic conflicts as a purely humanitarian matter regardless of the consequences for the state.

Perhaps the closest to an integrated theory is Boutros-Ghali's discussion in *An Agenda for Peace* of what he calls "post-conflict peacebuilding" as a way for UN intervention to restore states in the aftermath of ethnic conflicts. Even this, however, does not see ethnic conflict as related to the whole issue of state-building except in the sense that it poses a threat to the state-building process, which requires external intervention if the state itself is to survive. My aim, therefore, is nothing less than to create such an integrated theory.

In order to understand the interconnectedness of these three phenomena, two additional factors must be introduced: the impact of globalization and the consequences of structural changes to the international system associated with the end of the Cold War. The reason for their introduction is that it is not simply that the Cold War obscured some pre-existing relationship between ethnicity, the state, and UN peacekeeping. Rather, the interconnectedness which has become apparent in the post-Cold War era is itself intertwined with these changes and is at least in part a *result* of them. It is these wider changes which are driving the necessity for a paradigmatic shift. Concepts which resonated just a few years ago have become obsolete. Just as it is no longer possible in a world without superpower conflict to speak of ethnic conflict in terms of proxy wars or to speak of peacekeeping as a device for containing conflicts which might otherwise escalate into superpower confrontations, the Cold War mindset which gave rise to such notions needs to be cast aside in favor of a new way of looking at these phenomena which is consistent with new political realities.[2]

One difficulty with developing this sort of integrated theory, which also incorporates the impact of the wider context of globalization and international systemic change from a bipolar to a non-bipolar world, is that the number of interactive relationships makes explanation quite cumbersome. This raises the familiar problem in theory-building of balancing parsimonious elegance against distortions of reality. In the interest of simplifying as much as possible the process while at the same time retaining the explanatory power of the theory, these relationships will be discussed in a piecemeal fashion. As will become apparent, this is not intended to suggest that the "parts" can stand on their own independently of the whole. It is rather an analytical device designed to deal with complexity by gradually introducing these complicating elements in a manner which answers questions as they arise in each step of the theory-building process.

A good place to begin is with the identification of a focal point, which can serve as a kind of linchpin tying together all of the other strands. That focal point is the state. As indicated previously, the selection of the state is the product of a recognition that the state is still the single most important actor on the world stage and, therefore, the success or failure of the state seems to be related to all of the other parts of this puzzle. Consequently, the issue of state-building has the most explanatory power when it comes to understanding the set of relationships described earlier.

In an effort to develop an integrated theory, two key questions will be addressed: How do changes in the global setting or context (the phenomenon known as globalization) and in the structure of the international political system (the movement from a bipolar Cold War era to a unipolar (or perhaps multipolar?) post-Cold War era) contribute to the phenomena of state-building/collapse and the resurgence of ethnic identification/ethnic conflict? What impact do various forms of UN intervention ranging from traditional peacekeeping to peace enforcement in situations of ethnic conflict have upon the state-building/state collapse process and the likelihood that ethnic conflict will continue or cease to be an issue? The relationship that globalization and the end of the Cold War have to ethnic resurgence and the issues of state-building/collapse will be addressed in this and the next chapter. The impact of the UN will be discussed in *Chapter Seven*.

Before discussing the ways in which globalization and the end of the Cold War have contributed to both the resurgence of ethnic identification/ ethnic conflict and the building/collapsing of states, it is first necessary to lay the groundwork by establishing the relationship between ethnicity and the state. This is another way of saying that this chapter will move progressively from the less complex to the more complex. Once these linkages are understood, it will then be possible to describe how the wider issues of globalization and the end of the Cold War have impacted this relationship. Following this discussion, the ways in which various forms of UN intervention are believed to affect both the state and ethnicity will be laid out in greater detail.

ETHNIC RESURGENCE AND THE PROCESS OF STATE-BUILDING/COLLAPSE

What accounts for the apparent resurgence of ethnic identification and the proliferation of ethnic conflicts in recent years?

As the discussion of the literature in *Chapter One* indicates, this is an extremely complex question. A good place to begin the search for an answer to this puzzle is with the politico-territorial environment within which ethnic groups operate: namely, the state. To understand the growing tendency for individuals to define themselves in ethnic terms and to attach themselves to ethnic groups in a state-centric world, it is useful to consider first the condition or health of states in the contemporary period: the state of the state as it were. Specifically, one must look at whether a state is healthy and strong[3] or whether it is weak and failing or perhaps even collapsing. Broadly speaking, a healthy state may be thought of as one which possesses the governing capacity necessary to satisfy its population's needs for security at both the personal and collective levels and for economic well-being.

The concept of security can be disaggregated into both external and internal components. The external dimension consists of the ability of the state to provide protection against outside threats from other states. The internal dimension refers to the capacity to provide domestic order in accordance with Max Weber's notion of the monopolization of the legitimate use of force. A further component of this internal order is the existence of a system of justice capable of providing individuals with a sense of security against the possible excesses of their own government. The existence or absence of such a system is frequently used as one measure of the strength or weakness of a state's capacity to govern. In addition to these military, political, and judicial aspects, state strength is also a function of the state's capacity to provide at least some degree of economic security and well-being for its population. Given the multidimensional nature of state strength, it is better to conceptualize strength as a continuum rather than a dichotomy inasmuch as states may be able to provide some but not all of the above. State strength, therefore, should be thought of as a matter of degree.

The suggestion is that ethnic resurgence is most likely to occur in states which do not exhibit any of these capacities—in other words, failing or collapsing states. As Johua Bernard Forrest has pointed out, there is a considerable body of literature which addresses the question as to whether ethnic resurgence is a *cause* or an *effect* of state failure. In all probability, there is some truth in both propositions. Certainly, it is possible to find cases in which state failure produced the kind of insecurity within the population which resulted in ethnic resurgence and conflict of the sort identified by Chaim Kaufmann in his description of ethnic security dilemmas; likewise, it undoubtedly is possible to find cases in which the causal arrow points the other way and it is ethnic conflict which so taxes the capacities of the state that it becomes difficult or impossible for it to continue to function. Indeed, it may well be that the process of state failure is symbiotic such that each contributes to the other. If so, an analyst can break into the cycle at either point and believe that the causal agent has been discovered.

Having said this, it is important to note that in at least some, and perhaps most, cases, it is the failure of the state, due to a weak capacity for governance, to provide for the basic needs of its population which is responsible for the collapse of the state and the resulting search for some alternative source from which to receive these benefits.

Of course, this does not explain the reasons for the lack of capacity associated with state failure. In order to understand that, it is necessary to look at the changed environment within which states operate as well as the distinction between the way older states formed and the way in which post-colonial states came into existence. All of this will be dealt with in the discussion of globalization and the end of the Cold War.

For the moment, it is enough to understand that there is a relationship between state failure and ethnic resurgence, and that this relationship is in part, at least, a function of the declining capacity of ruling elites to govern effectively because of changes in the way in which traditional authority structures are perceived by those they seek to govern.

Along these same lines, James Rosenau has suggested that in the modern world, states are experiencing a crisis in their ability to exercise authority over their populations. As part of a process which he describes as "fragmegration" (simultaneous global fragmentation and integration associated with his concept of "turbulence"), the traditional criteria of legitimacy[4] have been replaced by the notion of "performance criteria," in which the ability to lead is increasingly tied to the ability of the state to satisfy public needs and wants.[5]

Ann C. Mason suggests that this shift to performance criteria weakens the state by making compliance conditional upon self-interest rather than the sense that those in power have the right to rule. The result is a transfer of allegiance to other actors including substate actors,[6] such as ethnic groups, which fill a void left by the state or serve a function as a way to gain control of the state apparatus.

This problem is particularly acute in weak states, which are already hard-pressed to satisfy the demands of their populations. The inability to do so can frequently result in total collapse.[7] It should be pointed out that the vast majority of these weak or collapsed states are also post-colonial states.

Thus far, the implication has been that the ethnic resurgence associated with state failure represents a retreat by the population of the failing state into primordial ethnic groups capable of performing tasks which the state no longer can. Undoubtedly, this is a piece of the story, but it would be an oversimplification to treat this as the entire picture. Among other things, it does not explain conflict between these groups. There is simply no reason to suppose that people looking to ethnicity as a substitute for the state must necessarily come into conflict with one another anymore than people looking to other non-governmental sources of support in the absence of state action, such as religious or charitable institutions, must necessarily come into conflict with one another.[8]

To understand the relationship between state failure and ethnic conflict (more specifically how state failure contributes to ethnic conflict), the constructivist and instrumentalist approaches to ethnicity described in *Chapter One* must be incorporated into this discussion. If state failure is related to the transition from traditional sources of authority and legitimacy to performance criteria, it is important to understand that this transition does not just happen. It occurs as a result of a transformation within society towards a greater degree of individualism and a correspondingly greater emphasis upon self-interest. As will be seen in the discussion of the impact of globalization and the end of the Cold War, individualism and the heightened concern with self-interest are related to both the social dislocations associated with urbanization and to the empowerment of individuals at the expense of traditional authority structures as part of the overall global restructuring currently underway. In other words, this transition to performance criteria is related to fundamental changes occurring *within* societies as a result of fundamental changes occurring worldwide. These changes are having important consequences for all states but especially for the most vulnerable ones.

The transition to performance criteria rooted in deeper societal changes is reminiscent of Emile Durkheim's notion of the transition from mechanical to organic solidarity.[9] Writing in the midst of the transition to modernity associated with industrialization and urbanization in France, Durkheim suggested that traditional societies were undifferentiated and held together by shared beliefs and values, such as a common religion. He referred to this type of societal cohesiveness as "mechanical solidarity." Modern societies, on the other hand, were characterized by differentiation and a division of labor. This differentiation made the existence of shared beliefs and values much more difficult to achieve. In such societies, the bond between individuals was not beliefs but the interdependence which grew out of the increasingly specialized division of labor. Durkheim referred to this bond as "organic solidarity." Throughout his work, he suggested that the movement from tradition to modernity was both personally and collectively destabilizing and characterized by a sense of rootlessness and normlessness, which he called "anomie." The destabilizing effects of anomie could be measured in such pathologies as the increasing rates of suicide.

There are several points of comparison between Durkheim's work and the theory being developed in this study. As was true of France in his time, societies across the globe, particularly countries that were once socialist and those previously referred to as members of the Third World, are undergoing a fundamental transformation with profound social and political consequences for their populations. Unlike France at the time in which Durkheim was writing, however, this time the transformation is not simply from agrarian to industrial economies. Although in many parts of the world a similar process of industrialization and urbanization is underway, this process is compounded by a parallel transformation from an industrial to a post-industrial (information-based) economy. Further complicating the situations in these countries are the fact that oftentimes these transitions are accompanied by a movement away from a centrally planned and toward a competitive liberal market economy, in which the government's role is diminished considerably. On top of all of this, there has been in recent years, in response to emerging international norms as well as internal pressures, a trend toward replacing authoritarian or totalitarian political systems with democratic forms of government. Thus, just as in Durkheim's day, although perhaps even more so, societies are facing significant restructuring.

Another point of comparison can be seen in the destabilizing effects which these societal transitions generate. In the case of this theory, however, the focus is not on the destabilizing effect which these radical changes are having upon *individual* behavior in the form of various pathologies but rather upon the *political* consequences in terms of the structure of the state as it struggles to satisfy the demands of its population—oftentimes without the necessary political and economic capacity to do so. The struggle to satisfy popular demands is directly related to the development of performance criteria for political legitimacy. This notion of performance criteria might be thought of as the contemporary political variant of Durkheim's concept of organic solidarity. Just as he suggested that a modern society is held together by interdependence (another word for mutual self-interest), the idea behind performance criteria is that a state is held together and continues to function by the satisfaction of the self-interested demands of its citizens.

Some states are able to successfully meet the demands of their citizens because they already possess all or most of the empirical attributes of statehood. In these strong states (usually those in either Western Europe or North America which have had time to develop these attributes relatively free of outside intervention),[10] one may observe expressions of ethnic identification and solidarity which bear a surface resemblance to those found elsewhere on the globe. Despite this surface similarity, however, the situations are fundamentally different. For the most part, political or economic demands associated with these expressions of ethnicity found in the more established states can be contained and channeled through existing democratic political structures so as not to pose any threat to the existence of the states themselves or their political systems.

In newer, post-colonial states, however, the situation is quite different. Various factors, including the existence of the idea of juridical sovereignty even in the absence of empirical statehood, have deprived these states of the historical opportunity to develop the tools for effective governance. Indeed, similar to Jackson and Rosberg, Christopher Clapham argues that the norms associated with juridical sovereignty as well as the ability of regimes, particularly in Africa, to rely upon the protection of either former colonial powers or the superpowers during the Cold War have removed war from the state formation process. This, however, has come at the price of undermining the development of internal state capacity in these newer states. In effect, the absence of war has resulted in state weakness.[11]

As a consequence of having it "too easy," to borrow a phrase from Clapham, these weak states have particular difficulty when it comes to meeting the demands of the population for personal security and economic well-being. In such states, the development of performance criteria as the standard by which legitimacy is measured poses a direct challenge to the survival of the state by threatening to overburden its already fragile institutions. Indeed, this is generally what is meant by the term state collapse. Since state collapse is merely a shorthand way of saying the collapse of the existing structures of authority, those in positions of authority obviously have a vested interest in finding some way to salvage these structures.

It is at this point that ethnicity and ethnic conflict reappear on the scene. The essence of my argument is that ethnicity as a social category and a powerful instrument for the mobilization of mass support is capable of performing the function desired by those seeking to retain power. It will be recalled that instrumentalist theories view ethnicity as a flexible social category crafted to meet a specific set of social circumstances; constructivist theories, on the other hand, take this a step further to suggest that such categories serve *a function in terms of the interests of particular political entrepreneurs*. Consistent with these theoretical approaches, my argument is that ethnic mobilization by state leaders represents an attempt *to transform the bases of authority* in weak, post-colonial states away from the idea of satisfying popular demands (self-interest), which the state lacks the capacity to satisfy, and towards a common cultural frame of reference (ethnicity).

My own thesis, however, departs from these theories in two important respects. First, it assumes that ethnicity is not infinitely malleable. This places constraints upon the efforts of would-be ethnic entrepreneurs to manipulate the concept by suggesting that there is, in fact, some primordial basis for ethnic identification. Second, by combining the constructivist concept of ethnic entrepreneurs with Durkheim's theories about social solidarity, the suggestion is made that the process of ethnic mobilization involves not simply elite manipulation of the masses for personal gain but rather efforts to transform the social structure of society in order to facilitate state capacity for governance, which, in turn, also serves the personal interests of those seeking to either maintain or obtain political power.

The movement from performance to ethnicity as the basis for state and regime legitimacy in some sense represents a reversal of Durkheim's model, which posited the transition from mechanical to organic solidarity. In this instance, political entrepreneurs seek to move the state away from the sort of cultural diversity found in ethnically heterogeneous postcolonial states and toward the ideal of cultural uniformity more likely to exist in ethnically homogeneous states. The aim of such a transition is to de-emphasize notions of individualism and the consequent preoccupation with the pursuit of self-interest while emphasizing instead in all aspects of life, including politics, conformity to a cultural norm embodied in the state itself, which identifies the state with a particular ethnic community.

The explanation for this reversal can be found in the difference between the Western European and the post-colonial state-building experiences. In Western Europe, as Charles Tilly and others have pointed out, the empirical aspects of state-building such as the territorial configuration of the state and the process of internal consolidation by state makers occurred *prior to, or perhaps concurrent with,* the development of juridical norms of nonintervention and the territorial integrity of states.[12] When these norms did develop, they served to *strengthen* these particular states by allowing them to consolidate control internally without outside interference from international or non-governmental organizations attempting some form of humanitarian intervention within the state. Thus, while it is clearly the case that many states did collapse along the way, those states which emerged from this often bloody process of war making and state making possessed the empirical capacity to govern a specific territory.

This situation is in sharp contrast with the circumstances surrounding the creation and existence of most of the states in the world today. As has already been discussed, in the newer, post-colonial (and one might even add post-communist) states, juridical norms preceded statehood. In terms of the state-building process, this reversal has had the opposite effect from that of their Western European predecessors: the prior existence of juridical norms served to weaken or undermine state capacity.

In his analysis of the issue of trusteeship, Robert H. Jackson comes to a similar conclusion. He suggests that under the UN trusteeship system, the original concept was that full membership in the international community was predicated upon one's *empirical capacity* for self-government. This changed beginning with the passage of UN General Assembly Resolution 1514 in 1960. From that point onward, the juridical *right to* self-government superseded the empirical *capacity for* self-government. The result has been the creation of an unequal international society characterized by strong states alongside weak, newer states.[13]

Gregory H. Fox explains this dichotomy by pointing out that juridical norms, which in the modern era also have come to include an expectation of respect by regimes for human rights and a process of democratization as part of the price of admission to the international system (norms with which Western Europeans did not have to contend in the building of their states), oftentimes have subverted empirical statehood rather than bolstering it.

Likewise, as noted previously, Christopher Clapham suggests in his summary of an entire body of literature dealing with state-building that the experience of state formation in the post-colonial state, with its pre-fabricated boundaries and state leaders who never had to engage in violent struggle either to assert their control over territory or their preeminence among rival sources of authority within that pre-existing territorial entity, had the perhaps unintended consequence of crippling the state's capacity to govern. Perhaps nowhere is this more true than in the case of the African post-colonial state.[14]

Now that the authority structures in these post-colonial states are facing serious challenges from popular demands that they perform in such a manner as to meet the needs of their people (performance criteria), they must go back and, in effect, re-create the Western European experience of developing empirical statehood. The first steps in this process are for state makers to define the territory of the state and to establish their capacity to exercise exclusive control within that territory in the face of potential rivals, who also seek to establish their preeminence. Without these two fundamental aspects of state-building, it is simply not possible to achieve any of the other stages in the state-building process such as nation-building, institution-building, or even democratization.

The central question in all of this is whether post-colonial states can re-create the *results* of Western European effective governance without re-creating the brutal *processes* which led to these results. This is rather like the old expression that everybody wants to go to heaven, but nobody wants to die to get there. One school of thought on this issue is skeptical of the ability of the post-colonial state to achieve this same level of success within the constraints of existing international norms and processes, which preclude the European path to state formation;[15] a second school, however, doubts that, even if they were to follow the path taken by Western European states, post-colonial states could achieve the same degree of success as their Western European counterparts because of the unique historical features of the European experience.[16] Although the suggestion may, at first glance, seem harsh, my own view is closer to the first school. The reasons for this will be explored in the context of the discussion of UN intervention.

As an aside, the problems associated with the post-colonial experience of state-building as a mirror image of the Western European experience are in some respects eerily reminiscent of the problems faced by twentieth century Marxists in their attempts to apply Marx' theories of proletarian revolution in mature capitalist societies to pre-capitalist societies without a significant proletariat. Both situations involved an attempt to reach a desired result without first establishing the prerequisites for that result. It would seem that just as the Leninist and Maoist attempts to skip the capitalist phase on the way to socialism have proven to be dismal failures, the attempt by the international community to require that post-colonial states skip the often violent antecedents to empirical statehood and rely instead upon international norms as a way to ensure both the existence and the viability of these states have likewise been a failure. Although this conclusion must, for the moment at least, remain tentative as this is the question that will be examined in the case study of Iraq, the earlier record of international attempts to build viable states in territories formerly under colonial rule through the League of Nations Mandate system and the UN Trusteeship system is not very promising. The question, of course, is whether contemporary forms of UN intervention will be any more effective in this regard.

Returning to the role of performance criteria in the discussion of ethnicity and post-colonial state collapse, it would seem that the failure to satisfy rising demands not only would explain the resurgence of ethnicity as a way to restructure society and the state around an organizing principle other than individualism and self-interest; it also offers valuable theoretical insights into the current phenomenon of ethnic conflict and so-called "ethnic cleansing." If cultural homogeneity is the new basis for claims to legitimate statehood, then only those individuals who aspire to create ethnically homogeneous states can lay claim to legitimate authority within the state. It follows from this that the reconfigured ethnic state cannot tolerate the presence of other ethnic communities in any significant numbers as such a presence would be irreconcilable with the foundational organizing principle of the state. The use of so-called "ethnic cleansing" in such newly created states as Croatia and Bosnia, the autonomous region of Kosovo, and in post-colonial states such as Rwanda or Sudan as a way to transform ethnically divided states into ethnically homogeneous states all support this thesis. Underlying each of these instances is a recognition that maintaining the demographic status quo in ethnically polarized, newer states (whose boundaries were initially determined without regard to ethnic composition) would pose the same sort of threat to the authority structures of the emerging ethnic state as performance criteria currently poses to weak post-colonial states.

Just as the logic of ethnically homogeneous states is clear from the perspective of governing capacity, it is equally clear that the effort to achieve this goal will require some form of population displacement ranging from relatively nonviolent attempts to encourage emigration all the way up to, and including, forcible population transfers. Indeed, ironically, efforts to impede this process may have the unintended consequence of *encouraging* genocidal warfare.

Particularly at the more violent end of the spectrum, these attempts to transform an ethnically heterogeneous state will necessarily entail conflict between communities. Conflict between communities also means conflict between rival ethnically-defined elites, each seeking to impose its definition of the ethnic state upon the same piece of territory. This generally violent form of conflict represents the final stages in the collapse of the post-colonial state as well as the gestation process for the development of the ethnic state. As such, it tends to mirror the logic behind the violent developmental process experienced at the start of Western European (as well as American) state-building. While it is true that the European case did not at this stage in its development have a specifically ethnic component to the violence (since the doctrine of nationalism and its link to an ethnic community had yet to develop), it is also true that the underlying logic of using force to establish the boundaries of the state and to subdue rivals or opponents within the state so as to consolidate the state maker's rule internally is the same. It is this similarity which Cohen, Brown, and

Organski identify as the underlying logic behind internal violence in their seminal article dealing with this issue.

Consistent with the argument by Tilly that early state making is a form of organized crime,[17] in which state makers extract resources from the population in order to facilitate their war making activities,[18] the creation of the ethnic state and the process of homogenization can also be understood as a variant of this theme in political economy. The use of ethnicity as an organizing principle for the state provides a powerful ideological basis for the mobilization of the members of society in defense of the ethnic state, which represents the tangible expression of the group's political identity. This mobilization is total. It may include a willingness on the part of the masses to serve in the armed forces in order to defend the new state. Alternatively, it may take the form of the adoption of military conscription. Likewise, there is likely to be a greater willingness to contribute economically to the support of the state whether through the assumption of heavy tax burdens for defense and/or the conversion of peacetime manufacture of consumer goods into wartime production of military hardware. Finally, the removal of ethnic rivals also facilitates the extraction of resources by would-be state makers through the expropriation of property left behind by members of the ousted community for use either by the state or by members of the dominant community.

A further consideration is that the transformation of the authority structures of society away from self-interested performance criteria and towards ethnic identification also has a basis in establishing the economic and political foundations of the state. By reducing popular expectations in the form of demands upon the state for social services, which would otherwise strain the capacities of weak states, the state is able to utilize these economic resources elsewhere. Since money is fungible, the resources saved in the area of social services can be re-directed towards the development of the military apparatus of the state, which, in turn, allows for the making of war and the expansion of the state. As Tilly pointed out, this war making and state making allows for the extraction of even more resources, without any loss of revenue in the process. Thus, the process of strengthening the state's capacity to govern through coercion and extraction is cyclical in nature.

The point of this discussion is neither to condone nor condemn this violence or the ends which it seeks to achieve. It is rather to gain some historical perspective so as to identify the function of ethnic conflict in the state-building process and to suggest that the oftentimes brutal process of ethnic homogenization represents the earliest stages in a process of establishing empirical statehood through the consolidation of control in those

parts of the world in which the establishment of juridical statehood interfered with this process.

The importance of this linkage will become apparent when the role
of UN intervention in ethnic conflicts is examined. The issue in that case
will be whether such intervention, while undoubtedly well-intentioned,
interferes with this rudimentary form of state-building by interfering with
the process of coercive consolidation by which the state develops the capacity to govern effectively and, ultimately, to satisfy the demands of performance criteria *at some future stage in the development of the state.*

Unless such intervention is capable of providing post-colonial states
with the governing capacity needed in order to satisfy the demands for performance coming from the population without resulting in state collapse
from system overload, it would seem that international efforts to artificially
preserve weak, ethnically heterogeneous, post-colonial states in accordance
with the principles of juridical sovereignty (principles which include guaranteeing the territorial integrity of states regardless of their viability) is only
offering false hope. It is not too dissimilar from those who would maintain a person on life support systems despite the absence of *any possibility* that the patient might regain consciousness. It may satisfy the moral
angst expressed by public opinion in the West (among people whose states
already share a large portion of the moral responsibility for this situation
through their own histories of colonialism, which, it can also be argued,
facilitated their own economic development and, therefore, state-building at
the expense of the very peoples whose plight is now the subject of so much
pious indignation), but it does little or nothing for the creation of empirically viable states capable of meeting the demands of their own people.

Tragically, the situation may have to get worse before it can get better.
The alternative is akin to inducing labor in a woman in the second trimester
rather than the third so as to spare her those extra few months of discomfort
and pain. While third party intervention would undoubtedly be motivated
by a compassionate desire to prevent pain and suffering and the process
would certainly be successful in meeting its stated objective, the developmental consequences for the premature newborn would likely be crippling
or possibly even life threatening. It is this which gives one pause when considering the *consequences* of well-intentioned conduct. One is reminded of
that ironic adage that the operation was a success, but the patient died.

GLOBALIZATION AND THE END OF THE COLD WAR

Before exploring the impact of globalization and the end of the Cold War
on state failure and ethnic resurgence, it is first necessary to digress for

a moment in order to understand the relationship between the phenom-enon collectively known as globalization and the end of the Cold War with the resulting demise of the Soviet Union. For reasons which will become apparent, without such an understanding, the attempt to relate ethnic con-flict, state-building/collapse, and UN peacekeeping/peace enforcement will inevitably miss the "forest" for the "trees."

The notion of globalization is actually an extension of an idea which has been around for decades in the field of international relations: inter-dependence.[19] The technological developments of the 1990s associated with the telecommunications revolution responsible for such innovations as the internet made it possible to think in terms of a global society with-out borders as not merely a philosophical concept but one with practical applications. In point of fact, however, globalization is not simply about the invention of a new technology. It is, instead, a collective term for a number of analytically distinct, but interrelated, phenomena[20] which tran-scend traditional state borders. These include, but are not limited to, the following: satellite technologies associated with the telecommunications revolution (which in addition to the internet would also include satellite dishes for television, cell phones, fax machines, etc.), threats to the global environment from industrial pollutants and radioactive nuclear waste, drug trafficking and other forms of transnational organized criminal net-works, international terrorist organizations and the networks which sup-port them financially, multinational corporations (MNCs), international financial organizations such as the International Monetary Fund and the World Bank, international trade organizations such as the World Trade Organization (WTO), transnational religio-political movements such as Islamic fundamentalism, the proliferation of weapons of mass destruction to an increasing number of states, and emerging supranational institutions such as the European Union (EU). While by no means an exhaustive list, these do serve as a representative sample of what have come to be seen as evidence of an increasingly integrated global community.

It is no accident that the end of the decades-long Cold War coincided with the onset of this phenomenon of globalization. Indeed the relation-ship between these two phenomena would appear to be symbiotic. Much as the relationship between state failure/collapse and ethnic conflict has a "chicken" and "egg" quality to it, the same can be said for the relationship between globalization and the end of the Cold War.

One way to view this relationship would be to see the transcendent nature of global technologies and economic forces as overwhelming the capacities of centrally planned economies and political systems found in socialist countries such as the Soviet Union and the countries of Eastern

Europe. The increasing tendency for economic development to be tied to participation in the global marketplace and the growing inability of centralized systems to control outside sources of information about the ever-widening gap between standards of living in the West and East mobilized populations in communist countries to demand more than their governments could or would provide (performance criteria).

The clearest examples of this would be the events in Tiananmen Square in May, 1989, which could only be managed by the Chinese government through a decision to employ overwhelming force to suppress the student-led movement, and the tearing down of the Berlin Wall later that year, which ended the division of that city and symbolically ended the Cold War.

Less dramatic in terms of a single cataclysmic event, but no less significant in terms of their impact upon the communist world, were the spiraling demands following the introduction of glasnost (openness) by Mikhail Gorbachev in the 1980s and his call for perestroika (restructuring). The pressures from below for both higher standards of living and greater autonomy for the Soviet republics (culminating in demands for independence and subsequently for ethnic secession from these republics as in the case of Nagorno-Karabakh) were also connected to a belated recognition by the Soviet leadership (or at least the General Secretary) of the linkage between political and economic liberalization and the need for both if the Soviet Union were to remain competitive in the new world economy.

This liberalization could not proceed without Soviet withdrawal from Eastern Europe. By that time, this region had come to be seen as a net economic loss for the Soviet Union as it was diverting precious economic resources away from the Soviet economy. Furthermore, the contradiction between domestic liberalization and external domination and repression in an era of increasing transparency in international relations was simply untenable. The peoples of Eastern Europe were becoming increasingly restless and the Western countries would not allow the Soviet Union to enter the world economy so long as it continued to engage in these policies. In the end, Soviet withdrawal of support for the regimes in Eastern Europe combined with popular mobilization in these countries due, in no small part, to the influence of outside information about economic and political conditions in the West resulted in the collapse of communism in Eastern Europe. The collapse of communism in Eastern Europe resolved, somewhat belatedly, the question which had bedeviled policy makers since the end of the Second World War by removing the original Cold War divide between East and West. Eventually, the contraction of the Soviet empire would result in the contraction of the Soviet state ending in the implosion or demise of the Soviet Union itself. Thus, one way to interpret events is that globalization accomplished something which forty years of military standoff could not: the end of the Cold War and the collapse of the Soviet Union.

A different way to view these events would see the end of the Cold War not as a *result* of globalization but as a *facilitator* of globalization.[21] From this perspective, global economic and political integration could not take place as long as the world was divided into hostile camps. Thus, globalization was actually a phenomenon of the post-Cold War era. According to this narrative, the withdrawal of the Soviet Union from Eastern Europe and the eventual collapse of the Soviet Union itself were not a function of the pressures of the global marketplace or transcendent information technologies beyond the control of states. These global forces could not develop until the path had been cleared by the retreat and collapse of the Soviet Union. Thus, political and economic liberalization under Gorbachev were not in *response* to popular demands from below brought on by exposure to life in the West; rather, they were *initiated* as state-sponsored efforts from above to improve the capabilities of the Soviet state.

As Gorbachev saw it, the problem for the Soviets at the time was not finding a way to enter the global market economy, which could have been achieved at any time by simply renouncing communism. Gorbachev made clear that his objective was not the downfall of socialism but its strengthening.[22]

In the midst of the Cold War, however, this objective forced the Soviets to deal with the proverbial problem of "guns versus butter." They would have to find a way to improve simultaneously the economy *while* competing militarily with the West in the face of President Reagan's determination to go forward with a massive arms buildup, which included his unshakeable support for the Strategic Defense Initiative (SDI). The recognition by the Kremlin that the military threat from the West could only be overcome by shifting already scarce economic resources from consumer goods to the development of enough ballistic missiles to compete with the American arms buildup and to overwhelm the proposed space-based program forced Gorbachev to the realization that the Brezhnev-era bureaucracy had to be reformed. Otherwise, it would be impossible to either maintain or improve the Soviet economy while at the same time engaging in a military build-up. In other words, glasnost and perestroika were not responses to popular demands from below for a restructuring of the society and the economy brought on by a restructured global economy which empowered Soviet citizens to demand reforms comparable to those sought by the students in the People's Republic of China; they were instead responses from above to a perceived military threat and to the inadequacies of an economic system left over from an earlier time.

If this view is correct, then the mobilization of various groups within Soviet society (something which would eventually bring down the system) was not brought on by global forces but by forces from within the Soviet Union itself—specifically, the decision to loosen centralized control.

The impact of Gorbachev's decision to open up the system needs to be understood in the context of nearly seventy-five years of centralized control. This system (particularly during the Stalinist period) had virtually eliminated any vestiges of non-governmental forms of association commonly referred to as civil society. In healthy societies and states, civil society inculcates certain norms or values into the population. As a result, individuals exercise a degree of self-restraint even in the absence of governmental oversight. The exercise of self-restraint makes limited government possible. The suggestion is that in the absence of this type of civil society, the lifting of governmental controls created a social and political vacuum in which societal behavior was without restraint and, therefore, out of control. The result was a mobilized Soviet public without any established rules of the game by which to express demands. In the absence of such rules, demands took the form of calls for secession by the various republics and by some ethnic minorities within those republics. The inability of the Soviet government to control what it had unleashed either by channeling it into some form of constructive policy program or by suppressing it caused the state to collapse. One consequence of this collapse was the growth of organized criminal networks, which operated in this environment of lawlessness associated with the collapse of the state.

The collapse of the Soviet state also brought to an end the Cold War. In the absence of this longstanding political bifurcation of the world, the door was opened to a process of greater global integration. Thus, for example, one of the clearest symbols that the Cold War had ended and a global era was beginning was the opening of McDonald's in Moscow (as a symbol of the penetration of American-style capitalism in the heart of the former communist world). This would have been unimaginable during the Cold War. Similarly, the disappearance of Cold War tensions from the UN Security Council (as evidenced by the far more assertive role of the Council beginning with the 1991 Persian Gulf War and in the years since the end of the Cold War) and the expansion of NATO (a Cold War alliance formed specifically to meet a potential threat from Eastern Europe) into Eastern Europe all point to a level of cooperation and integration which were simply not possible in a bipolar world. Thus, a strong case can be made that globalization was a *result* rather than a *cause* of the end of the Cold War.

As with the question of whether state failure causes or results from ethnic resurgence, there is no doubt an element of truth in both of these interpretations of the relationship between globalization and the end of the Cold War. Both can be supported by evidence from the historical record. Unlike historians, however, who are primarily interested in documenting the sequence of events correctly, the goal of political scientists engaged in theory-building is to try to develop an explanation not merely for a particular sequence of events but which is useful as a way to explain an entire category of events such as state failure or ethnic resurgence. The important question to ask, then, is not simply what was the precise order of events which led to the failure of the Soviet Union and the resurgence of regional and ethnic separatist demands? That is a question with which historians must wrestle. The important question for political scientists to ask is rather: how and why are these twin phenomena of globalization and the end of the Cold War related to the proliferation in the number of state failures and the increasing tendency of greater numbers of people across the globe to identify with their ethnic communities and to be mobilized on their behalf in recent years? As part of the endeavor to understand this complex relationship, the factual pattern in cases such as that of the Soviet Union become instructive without necessarily being definitive.

While both interpretations of the relationship between globalization and the end of the Cold War can be defended historically, the former is more useful for a study of this sort. Unlike the latter, its explanatory power transcends the particular circumstances which existed in specific countries in the late 1980s and early 1990s.

The next chapter will pick up on this point by focusing in greater detail upon the impact that both globalization and the end of the Cold War had upon the increasing number of cases of state failure/collapse and the resurgence of ethnic identification and conflict in weak, post-colonial states.

Chapter Six

Globalization, the End of the Cold War, Increasing State Failure, and Ethnic Mobilization

INTRODUCTION

Up to this point, the argument has been that post-colonial states have been precluded from developing the empirical attributes of statehood necessary for the fulfillment of the rising expectations which occur when the focus of state legitimacy shifts to performance. Although valid, this explanation is only partial and leaves certain questions still unanswered.

It does not, for example, explain the impetus for this transition. Clearly, societies have not always linked the notion of legitimate political authority to the satisfaction of individual self-interest. Indeed, as Max Weber observed long ago, most societies throughout the greater part of human history have linked authority to other criteria such as heredity or personal attributes, which he referred to as charisma. This is not to suggest that self-interest played no role in political loyalty until recently. For example, urban political machines in the United States at the start of the twentieth century derived their political strength from their ability to meet the needs of their constituencies. Indeed, one can go back even further. Tilly has argued that an important element in the early process of consolidation of state power by state-makers in Western Europe centuries ago involved the co-opting of relevant political elites by offering certain tangible benefits in exchange for their loyalty.

At the same time, however, it is worth pointing out that this ability of early state-makers to satisfy demands was largely limited to the upper strata of society. Likewise, in the case of urban machines, it is important to note that, while connected to the political process, they operated outside of the formal machinery of government and in large part were a substitute for institutionalized governmental activity in the area of social welfare. Consequently, for most of the members of society, the welfare state concept simply did not exist until fairly recently. In fact, in what now would appear to be in some important respects a precursor to the development of this notion of performance criteria, Samuel H. Beer discussed the comparatively recent decline of the deferential society in Great Britain. In this regard, it is worth noting that, for Beer, this deferential society had imposed an element of self-restraint upon the public. In *Britain Against Itself*, he linked the steadily increasing set of popular demands upon the government for public services to the rise of the welfare state. This tendency transformed national politics from the idea that *each exists to serve all* to the idea that *all exist to serve each*. He goes on to argue that this shift had profound effects upon the capacity of the British government to continue to govern effectively.[1]

In this fascinating study of British politics, he argues that the so-called "contradictions of collectivism"[2] led to the emergence of interest group politics, in which politics came to be based upon *self-interest* rather than some understanding of the common good. In his view, the demands generated by this development continued to spiral out of control until eventually they overloaded the capacities of the British political system to deliver.

While some of the specific causes for this transition in Britain may differ from those found in more contemporary examples of societies undergoing a transition in their concepts of political legitimacy, the important point is the suggestion that the decline of deference had a number of negative consequences for the *capacity* of Great Britain to continue to govern itself. The parallels suggest that what sometimes had been referred to as the "British disease" during the period of the 1960s and 1970s may, albeit in a much milder and arguably more manageable form, presage the far more serious consequences for governance in post-colonial states as a consequence of the introduction of performance criteria for political legitimacy and the resulting rise of the politics of self-interest.

One question, then, which needs to be answered is: why are traditional sources of authority increasingly being replaced by demands for performance? A related, but arguably even more important, question in terms of this theory is: how do globalization and the end of the Cold War contribute to the development of performance criteria as well as to the collapse of post-colonial states and the resurgence of ethnic identification and conflict? The answer to this question will bring this discussion considerably closer to the development of an integrated theory capable of solving the ultimate puzzle of the relationship between ethnic conflict, state-building/collapse, and UN peacekeeping/peace enforcement.

The transition to performance criteria by itself cannot explain state failure and ethnic resurgence. While Rosenau's theory posits that all states in the modern world are undergoing this transition, Mason makes clear that it is weak states (which generally refers to post-colonial states) which are most in danger of collapse. Clearly, then, more is necessary than a demanding public in order for a state to collapse. It is also necessary to look at the *capacity of a state to satisfy these demands.*

A key element responsible for this lack of capacity is the failure of post-colonial states to develop the attributes of empirical statehood as a result of the introduction of norms associated with the idea of juridical statehood. The problem, however, is that this explanation treats the state as if it were a self-contained or isolated entity rather than a unit existing within a wider global context, which includes a particular international system with its own specific structural features.[3] To better understand the problem of state failure/collapse, it is necessary to draw upon the discussion of globalization and the end of the Cold War. Of particular interest is the impact that these twin developments have had upon post-colonial states. This discussion will make it possible to understand not only *how* and *why* but also *when* state failure/collapse and ethnic resurgence are likely to occur. After all, it should be remembered that these same post-colonial states, which are now failing, continued to exist for decades after independence even without the empirical attributes of statehood. What, then, accounts for the seemingly sudden change?

The answer would seem to be that the international norms associated with juridical statehood, which once sustained these otherwise failing states, are themselves undergoing a transformation. In the process, the existence and/or the territorial configurations of states are no longer held to be sacrosanct. This normative transformation and its impact upon weak post-colonial states are best understood in terms of the impact of globalization and the end of the Cold War.

Ironically, it is through a careful study of the factors which account for state failure that a theory of state-*building* can begin to take shape in much the same way that the first step in the development of a cure is to study the disease. This theory will seek to establish, through both logical and empirical analysis, that this erosion of certain international norms has made it both possible and necessary for ethnic identification and ethnic conflict to lay the foundations for empirical statehood in those states which have been historically disadvantaged by their late entry into the states system.

My premise is that a resurgence of ethnic identification, and the resulting conflict pursued to a military conclusion, in ethnically heterogeneous societies is integral to the development of state capacity in weak post-colonial states. The converse of this counterintuitive statement is that outside interference with this sort of conflict, which prevents a military resolution from taking place, will result in state failure/collapse or the inability of the state to exercise sovereign control over its own territory. As stated earlier, since the ability to control the population within one's own territory is fundamental to statehood, ethnic resurgence and uninterrupted ethnic conflict should properly be understood as an initial stage of the state-building process.

The linkage between the notions of uninterrupted and interrupted ethnic conflict suggests that it is useful to think of ethnic conflict as a variable. Sometimes this phenomenon is allowed to run its course without interruption while on other occasions there is outside interference designed to stop the killing before one of the belligerents has been able to achieve a military victory. The presence of both sets of occurrences makes it possible to establish a *causal* relationship between ethnic conflict and the capacity of a state to exercise effective governance. Any correlation between the two might be nothing more than a coincidence. If, however, cases can be identified in which uninterrupted ethnic conflict preceded the development of state capacity alongside cases in which the interruption of ethnic violence preceded either state failure/collapse or a stalemate in which the state was unable to exercise sovereign control over its own territory, this would provide a basis upon which to suggest that external intervention in internal (ethnic) conflicts serves to undermine the state-building process in post-colonial states.

Accordingly, this chapter will close with a discussion of the changing nature of UN intervention in the post-Cold War era and its impact upon both ethnic conflict and the state-building process. This discussion will draw upon previous experiences to complete the development of an integrated theory of the relationship between ethnic identification/conflict, state-building, and UN peacekeeping/intervention in post-colonial states in a post-bipolar era of globalization. Once this theory is developed, it can be tested against the more detailed case study of Iraq in order to see whether (and to what degree) it holds up to closer scrutiny.

RISING EXPECTATIONS AND DECLINING STATE CAPACITY: THE IMPACT OF GLOBALIZATION

How and why are globalization and the end of the Cold War related to state failure and ethnic resurgence? It would seem that the concept of juridical sovereignty as an explanation for the virtual absence of state failures during the Cold War is useful but a bit too simplistic. While perhaps an indispensable element, it alone cannot explain the relative absence of authority crises (certainly compared to the post-Cold War era) associated with performance criteria. Nor, for that matter, does it provide any reasons for the recent emergence of the politics of self-interest and rising expectations. In order to develop such an explanation, it is necessary to take into account the ways in which the worldwide dissemination of information (one would have to go back perhaps to the invention of the printing press to find a comparable example with similarly destabilizing consequences in the form of the Protestant Reformation and ultimately the collapse of the Holy Roman Empire) have empowered individuals. Correspondingly, the capacities of all states, but especially the weakest among them, have been continually eroded by their declining ability to control the flow of information within their borders.[4] The resulting increase in awareness of both material prosperity and opportunities for political participation elsewhere in the world has generated growing demands for these same things at home. *In this environment, rising popular expectations find themselves on a collision course with diminishing capacities on the part of governments*, whose ability to control their own borders and populations already has been circumscribed by their inability to control the flow of information across state boundaries. In the absence of some resolution, these intersecting trajectories are a recipe for crisis and eventual collapse.

It would seem that the only ways to avert this crisis are either to lower public expectations for state performance and/or to increase the capacities of states to meet these growing demands. In an era of globalization, these options pose a dilemma for state makers. In order to lessen the pressure on the post-colonial state on the demand side, there would need to be a drastic reorientation of society away from the sort of "organic solidarity" described by Durkheim. This would entail a fundamental change in the organizing principle of society. Individualism and the politics of self-interest (performance) would have to be replaced by some other organizing principle for society and the state (such as the norm of cultural conformity associated with ethnic identification, for example). Unless such a transformation occurs, the first option of lowering public expectations, and, therefore, pressure upon weak states to perform, is unlikely to occur.

The alternative would be to address the growing demands within societies from the supply side by increasing the capacities of newer states to meet these challenges. This, however, would require that obstacles to the development of state capacity be removed. Since both the preservation and the weakness of post-colonial states are largely the result of a set of international norms involving the Cold War era notion that state boundaries are sacrosanct and may not be altered by force,[5] the prospect that the second option of increased state capacity will occur remains unlikely unless a new consensus develops under which these international norms would be temporarily deferred during this interim phase of state reconstruction.

Further complicating this issue of developing state capacity so as to meet the demands of the population for government performance are the introduction of various post-Cold War international norms. These include the requirement that international recognition of a state's legitimacy be made conditional upon the regime's respect for so-called "universal" human rights and the widely-held insistence that states undergo a process of democratization. Even the most politically developed states are often-times hard-pressed to satisfy these noble, but frequently unrealistic, expec-tations. It is reasonable, therefore, to inquire as to whether placing such added burdens upon the still fragile state structures of post-colonial states (something which was not imposed upon Western states at a comparable stage in their own political development) may have unintended conse-quences. These added responsibilities imposed upon states still struggling to achieve control over their territories and populations without the protec-tions afforded by juridical statehood more than likely will lead to system overload and political collapse. If so, then these international expectations would be a recipe for anarchy and bloodshed rather than human rights and the development of stable, functioning democracies. Under the cir-cumstances, the tragic irony is that norms which were developed in order to protect the population of a state may, and frequently do, end up posing the gravest threat to that population. In this instance, the cure may be even worse than the disease since arguably even bad government is less danger-ous than no government.

In this regard, the evidence suggests that normative changes are underway—albeit, not necessarily ones which would facilitate state recon-struction. While the norms of human rights and democratization have been strengthened in the post-Cold War era, there do seem to be indica-tions from the greater frequency of shifting territorial boundaries that ter-ritorial integrity as an international norm has weakened in recent years. These normative changes in the international system would be consistent with the Realist notion that such changes are a byproduct of the re-distri-bution of power among states and the Neorealist emphasis upon systemic structure and the restructuring of the international system associated with the end of bipolarity.

Up to this point, the linkages between these phenomena have been described only in broad strokes. The question arises, however, as to the precise nature of the relationship as an explanation for state failure and ethnic conflict in a post-bipolar age of globalization. The answer to this rather complex question will explain how it was that the post-colonial state was able to function during the Cold War, what went wrong, and in what direction it is currently headed.

As was mentioned, the global dissemination of information helped to create rising expectations. In the process, largely traditional societies based upon some specific variation of Durkheim's principle of mechanical solidarity have been transformed into more individualistic, mobile, and demanding societies. These societies seek the same material possessions and creature comforts found in the more economically and politically developed countries of the world. This represents a significant change. When information about the outside world was scarce and generally controlled by governments, it was possible for people to be satisfied living the same kind of lives as their ancestors had for centuries.

The absence of an increasingly educated general population and a growing professional class meant that for a long time after independence, there were comparatively few demands upon the state. Those which did exist were usually within the capacity of the state to satisfy. According to Mohammad J. Kuna, this was accomplished through programs of state-sponsored economic development, which were a primary focus of the early post-colonial state particularly in Africa.[6] If popular demands exceeded the domestic capacities of post-colonial states, economic assistance generally was available from superpower donors eager to obtain client states during the Cold War.

Thus, whether through domestic or international initiatives, post-colonial states were able to respond to rather limited popular demands for improvements in the standard of living. Whatever residual demands (if any) existed which could not be satisfied either through domestic policies or through foreign assistance could be suppressed using weapons obtained from superpower benefactors. In this comparatively demand-free society, authority was not seen as deriving from one's capacity to satisfy popular demands. Instead, it was based largely on traditional criteria such as heredity or perhaps religion in a manner reminiscent of the European notion of Divine Right of Kings.

The transition to performance criteria is largely a function of the related trends of modernization and globalization. In addition to easier access to unfettered information about the outside world made possible by globalization, the increasing mobility of populations is another aspect of the transition taking place in much of the world today. In this instance, the problems for traditional societies associated with urbanization and industrialization are all too familiar to modernization theorists. The large-scale uprooting of the peasant class in agrarian societies (whose minimal needs for food, clothing, and shelter were usually taken care of by wealthy landlords) to cities unprepared for this massive influx creates demands for such things as adequate housing, sanitation, health care, as well as decent wages and working conditions. These demands (which traditionally have taken the form of political and economic organization and mobilization) become all the more necessary now that the traditional support system which existed in a land-based agrarian economy is no longer present to provide for these new city-dwellers. Unfortunately for these new residents, the rapid transformation of traditional cities into vast urban centers in places such as Mexico City or Cairo usually occurs at such a pace as to overwhelm the existing capacities of the urban administrations necessitating some form of action at the national level.

The post-colonial state, however, is generally no better equipped to deal with this situation than are local governments. On the demand side, the reason has to do with the temporal conflation of the analytically distinct, but nevertheless related, processes of modernization and globalization (developments which occurred sequentially in older states). These have produced in post-colonial states both the societal dislocations common to earlier modernizing societies brought on by the loss of traditional support networks as well as a greater awareness than that which existed in earlier modernizing societies of standards of living elsewhere. The result is a rather volatile combination of rising expectations alongside growing impatience with traditional state structures, which simply lack the means to satisfy these demands partly because these states are themselves still in the midst of struggling to complete the transition to modernity through industrialization. As if this were not difficult enough to manage, the transition to modernity is made all the more difficult by global environmental constraints not confronted by earlier industrializing societies, which have given rise to calls for so-called "sustainable development."

The demand side is only part of the problem, however. It can explain the shift to performance criteria for state legitimacy, which undermines traditional state structures as loyalty becomes tied to those best able to satisfy growing demands. By itself, however, it cannot explain the lack of state capacity and the failure of the state to provide for the needs of its people with the resulting political crisis which this creates for the post-colonial state.

This brings the discussion to a closer look at the issue of state capacity. Unlike older states, which also had to contend with the dislocations associated with the transition to modernity, the problem is infinitely more acute in newer states as the problem is not merely one of completing the industrialization process—although that no doubt would ease the burden somewhat. Ironically, the reason for this far more complex problem is rooted in the same globalization process which plays such a pivotal role in escalating societal demands as well as the systemic change which occurred with the ending of the Cold War.

Globalization has been a major factor responsible for undermining the governing capacity of already weak states. The fundamental challenge to state capacity is that various functions which were traditionally seen as matters of state responsibility such as law enforcement, environmental control, and economic development, to name just a few, are increasingly operating at a level beyond the scope of the state. One need only consider some examples of this phenomenon to grasp the wider point: the telecommunications revolution has seriously weakened the ability of even the most totalitarian states to control the flow of information within their borders;[7] the growth in the number of international non-governmental organizations concerned with human rights issues introduces the notion of transparency, which greatly limits the ability of states to determine what information is received by the outside world (while few would object to this on moral grounds, the issue here is not morality but state capacity) thereby complicating the exercise of sovereign control within a state; the problem of coping with international networks engaged in criminal activities such as drug trafficking and/or terrorism increasingly links a state's ability to provide for the safety of its own people (arguably the primary responsibility of any government) to decisions made beyond the territorial control of that state and to the capacities of other states to control criminal activities within their borders;[8] the increasing willingness by the international community to countenance the use of UN or other external troops to address internal conflicts has pre-empted the state's traditional control over its population as a fundamental attribute of its sovereignty and produced a growing dependence upon external security forces, which may even have the unintended effect of encouraging those with grievances to challenge the state's authority by force, if necessary, in the belief that they will enjoy international protection in their efforts; the global trend towards economic liberalization[9] in the form of the removal of trade barriers by the WTO (World Trade Organization) weakens the ability of states undergoing the process of industrialization to protect domestic manufacturers and jobs by controlling the flow of goods into the country; and structural adjustment[10] or austerity programs imposed by the IMF (International Monetary Fund) and the World Bank as conditions for providing economic assistance to newly industrializing countries struggling to cope with the debt crisis of the 1970s restrict the ability of governments to provide a safety net in the form of jobs programs or social welfare programs to those workers who become unemployed as a result of the inability of domestic manufacturers to compete with foreign competitors. It also limits the capacity of states to utilize patronage as a way to solidify control within the state.

As globalization increasingly preempts the traditional functions of states which are basic to people's lives at precisely the moment when individuals are coming to expect more and more from their governments in exchange for their loyalty, *the widening gap between expectations and performance* poses an ever-increasing challenge to the stability of existing state structures. Again, the problem is one faced by all states, but is particularly serious in post-colonial states due to their failure to undergo the painstaking, and usually quite painful, process of building empirical statehood.

SYSTEMIC CHANGE: WEAK STATES IN A POST-BIPOLAR WORLD

As if the problems for state capacity in weak states associated with globalization were not enough, they are further compounded by the end of the Cold War. Contrary to popular expectations that the post-Cold War era would be one of peaceful economic development through the spread of capitalism and democratization,[11] this period has proven instead to be a time of considerable violence and instability. It would appear that few at the time of the Cold War fully appreciated the extent to which the stability of state boundaries and regimes were tied to the existence of bipolarity in the world. Even Jackson and Rosberg failed to make the connection between the norm of juridical sovereignty and the underlying systemic structure of bipolarity. Since the vast majority of modern states came into existence concurrently with the Cold War, owing to the chronologically parallel process of decolonization of Western empires, it is only in the aftermath of the East-West struggle that it has become possible to appreciate more fully the role which this global competition played in sustaining otherwise non-viable states. This can be accomplished by looking at the impact of the termination of this conflict upon state capacity for governance in both post-colonial and post-communist states (some of which, such as Yugoslavia or perhaps Czechoslovakia, might also be thought of as post-colonial states inasmuch as they were created out of the former Austro-Hungarian empire by the victorious Allies following the conclusion of the First World War).

In some ways a precursor of developments in post-colonial states following the Cold War, the Soviet decision to contract its foreign policy commitments in the late 1980s had demonstrable effects upon the regimes and states of communist Eastern Europe. Long sustained by Soviet military and economic assistance, these regimes proved to be lacking in any significant degree of domestic support. In part, this lack of support stemmed from the fact that, with the exception of Tito in Yugoslavia, most of these regimes were imposed by external force as opposed to coming to power as the result of indigenous processes.

Equally, if not more, important, however, was the fact that these states were incapable of competing economically with their counterparts in Western Europe. Once the twin pillars of Soviet military and economic assistance were withdrawn and the peoples of Eastern Europe became aware of these economic disparities through travel and liberalization of controls on information from the outside world, the communist political systems in Eastern Europe came crashing down. These events in 1989 represent early examples of the crisis brought on by the collision between declining state capacity and rising public expectations (performance criteria).

An examination of these events reveals, however, that it was not only the regimes which collapsed. Closely related to the collapse of these communist regimes was the breakup of certain artificially created states: Czechoslovakia and Yugoslavia. Carved out of what had been the Habsburg Empire at the end of World War I, the boundaries of these states were not the result of internal state-building processes. Consequently, they bore no relation to any single identifiable national community.

In this regard, their situation is reminiscent of a recurring phenomenon which challenged the legitimacy of many post-colonial states in Africa.[12] In the case of Yugoslavia and Czechoslovakia, it was the victorious Allies who were responsible for the creation of these states ostensibly to further the goal of national self-determination. It can be argued, however, that, as in the case of the African colonies/states, these newly created Eastern European states bore little relation to demographic conditions on the ground and instead represented efforts by the great powers to dismember Germany's Austro-Hungarian ally in an attempt to contain Germany's growing influence on the continent.

During the communist period following World War II, efforts were made to utilize the transcendent ideology of communism as a substitute for sentiments of national solidarity in a manner similar to efforts undertaken in the Soviet Union. Perhaps the clearest example of substituting communism for nationalism would be the case of the German Democratic Republic, whose existence as a distinct entity was tied exclusively to ideology inasmuch as there was no other reason for there to be two German states.

In a different, but no less important way, communism was also important as an organizing principle for ethnically diverse states such as Yugoslavia.[13] As was mentioned, however, the lack of legitimacy of these communist regimes (in the case of Yugoslavia, it was less a result of Soviet withdrawal of support and more the result of the inability of the country to compete economically combined with the collapse of communist regimes in surrounding countries) resulted in the collapse of the political systems and the discrediting of communism as the ideological foundation for these states once external support was removed. This collapse created a political vacuum. Without some overarching political ideology to justify the continued existence of states which were not the product of empirical processes of state formation, it was only natural that the question of appropriate state boundaries should arise once the ideological underpinnings had disappeared. Indeed, the more surprising fact is that state collapse in Eastern Europe was limited to only these cases plus the special case of the German Democratic Republic, whose existence was solely a function of the Cold War divide in Europe and whose collapse was a natural result of the end of that struggle.

Interestingly, a good case can be made that the reason why widespread *regime* collapse did not produce more cases of *state* collapse in Eastern Europe was due to the number of ethnic population transfers (today these would be called "ethnic cleansing") which had occurred in this region during the twentieth century.[14] The net effect of these transfers was to create a closer fit between the nation and the state than that which had existed in these states at the end of World War I.[15] Indeed, this was the very rationale behind these transfers.[16]

It, therefore, should come as no surprise that the cases of state collapse in Eastern Europe at the end of the Cold War occurred in those states which had *not* experienced these transfers of population. Seen in this context, the use of the practice widely known as "ethnic cleansing" in the former Yugoslavia after the fall of communism should be seen as merely the latest in a long series of such transfers responsible for the creation of more homogeneous and stable states: "As a war strategy pursued by Croats and Serbs alike in Croatia and in Bosnia-Herzegovina, however, the association between persons and rights to land became a deliberate policy to clear a territory of all those who were considered not to belong in their national territory and who might be suspected of disloyalty. In Bosnia-Herzegovina, 'random and selective killing,' detention camps as way stations with 'inadequate shelter, food, and sanitation,' and even massacres were reportedly used as 'tools' to remove populations."[17]

Susan L. Woodward goes on to point out that the underlying logic of this policy was political in nature: "The basis of this policy of ethnic cleansing lay not with primordial hatreds or local jealousies, but with political goals."[18] These goals are defined as " . . . to consolidate ethnically pure territories that would vote correctly in a referendum on sovereignty and in future elections and to justify government administration by their national group. . . ."[19]

It would seem that her conclusion is consistent with my contention that the creation of ethnic states, albeit oftentimes a brutal process, represents an attempt by state makers to utilize ethnicity as opposed to individual economic self-interest associated with performance criteria as an organizing principle for the state.

Furthermore, it is worth emphasizing that such events are not limited to the contemporary period. As Jennifer Jackson Preece points out, they have been part of the nation-state creation process for at least much of the twentieth century. The only reason why they have come under such international scrutiny and disapproval is that a shift occurred in international norms after the Second World War. This normative change caused the practice of population transfer, *once thought to be a means of creating international order and stability*, to be viewed instead as a threat to both international order[20] and, since the end of the Cold War, to human rights.

Similar to the relationship between the Soviet Union and Eastern Europe, many post-colonial regimes and states in the so-called Third World were sustained in large part through the existence of a patron-client relationship with one or the other superpower. The end of the Cold War undermined the logic of this relationship and resulted in the withdrawal of support by the major powers.[21] Already overburdened by the problems which globalization created for their weak governing structures, the consequences for post-colonial states and regimes of this removal of support at the end of the Cold War demonstrated just how dependent many of them had been upon the international structure of bipolarity. In its absence, the capacity of these regimes to govern (indeed of the states themselves to continue to exist!) was increasingly in doubt.

INTERNATIONAL STRUCTURE, NORMS, AND STATE CAPACITY

Any notion that the relationship between the end of the Cold War and state failure can be explained *solely* through the withdrawal of major power support, however, would be a gross oversimplification. Another factor which needs to be understood is how *structural* changes in the international system away from bipolarity produced *normative* changes and, in turn, how these normative changes contributed to the weakening of the governing capacities of post-colonial states.

The Realist tradition,[22] and more specifically hegemonic stability theory, have long held that international norms, institutions, and organizations are rooted in the power and interests of a dominant state or group of states and/or the overall structural distribution of power within the international system.[23] Viewed in this manner as epiphenomena of the structure of power,[24] it would seem to follow that changes in the power structure of the international system would be reflected in changes in the normative bases of international relations.[25]

In order to relate this discussion of norms and power to the issue of state capacity and state failure, it is necessary to recall that for many post-colonial states, their continued existence was not a function of empirical statehood but of the juridical norms of state sovereignty, nonintervention in internal affairs, and the preservation of territorial integrity. As Hans-Henrik Holm observes, these norms served the power interests of the competing centers in the bipolar system during the Cold War inasmuch as the admissibility of external intervention or the shifting of state boundaries[26] by force would have threatened each superpower's projected sphere of influence and also increased the likelihood that local or regional conflicts would spill over into superpower confrontations[27] in those areas in which the political status of a state was up for grabs.[28]

The end of the Cold War has removed these concerns from the international agenda. Consequently, the shift in the underlying power structure of the international system has made it possible to relax certain norms associated with juridical sovereignty[29] which can no longer be said to serve the same function as they once did. The problem, however, is that weak states depended upon these norms to serve as a substitute for the development of an empirical capacity to govern. Thus, another part of the explanation for the relationship between the end of the Cold War and state failure must be this new international willingness to accept challenges to the survival and territorial integrity of the state. These challenges would have been impermissible at an earlier time when the international system operated under a different structure. Given the historical coincidence between decolonization and the emergence of juridical sovereignty as a *substitute* for empirical sovereignty in these newer states, the relaxation of the very international norms which undergirded otherwise weak states can only serve to undermine already fragile state structures.

Even this, however, is only a partial explanation for the post-Cold War phenomenon of state failure. A more complete explanation also would have to take account of the proliferation of weapons to non-state actors following the collapse of the Soviet Union. Once able to control the flow of arms, the combination of the collapse of communist central governments across Eastern Europe and parts of Asia, the creation of organized crime networks with access to weapons, and the desperate need for cash in failing economies in Eastern Europe and the new states of the former Soviet Union have all contributed to the greater ease with which challengers to state leaders are able to acquire military hardware.[30] As these weapons find their way into the hands of non-state actors challenging the claims of state elites either for control of the central government or as part of an effort at secession from the state, the capacities of weak states are further strained by the loss of the monopolization of the legitimate use of force.

Further compounding the problems of post-colonial states in the post-Cold War era is the emergence of the global norm of democratization, which reflects the values and interests of the Western powers as the unrivaled leaders of the new international system. Unlike the Cold War era, when this norm was contested and states could opt for Soviet-style authoritarian/totalitarian regimes, one consequence of the end of the Cold War has been the discrediting of autocratic models both as viable paths to economic development and as politically legitimate forms of governance. The linkage of democratization and state legitimacy has created a serious problem for weak states. Already stripped of the protection which juridical sovereignty once provided and deprived of the Cold War patron-client support system, these states, which lack legitimacy due to both the artificial nature of their inherited boundaries and to their poor economic performance as a consequence of late industrialization amid mounting debt crises, are nevertheless expected to meet the same democratic standards as their more politically and economically developed Western counterparts.

Without an underlying empirical basis for statehood, calls for democratization only serve to increase political instability. It must be remembered that these calls are coming at a moment in time in which a number of developments are all occurring simultaneously in such a manner as to produce what has been referred to as a "cumulation of crises." These "crises" or converging developments include the following: the absence of a firm basis upon which to define the nature of the political community (territorial (civic) nationalism or perhaps ethnic nationalism); the existence of structural adjustment programs, which, at least in the short-term, heighten economic disparities within the population by reducing or eliminating government social safety nets and patronage networks designed to ease the transition to an industrial economy and preserve loyalty to the regime in power;[31] and the increasing political mobilization of the population. This mobilization is partly a response to industrialization and urbanization but also to advances in telecommunications technology as well as the presence of intergovernmental and non-governmental organizations pressing for democratization and protection of human rights for those who challenge the regime.

This "cumulation of crises" would strain the capacities of even the most stable states. For those with little or no empirical basis, the problem seems almost insurmountable. Echoing the views of Ayoob, Holm discusses the enormous burden which is placed upon post-colonial states: " . . . Third World states have to accomplish state building in a much shorter time than it took the West to do. The process is complicated by the fact that they have to perform the task of state building 'in a humane, civilised and consensual fashion in an era of mass politics'. The frequency of state failure in the Third World is, therefore, hardly surprising."[32]

The problems associated with this conflation of state-building processes and the narrow constraints of time in which they must be accomplished[33] have been aggravated further by the increasing willingness of the international community in the post-Cold War era to utilize UN forces for the purposes of intervention in cases traditionally defined under Article 2 (7) of the United Nations Charter as falling within the domestic affairs of states. While ostensibly authorized for the purpose of providing humanitarian assistance and/or the promotion of a peaceful resolution of internal conflicts, a key point to be considered is that such missions may complicate the already monumental task of empirical state-building. Briefly stated, the argument is that the more muscular and intrusive nature of these missions as compared to their Cold War era counterparts have a number of counterproductive consequences for the state-building process. One of these is the erosion of state capacity or perhaps the failure to develop such capacity. The use of UN troops for the provision of vital functions, such as law enforcement and the preservation of order within a state, may be intended to assist states until they can develop or restore governing capacity. It is far from clear, however, that external assistance is a useful approach in the provision of these functions, which are normally regarded as the responsibility of states rather than international organizations. As discussed earlier, this type of assistance may have the *opposite* effect. It may actually increase dependence upon the outside world similar to the experience of patron-client relationships during the Cold War. Such dependence is counterproductive to the goal of enabling otherwise weak, post-colonial states to develop their own internal capacities.[34] Following the line of reasoning developed by Tilly and elaborated by those such as Clapham or Jackson and Rosberg, it is equally plausible to argue that states only develop the capability to exercise effective control over their territories in response to some threat (whether it be generated externally or internally) and not as the result of some form of international assistance—however well-intentioned.

Another consequence of external intervention, especially humanitarian intervention, comes in the form of the creation of so-called "safe havens" and the provision of various forms of humanitarian assistance to the civilian victims of war. Again, while quite possibly the product of the highest of motives, it may also be that such assistance will result in the interruption of a process of ethnic consolidation, which, as suggested previously, is an important element in the development of empirical capacities in otherwise ethnically divided post-colonial states.

In accordance with the law of unintended consequences, the argument can be taken a step further to suggest that such interventions may inadvertently encourage ethnic conflicts by failing to distinguish between *political* and *natural* crises. As a result, a humanitarian response is offered which ignores the *political* roots of the situation at hand. Arguably, one constraint upon potential ethnic entrepreneurs tempted to mobilize segments of the population of a post-colonial state against the existing regime is the danger that such mobilization, and the ethnic conflict likely to follow, will result in widespread bloodshed as the regime unleashes its full repressive capacity. As the expectation of humanitarian intervention gains wider acceptance, however, the risk to these potential ethnic entrepreneurs is reduced accordingly since they now can attempt secession or violent overthrow of the government and still look to outside intervention for protection and humanitarian assistance.

Ironically, therefore, by reducing the potential risks to ethnic entrepreneurs, the danger exists that outside interference may actually *increase* rather than decrease the likelihood of conflict erupting. There are essentially two reasons for this. As indicated above, one is that the assurance of external intervention reduces the cost involved in pursuing secessionist struggles or struggles for control of the central government.

In addition, as seen in the case of the French mission Operation Tourquoise during the conflict in Rwanda, a second reason is that humanitarian intervention, which by its very nature tends to ignore political considerations, also has a tendency to preserve rebel forces until they are strong enough to undergo another round of fighting. Thus, the unintended result of this humanitarian "band-aid" oftentimes turns out to be the *prolongation* of the conflict rather than the alleviation of human suffering.[35]

Finally, the relaxation of juridical norms against intervention have clearly weakened the state's claim to juridical sovereignty. By itself, this would not necessarily pose a problem if one accepts the thesis that juridical sovereignty during the Cold War not only preserved weak states artificially but also made it unnecessary for them to develop their internal capacities because of the existence of an international safety net upon which they could depend for their survival. If, in turn, these states were able to utilize this relaxation of juridical norms to develop, somewhat belatedly, the capacity to govern associated with the idea of empirical statehood, it might be argued that this post-Cold War tendency has actually contributed somewhat belatedly to the strengthening of otherwise weak states. The problem, however, is that it is not at all clear that the relaxation of international norms in this instance has done anything to improve states' empirical capabilities. It is at least as plausible to argue that denial of a state's *exclusive* control over its own territory by permitting external intervention in support of human rights, democratization, or various other praiseworthy humanitarian objectives has had exactly the opposite effect. It has only contributed to the further erosion of state capacity.

DECLINING STATE CAPACITY AND ETHNIC RESURGENCE

It should come as no surprise that ethnicity and ethnic solidarity should emerge at this point in time as a response by weak states to their inability to cope with the numerous burdens imposed upon them by globalization and the structural changes to the formerly bipolar international system. The restructuring of societies away from individualism and self-interest and towards a more collectivist model based on cultural conformity not only serves the interests of ethnic entrepreneurs interested in exploiting ethnicity as a way to maintain or acquire power, as constructivists would argue; it also serves to provide weak post-colonial states with an opportunity to begin the long and arduous path of empirical state-building through ethnic conflict.

There is some reason to be optimistic that states emerging in a reconfigured form as ethnic states will in time evolve into healthy functioning democracies. This would be consistent with a line of reasoning dating back to John Stuart Mill, who saw democracy as related to national unity and as being unworkable in ethnically divided societies.

James Hughes and Gwendolyn Sasse explain that Mill is by no means alone in this regard; a significant body of literature has developed more recently in the field of comparative politics which shares Mill's view and suggests that national unity is a *prerequisite* to successful democratization. It follows from this argument that deeply divided societies (a condition all too common in the case of post-colonial states, given the arbitrary nature of the way colonial boundaries were initially drawn from the point of view of the indigenous cultures) are far less likely to develop along democratic lines. They observe further that ironically the national unity necessary for successful democratization is itself sometimes the

unintended result of brutal policies of forced homogenization which eradicate the problem of deeply divided societies by either expelling or exter-
minating ethnic minorities.[36]

Before concluding this discussion of the relationship between globalization, the end of the Cold War, and the resurgence of ethnic identification, it is necessary to go back to an issue raised in the first chapter and
explain the appeal of ethnicity to the masses at this moment in time. Up to
this point, the appeal of ethnicity has been merely assumed and the emphasis has been instead upon the efforts by ethnic entrepreneurs or potential
state makers to utilize ethnicity to restructure society.

While the theory developed in this study argues that a combination of
constructivist notions of ethnicity and Durkheim's approach to social solidarity is the driving force behind the ethnic resurgence at this particular
historical juncture in the development of the state,[37] this process does not
operate in a social or political vacuum. As suggested previously, attempts
by ethnic entrepreneurs to sow the seeds of ethnic identification would be
useless unless there were already in place a fertile ground for this appeal.
Thus, it needs to be understood that other interrelated processes are working in tandem with these activities by entrepreneurs to reinforce the appeal
of ethnicity among the members of society. While not the central focus of
this particular study, these processes are nevertheless important inasmuch
as they provide a context within which to understand the theory developed
here. That context is related to the phenomena of globalization and the
end of the Cold War.

The breaking down of cultural and informational barriers in this new
era tends to encourage ethnic identification by offering what is sometimes
referred to as a "demonstration effect," whereby people in one part of the
world are able to witness events in other parts of the world *as they unfold*.
In this case, these events would include the breakups of the Soviet Union,
Yugoslavia, and Czechoslovakia and the reaction of the rest of the world
to these developments.

The idea of a "demonstration effect" suggests that the fact that outside actors permit such events to occur in one part of the globe establishes
a series of precedents. These, in turn, serve as role models for those potential state makers elsewhere who otherwise might not have considered the
possibility of pursuing demands for secession at another time when international norms such as the territorial integrity of states were considered
to be inviolable. In this regard, it is worth considering that during the
nearly half century of the Cold War, there were only two internationally
recognized successful cases of secession: Bangladesh and Eritrea. Clearly,
the message to would-be rebels at the time was that efforts at secession

were more likely to meet the unhappy fate of Katanga in the Congo or Biafra in Nigeria.

It can be concluded from this discussion that the notion of a "demonstration effect" suggests that the breakup of states and the resurgence of ethnic demands at the present time are not simply a result of the relationship between international norms and the structure of the international system. They also are affected by what economists refer to as a "multiplier effect." In other words, each event becomes a precedent for the next event, which, in turn, serves to further relax the international norms against these occurrences. This accelerating relaxation results in the increasing frequency of such activity in what might be described as a downward spiral. Thus, each successful ethnic secession not only encourages others to consider the same option; it actually makes it easier for them to succeed than their predecessors because, with each breach, it becomes increasingly difficult to defend the norm.

At the same time, as was discussed at some length in *Chapter One*, the increased opportunities for contact between individuals representing different cultural communities (due to the end of the Cold War and the integrating effects of information technologies and global capital, which have spread to the former Soviet bloc and its client states in what used to be called the Third World) raises the specter of cultural domination. This, in turn, produces a tendency on the part of those in a more vulnerable position to feel increasingly threatened by what seems to them to be a form of cultural imperialism designed to obliterate their own cultural traditions. Thus, whether it is xenophobia in the Russian Federation (as expressed in the Great Russian nationalism of individuals such as Vladimir Zhirinovsky and his supporters), militant Serbian nationalism and calls for a Greater Serbia by those such as Slobodan Milosevic, increased militancy across much of the Islamic world including the mullahs in Iran, Islamic organizations in Lebanon, Egypt, the areas controlled by the Palestinian Authority, or the case of Afghanistan under the leadership of the Taliban, the tendency to emphasize that which makes one's own culture distinct reinforces the perceived need for cultural identification. In a global climate in which non-Western cultures are seen as increasingly threatened by Western values, which emphasize the importance of materialism, individualism, sexual permissiveness, and a general lack of respect for traditional sources of authority (the notion of "Jihad versus McWorld" as articulated by Benjamin R. Barber), the popular desire for ethnic exclusivity in the form of efforts to establish independent ethnically-based states and/or to eliminate all traces of another culture from within one's own state becomes understandable as an attempt at cultural self-preservation. Taken together, these processes create a fertile environment for the use of ethnicity by ethnic entrepreneurs.

Interestingly, there is a certain irony in this ethnic resurgence. It would appear that the widely perceived heightened need on the part of large numbers of individuals to identify with the ethnic group, which is related as both cause *and* effect to the weakening of the post-colonial state in a post-Cold War era characterized by globalization, should itself become the basis upon which state makers would attempt to reconstitute and revitalize the state. The argument has been throughout, however, that this irony is rooted in the distortions created by the historical reversal of the state-building process in the post-colonial world. It is these distortions which placed juridical statehood ahead of the issue of state viability. Thus, in order to develop the empirical attributes of statehood, the problems created by the juridical state, such as the norms which preserved otherwise non-viable states, must be jettisoned. In the context of this inverted situation, ethnic conflict leading to the development of the ethnic state becomes the *means* by which the goal of empirical statehood is achieved.

CONCLUSION

In an effort to lay out the theoretical foundations for the notion of the relationship between ethnic conflict and state-building in the post-Cold War era, the discussion up to this point has for the most part avoided addressing the issue of UN intervention. Instead, the focus has been upon the relationship between ethnic conflict and the collapse of post-colonial states. The reason for this focus is the belief that more can be learned about the requirements for effective state-building from an examination of its failures than its successes.

One conclusion to emerge from this discussion is that a significant contributing factor to the rising number of failing/failed post-colonial states has been the many burdens imposed upon these weak states in a post-Cold War era characterized by an increasing trend towards globalization and a relaxation of the juridical norms which had previously sustained these states.

Having missed the historical opportunity to develop cohesive political communities and strong state capacities through the process of war-making, as happened in older more stable states, one suggestion to emerge from this discussion has been that the rising number of ethnic conflicts raging in the post-Cold War era in post-colonial states is organically related to the earliest stages in the process of building empirically viable, politically cohesive states. Consistent with this line of reasoning, ethnic conflict accomplishes this objective through the mobilization of human and material resources within an ethnically-defined political community, whose energies and talents are directed toward providing for the survival of that group. Once mobilized, the members of this community under the leadership of would-be state makers (a/k/a ethnic entrepreneurs) seek to reconfigure the juridically determined territorial boundaries of the post-colonial state by drawing upon these human and material resources for a campaign of military conquest reminiscent of the early stages of Western European state formation described by Charles Tilly.

Occurring simultaneously with this process of military conquest is a process of political consolidation within the territories held through the removal and/or suppression of rival state makers and their ethnic communities. This exercise is reminiscent of the argument made by Cohen, Brown and Organski in their seminal work on the relationship between internal violence and the creation of political order. In a similar manner, the boundaries of the newly reconfigured state become synonymous with the territory within which a political leadership is capable of exercising physical control in place of lines arbitrarily drawn to reflect the needs of colonial powers with little or no thought given to the eventual capability of an indigenous elite to govern effectively.

While the above represents an interesting theoretical discussion, it remains to address the policy implications for the international community of this phenomenon of ethnic conflict and state-building: Should the international community intervene in these situations or should it step back and allow the process to unfold whatever the human cost to civilians? If it should intervene, what should be the policy objective of such intervention? Should it be limited to ending the violence? Should it go further and provide humanitarian assistance designed to ease the suffering of the victims of war? Should it go further still and revive the now defunct concept of trusteeship in an attempt to influence the future course of political developments within the country by undertaking the responsibility for (re)building states torn apart by civil war?

Alongside the question of the *ends* which the policy should serve is that of the appropriate *means* by which to achieve these goals. After all, there is little point in defining the goals of a policy if the means chosen fail to accomplish these purposes. International actors must, therefore, also grapple with the following questions: If there is to be an outside presence, what form should it assume? Should it be limited to traditional, lightly armed observer or peacekeeping missions? Alternatively, should a more muscular and assertive posture in the form of heavily armed enforcement operations with more robust rules of engagement be undertaken?

Of course, even if one starts from the premise that intervention is preferable to non-intervention, there need not be a one size fits all approach to this issue. At the same time, however, further consideration of the types of conditions which would warrant one or the other type of intervention is necessary. Otherwise, the results of a mismatch between conditions on the ground during a conflict and the type of intervention chosen could be disastrous.

In order to do justice to these questions and to integrate this discussion into the discussion of ethnic conflict and state-building, these issues will be addressed in greater detail in the next chapter.

Chapter Seven

Ethnic Conflict, State-Building, and UN Peacekeeping

An Integrated Theory for the Post-Cold War Era

INTRODUCTION

The suggestion that international norms concerning such things as human rights and democratization should be held in abeyance in the case of post-colonial states until such time as they have been able to achieve a level of political development at which the kinds of fundamental questions of state formation discussed earlier have been sorted out runs directly counter to the course of events in the period since the end of the Cold War. Instead of allowing ethnic conflicts to proceed uninterrupted on the theory that they constitute an area within the domestic jurisdiction of states protected by Article 2(7) of the UN Charter against outside intervention, the Security Council has assumed a more interventionist posture with regard to conflicts within states. This posture reflects a more expansive reading of the provision in Article 1(1) of the Charter regarding the preservation of international peace and security. The growing recognition that violence *within* states has the potential to threaten international peace and security as a consequence of massive population displacement into neighboring states has resulted in a changed understanding of Article 1(1). Once thought of as referring to acts of aggression *across* state boundaries, it now has come to be understood as also encompassesing violence *within* state boundaries.

This looser construction of the notion of threats to international peace and security corresponds to a wider range of responses to conflicts (especially internal conflicts) in the post-Cold War era. Previously the principal response came in the form of what is now referred to as traditional peacekeeping.[1] In the post-bipolar world, however, the fact that smaller conflicts no longer have the potential to escalate into superpower confrontations combined with the reduced likelihood that the veto will be used by one of the Permanent Members in a less ideologically polarized Security Council have had the effect of emboldening the UN to pursue more intrusive and more muscular forms of intervention. Unlike traditional peacekeeping operations, these types of intervention (which include operations described by former UN Secretary-General Boutros Boutros-Ghali as humanitarian intervention,[2] peace enforcement,[3] and post-conflict peace-building[4]) frequently occur without the consent of one or more of the belligerents even in situations in which one of those belligerents is the host government.

The issue of consent to the presence of outside forces is not the only difference between the newer and older forms of UN operations. Traditional peacekeeping was designed to offer the parties, who in all likelihood would be distrustful of one another, a way to separate themselves for the purpose of stopping the killing. As discussed previously, it was hoped that, at least in some cases, this cooling off period would contribute to the resolution of differences by the parties themselves. These newer forms of intervention, however, are designed to do more than simply stop the fighting or give the parties an opportunity to resolve their disagreements. The purpose of these operations is to *impose* a solution upon the parties.

This difference between older and newer forms of UN intervention raises the issue discussed in *Chapter Three* dealing with the question of identifying the criteria for a successful mission. It will be recalled that this question centers around the issue identified by William J. Durch as to whether a mission is successful merely by stopping the killing or whether success should be defined in terms of resolving the underlying causes of the conflict. Unfortunately, neither the idea of simply stopping the killing nor the idea of addressing some vague notion of "underlying causes" offers an adequate answer to the question.

In a certain sense, therefore, the task of this chapter and of this entire study is to develop a clear and consistent standard against which post-Cold War UN operations may be judged to be either a success or a failure. The development of such a standard must meet the test of allowing analysts to assess in a rational and dispassionate way whether or not a particular mission is furthering or hindering a previously articulated progression of events in a manner which will bring one either closer to, or further away from, the goals outlined. A central purpose, then, of this chapter is to replace the rather vaguely defined, and often ad hoc, notion of "underlying causes" with a clearer and more precise objective against which progress can be measured.

In keeping with the goal of developing an integrated theory of ethnic conflict, state-building, and UN peacekeeping, the yardstick for measuring the success or failure of any operation dealing with ethnic conflicts in post-colonial states should be the degree to which it either advances or retards the process of building a viable state capable of managing its own affairs and, therefore, of preventing a return to the violence. This would involve the consolidation of power within the state presumably through the creation of an ethnic state in place of the ethnically divided post-colonial state. Thus, for example, some sort of internationally sponsored initiative designed to facilitate the creation of ethnically homogeneous states similar to that recommended by Chaim Kaufmann or of the kind which took place between Greece and Turkey in the 1920s would seem to meet the criteria for success as an alternative to the model of uninterrupted ethnic conflict leading to the building of viable states. Of course, in terms of the question of success or failure, a great deal would depend upon how such an initiative was executed.

The emphasis upon the building of states as a way to measure the success of both older and newer UN missions allows for a common standard to be applied which is consistent with the state-centric approach to international relations discussed earlier. Until such time, if ever, as the world should move beyond the states system, a focus upon state-building would seem to be not only consistent with international norms of state sovereignty as articulated in the Charter of the United Nations but also a way of logically linking together the seemingly distinct phenomena of peacekeeping, state-building, and ethnic conflict.

In this regard, the priorities of the UN (particularly, but not exclusively, in the post-Cold War era) have been precisely the opposite of what they should be. Instead of identifying the issue of state-building as the primary consideration and recognizing that this, in turn, will result in a quicker end to the violence with ultimately fewer lives lost,[5] the notion of saving lives in the short-term has been given the highest priority while any consideration of building states with the capacity to govern themselves has been addressed only secondarily, if at all.

Of course, given what has been said earlier about the violent nature of the state-building process, the logical implication of this argument that the building of viable states should take priority over saving lives is that generally speaking the best response that the UN can offer in these situations is to step back and offer no response at all or, to use Edward N. Luttwak's phrase: "give war a chance."[6] This notion requires that some discussion be given to the consequences for the state-building process of the alternatives of nonintervention and of the various types of intervention undertaken by the UN.

COMPARING CASES OF INTERVENTION AND NONINTERVENTION: THE POSITIVE AND NEGATIVE EFFECTS UPON STATE-BUILDING

The idea that nonintervention[7] is preferable to intervention when it comes to state-building is based upon more than just a logical inference from the theory that state-building is by its very nature a violent process. It is rooted also in a variety of experiences spanning both time and geography. Taken together, these experiences offer a strong prima facie case for the suggestion that the determination of state boundaries and the accumulation of power within those boundaries, which are both central to the state-building enterprise, are achieved most effectively in the absence of external intervention. A few examples will illustrate the point.

In addition to the cases of state formation in Western Europe addressed by Tilly, the discussion of the American Civil War in *Chapter Two* of this study points to a similar conclusion regarding the potentially harmful effects of outside intervention.[8] Clearly, the present boundaries of the United States are in no small measure the product not only of the Civil War but also of a series of uninterrupted wars waged by the government against Native Americans (which resulted in the expulsion of Native American peoples and the opening up of their lands to settlement by the white population)[9] and against Mexico. The latter resulted in the acquisition of vast territories and turned the US into the most powerful state in the Western hemisphere. Thus, a good argument can be made that the current continental dimensions of the US and its status as a global superpower are largely due to the absence of any international organization during the nineteenth century comparable to the United Nations capable of intervening to stop the carnage. If there had been such an organization during the nineteenth century instead of the rather loosely organized Concert of Europe, the likelihood is that the United States today would consist of little more than the area from Maine to Washington, D. C. and perhaps portions of the upper Midwest.

An interesting counterfactual thought experiment would be to consider the fate of such a truncated country if the same sort of humanitarian norms had been imposed back then. On the positive side, it seems clear that many lives would have been saved *at the time*. For those who may be inclined to take this rather short-term view of humanitarian considerations, however, the following question is worth considering: Would a considerably smaller US have been able to provide the so-called "Arsenal of Democracy" as described by Franklin Roosevelt,[10] which made possible the defeat of Hitler or might Germany have emerged victorious in the Second World War? This hypothetical, but plausible, exercise raises disturbing moral questions about how to balance present actual casualties against a possibly even greater number of potential future casualties in a world fraught with unintended consequences.

Taking this out of the realm of the distant past, some more recent examples of what might be described as successful state-building (at least in terms of the initial criteria for state-building addressed in this study) would include the Nigerian suppression of the Biafran revolt in the late 1960s, the eventual unification of Vietnam by force following the removal of US troops in 1973, and the suppression of Chechen resistance by the Russian Federation. While none of these cases can be said to be pretty, the common feature in all of them is the fact that it was the absence of out-side intervention in the form of peacekeeping or peace enforcement troops which made possible the consolidation of power in the hands of a govern-ing authority.

As a way to understand the impact of uninterrupted violence upon the state-building process, the case of Palestine/Israel is perhaps one of the most instructive as it involves an early case of the transition from a colony/Man-date (Palestine) into what can only be described as an ethnic state (Israel). Accordingly, it deserves to be considered in somewhat greater depth.

Following the passage of General Assembly Resolution 181 in November 1947 calling for the partition of Palestine into independent Jew-ish and Arab states with Jerusalem as a corpus separatum, civil war broke out between rival Jewish and Arab militias within Palestine.[11] In the wan-ing days of the British Mandate (itself a form of intervention which had done little to prepare the area for independence or to resolve the tensions between Arabs and Jews and may be seen instead as one of the principal *sources* of those tensions through its oftentimes conflicting promises), the struggle to fill the political vacuum created by the imminent departure of the British consisted of what today would be characterized as an ethnic conflict. In preparation for the implementation of the UN partition resolu-tion, each side attempted to press its advantage militarily in an effort to create by force of arms defensible borders containing an ethnically homo-geneous population.

While there was some diplomatic activity during the six month period of time between the approval of General Assembly Resolution 181 in November of 1947 and the declaration of independence by Israel in May of 1948 (including even the suggestion in April that the resolution be rescinded and Palestine be placed under the administration of the UN Trusteeship Council), the fighting on the ground between rival Palestinian Jewish and Palestinian Arab militias continued uninterrupted.

The UN does not begin to play a more active role in the conflict until the internal civil war is internationalized immediately following the establishment of the State of Israel on May 14, 1948 and the decision by the neighboring Arab states to invade the new country the very next day. It is only at this point in the conflict that the UN begins calling for a cease-fire and that armistice negotiations begin first under the leadership of Swedish diplomat and UN Mediator, Count Folke Bernadotte, and, later, under his American successor, Dr. Ralph Bunche.

The negotiations between Israel and its neighboring Arab *states* would lead eventually to the conclusion of truce agreements in 1949 and the establishment of the United Nations Truce Supervision Organization (UNTSO). UNTSO consisted of unarmed observers whose responsibility was to monitor the armistice lines between the parties to the negotiations and report on any violations of the armistice agreements. Since UNTSO was unrelated to the internal Palestinian phase of this conflict, however, it is fair to say that the earlier portion of the war involving internal conflict within Palestine was conducted without intervention by outside forces. This earlier phase, therefore, can be examined as an example of the effects of nonintervention upon the state-building process in situations involving ethnic conflict.

In terms of the issue of ethnic conflict and state-building, the consequences of nonintervention were mixed. This is not surprising given the conflict model of state-building developed in this study. Such a model views state-building as a process with both winners and losers. As Tilly observed in his discussion of the forcible consolidation of hundreds of smaller entities into approximately twenty-five modern states in Western Europe, *state-building* for some also necessarily entails *state-destroying* for others. After all, conquest and subjugation also involves those who are conquered and subjugated.

From the perspective of the Arabs of Palestine, the consequences of nonintervention were negative. The absence of outside intervention meant that they lost everything. Not only did they lose their homes in that portion of the country which eventually became Israel, but they were not even able to set up an independent state in whatever remained of the areas allotted for an Arab state under Resolution 181. These areas eventually came under the control of Transjordan (the West Bank) and Egypt (Gaza).

Another negative consequence of nonintervention by the UN during the civil war phase was that it all but guaranteed that eventually the conflict would become internationalized by changing the dynamic from a *Palestinian* ethnic civil war between Arabs and Jews within the British mandate into an interstate war between Israel and the neighboring Arab states. The failure on the part of the UN to intervene before May 1948 to either resolve or, at least contain, this conflict led to intervention by the Arab states after the creation of Israel. This internationalization of what started as a civil war was not only the result of sympathy in the Arab world for the plight of the Palestinian Arabs. It was also a function of the de-stabilizing impact of the flow of refugees from Palestine upon the economies and societies of newly independent Arab states still struggling with issues of decolonization and economic and political development. The consequences of this de-stabilization can be seen in both the 1970 Jordanian civil war (which in some ways was reminiscent of the 1947–1948 Palestinian civil war in terms of the exodus of Palestinian Arabs except that this time it involved the consolidation of *Hashemite* control over Jordan rather than *Jewish* control over Palestine/Israel) and the protracted civil war in Lebanon (from which the Palestinians also eventually were expelled) during the 1970s and 1980s.

In contrast to the experience of the Palestinian Arabs, the consequences of nonintervention when viewed from the vantage point of the newly created State of Israel were generally positive. During the Palestinian civil war phase of the conflict in 1947–48 and the subsequent 1948 war between Israel and the surrounding Arab states, the Yishuv (the Palestinian Jewish community) was able to expand by force of arms the area of its control beyond the territory allotted to the proposed Jewish state by Resolution 181[12] and to effectively remove (whether by forcible expulsion or intimidation)[13] the bulk of the Arab population from those areas controlled by Jewish forces.

On this point, there remains disagreement as to the causes and, therefore, the responsibility, for what has become known as the Palestinian refugee problem. The official Israeli position has always been that the Palestinian Arabs fled at the encouragement of various Arab leaders in order to clear a path for what were supposed to be the invading armies of the Arab *states*. For their part, the Arabs have always maintained that the Palestinians were driven out by Zionist forces employing terrorist tactics, such as those utilized during the infamous massacre at the village of Deir Yassin[14] on April 9, 1948.

It is beyond the scope of this analysis to assess the veracity of these competing claims. Wherever the truth may lie on this question, however, there can be no doubt that, in the final analysis, the Arabs in Palestine/Israel went from being a majority of the population to becoming a minority. This outcome, which today some might refer to as "ethnic cleansing" (although, due to the pejorative nature of the term, its application to this situation would itself be a matter of some controversy), undeniably enabled the Zionist/Israeli establishment to solidify its control over the territory within the new state and also allowed it to establish a functioning democracy. Given the Arab majority in Palestine in the late 1940s just prior to Israeli independence, a democratic *and* Jewish state would have been impossible without a resolution to the problem of a society deeply divided along ethnic lines.[15] The alternative to the creation of a largely homogeneous state would have been the very real possibility, indeed probability, that an Arab majority living within a "Jewish" state created by the UN might simply vote the Jewish state out of existence. Thus, without the removal of a significant portion of the Palestinian Arab population, it is inconceivable that Israel (a Jewish state whose very reason for being included the need to end the homelessness of Jewish survivors of the Nazi holocaust still living in Displaced Persons camps) could have developed into a democracy unless it chose to adopt a system of disenfranchisement of the Arab population similar that which existed under the apartheid system in South Africa.

The importance of this de facto removal of most of the Palestinian Arab population from what would become the new Jewish state to the process of building not only a Jewish state but a *democratic* Jewish state can be seen by contrasting the situation in the late 1940s with that which occurred after June 1967. While the pre-1967 territorial configuration of the country had left Israel vulnerable to the threat of outside attack from hostile neighbors, the existence of an overwhelmingly Jewish population meant that the internal situation was one in which the country was able to consolidate its control within its borders and develop and operate democratic political institutions without compromising the Jewish character of the state.

The situation changed dramatically following the 1967 war and the expansion of the country's frontiers. The newly acquired territories arguably offered Israel greater strategic depth[16] and military security against the sort of threats to its survival posed by traditional interstate wars. Thus, for example, the crossing of the Suez Canal by Egyptian military forces in October 1973 produced a significant number of Israeli military casualties, left long-term scars upon the Israeli national psyche by shattering its sense of invincibility, and resulted in bitter recriminations against the political leadership of Prime Minister Golda Meir and Defense Minister Moshe Dayan, but at no time did these Egyptian forces pose any serious *military threat* to Israel's population centers or to the survival of the state itself.

While Israel enjoyed a greater degree of security against traditional interstate threats, the post-1967 situation within the country was also markedly different. Unlike the events surrounding its creation in the late

1940s, the 1967 war and military occupation resulted in a situation in which Israel now controlled territories with an Arab majority. This time the Palestinian Arabs were unwilling to repeat the experience of 1948 by leaving the areas under Israeli rule. Despite the calls of some within the Israeli establishment in the years since the 1967 war for "transfer" (a euphemism for "ethnic cleansing"), no such policy was ever carried out. Indeed, if such a policy had been carried out in the period after 1967, it no doubt would have resulted in an escalation of the conflict and even the possibility of superpower intervention during the Cold War.

From the perspective of the building of the Israeli state, however, it can be argued that the price of this failure to remove the Arabs again from within the now expanded state frontiers was a return of the situation to one resembling the pre-independence status quo ante. Under these new conditions, and given the higher birthrates among Palestinian Arabs as compared to Israeli Jews, the country faced a difficult dilemma which came to be known as the "demographic dilemma": it could not remain for the indefinite future simultaneously a Jewish state, a democratic state, and an occupying power. It could have any two of the three but only if it were prepared to give up the third.[17]

Thus, if the country wished to remain both a *Jewish* state and a *democracy* without removing the Arabs living in what came to be known as "the territories," it would be necessary to relinquish control over this area and return to what had been less defensible borders; if the country wished to remain a *Jewish* state and retain these more defensible borders, then it would have to sacrifice its *democratic* character by adopting a policy of disenfranchisement; if it wished to remain a *democracy* and retain the territories, then it would have to eventually surrender its *Jewish* identity. Only the political fiction that the occupation was a temporary situation until such time as there would be peace with the neighboring Arab states allowed Israel to maintain the illusion of avoiding this painful choice while at the same time denying the Arabs living inside the territories voting rights as Israeli citizens. The first Uprising, or Intifadah, of the late 1980s demonstrated, however, that choosing from among the options listed above could not be postponed indefinitely. Indeed, it is no accident that the Madrid, and later Oslo, processes occurred shortly after the Intifadah.

In terms of the issue of immediate concern here, namely intervention versus nonintervention, the Palestinian Arab migration of the late 1940s, whatever its causes, would certainly qualify by today's standards as a humanitarian crisis. Applying current standards for humanitarian intervention retroactively, one can easily see that a good case certainly could have been made back then for some sort of external intervention, by force if necessary, designed to stop the exodus from occurring. Such an intervention might have assumed a form similar to the creation of safe havens during the Bosnian war following the breakup of Yugoslavia or perhaps those created in northern Iraq following the Kurdish uprising in 1991.

It is incumbent upon any discussion of humanitarian intervention, however, to consider whether such intervention, in this case to stop the Palestinian refugee problem from occurring, would have produced a more salutary outcome measured either in humanitarian terms or in terms of the creation of a stable (democratic) state in Palestine/Israel. Given what has been said above, it is possible to contrast the actual outcome with some likely alternatives or counterfactual ones.

If applied to the Palestinian case in the late 1940s, the type of humanitarian intervention which occurred in Bosnia or Iraq almost certainly would have meant that Israel, which was created as a *Jewish* state in large measure to provide a solution for the humanitarian crisis created by the displaced Jewish survivors of the Nazi holocaust, would have become instead some version of a secular or binational state. The unwillingness of the Palestinian Arabs to accept unlimited Jewish immigration even during the period of Nazi atrocities during the Second World War would have meant, however, that the humanitarian problem of European Jewish homelessness after the war most likely would not have been resolved. In part, this was due to the unwillingness of other countries to accept these refugees and also in part to their desire to go to Palestine/Israel. Thus, had the UN or any other international organization made the decision to intervene to prevent the creation of a clear Jewish majority in Palestine/Israel, the most likely result would have been to prevent one refugee problem (Palestinian Arab) by perpetuating another (European Jewish).

To be sure, it is possible to contemplate an alternative counterfactual scenario. Under this set of circumstances, a Jewish state would have come into existence alongside an Arab state in Palestine as originally was envisioned by General Assembly Resolution 181. If history had taken this course, the area allotted for the Jewish state would have contained nearly as many Arabs as Jews. Consequently, the only way to ensure the existence of a *Jewish* state as a haven for those living in Displaced Persons camps would have been to restrict full citizenship rights to members of the Jewish community. Such a decision would require, in turn, that the new state severely curtail its democratic form of government through disenfranchisement of its Arab population. Thus, if the UN had acted in the 1940s the way it acted in Bosnia and northern Iraq in the 1990s so as to prevent the displacement of the Arab population at that time, ironically, the only way that Israel could have fulfilled one part of the mission for which it was created (to be a humanitarian response to the inhumanity of Nazism) would have been to assume the inhumane character of an undemocratic, apartheid state!

Indeed, this conclusion is not mere idle speculation or counterfactual analysis. A good argument can be made that this is precisely what *has occurred* in the occupied/disputed territories in the period since 1967. The absence of a second Palestinian exodus comparable to that which occurred in 1947–48 has created within Israel a demographic situation very similar to that which would have prevailed within the State of Israel proper in the late 1940s but for the creation of the Palestinian refugee problem in the late 1940s. It is no accident, therefore, that within these territories, Palestinian Arabs are denied Israeli citizenship in marked contrast to the situation which exists for the so-called "Israeli Arabs" living inside what is often referred to as the "Green Line."

It has often been stated that hard cases make bad law. Based upon this line of reasoning, one might object that the situation in Palestine/Israel is an anomaly and, therefore, that one should not attempt to draw general conclusions from this very difficult case. The problem with this argument, however, is that, when it comes to humanitarian intervention in ethnic conflicts, *virtually all cases are hard cases.* They involve difficult tradeoffs. In addition, given the oftentimes zero-sum nature of such conflicts, humanitarian action in one sphere may lead to unintended, and perhaps even inhumane, consequences in another.

Accordingly, it is incumbent upon those who might advocate intervention in contemporary conflicts so as to prevent the sort of humanitarian crisis which unfolded for the Palestinian Arabs in the 1940s from recurring today to consider very carefully some very difficult questions regarding this historical example: If intervention in the Palestine conflict had resulted in the creation of a secular or binational state rather than the creation of the State of Israel as a haven for the European Jewish victims of Hitler, would the perpetuation of Jewish homelessness as opposed to Palestinian Arab homelessness have been a more humane solution to the problems which have given rise to more than a half century of conflict? If, on the other hand, intervention in the Palestine conflict to prevent the exodus of the Palestinian Arabs had resulted in the creation of a Jewish state in which nearly half the population consisted of Palestinian Arabs, would the undemocratic denial of citizenship rights to this vast Arab population in order to ensure the country's continued Jewish character have been a more humane solution to the humanitarian/political crisis than the creation of a vast refugee population? What is the moral calculus by which such determinations are to be made when deciding as to which outcome would be more humane?

In addition to the moral dilemmas regarding humane outcomes, another question which needs to be considered is a political question with humanitarian overtones involving the issue of state-building. Since there was virtually no support for the idea of a binational state within the Palestinian Arab community and support within the Palestinian Jewish community was relegated to a political fringe, it is worth contemplating whether a binational state without the support of either community in Palestine as an alternative to population displacement would have been a viable political entity? The experiences of other countries such as Cyprus with its (Greek-Turkish split) and Lebanon (with its Chrisitan-Muslim split) indicate the fragile nature of such binational entities and the likelihood that the result will be civil war when such political arrangements do not enjoy widespread popular support.

The prima facie case in favor of nonintervention is strengthened even further when this option is compared with examples of intervention during the Cold War such as Korea and Cyprus. Unlike the cases mentioned above, in which a state was able to consolidate its control over territory through a ruthless campaign designed to eliminate competitors, the failure to resolve the Korean question and the continued division of the Korean Peninsula more than fifty years after the end of the Korean war is directly related to the presence of large numbers of outside forces along the demilitarized zone. To be sure, it did serve a purpose in averting a possible escalation of the conflict during the Korean War, but even this argument is considerably less compelling in a post-Cold War world.

Likewise, the existence of UN peacekeepers inside Cyprus as well as the continued presence of military forces from Turkey separating the Republic of Northern Cyprus from the rest of the island following the 1974 civil war appear to have contributed to the persistence of the conflict[18] and served as a barrier to unification. Their presence indicates that while intervention may be successful in stopping the bloodshed, it is not likely to contribute to the state-building process.

Indeed, the evidence from these cases suggests that it may actually complicate such a process thereby making the development of a viable state an even more remote possibility. If, as has been suggested, state-building is, at least in part, a violent process, then efforts to interfere with that violence are likely to cripple the ability of would-be state makers to develop effective state apparatuses capable of exercising control over a given territory. While such interference may be understandable in terms of other concerns, such as global strategic or humanitarian considerations, the problem from a state-building perspective is that it is likely to result in the presence of an interposition force for an indeterminate period of time. This force will find itself on the horns of a dilemma as it can neither resolve the issues which led to the conflict nor extricate itself from the situation. To the extent that the continued presence of this peacekeeping force prevents the parties from resolving the underlying conflict through the consolidation of state power its very presence on the scene can be said to act as an impediment to the creation of a viable state. The result is a vicious cycle: *the presence of external actors prevents the state makers from developing the capacity to govern effectively by consolidating their control over territory; the failure of these state makers to develop this capacity makes the presence of external actors necessary in order to preserve some kind of order and prevent bloodshed; the ongoing presence of this external force continues to undermine the ability of state makers to develop the capacity to govern the state.* Thus, the conflict remains frozen in place while the symbiosis between peacekeeping and state weakness continues ad infinitum without any resolution in sight.

From the perspective of state-building, it would seem that the record of the use of more muscular and intrusive forms of UN intervention in the post-Cold War era has offered little in the way of cause for optimism. The comparatively new concept of humanitarian intervention actually involves two distinct types of operations, which sometimes go hand in hand. The first type involves the use of outside military forces as a way to offer protection to humanitarian relief workers engaged in the work of dispensing food, medical care, and supplies to civilians who find themselves caught in the crossfire of internal warfare. These workers are sometimes themselves the objects of threats or hostile activities by combatants. The parties to the conflict use these desperately needed supplies as weapons against the civilian population. The aim is to gain leverage in their ongoing struggle against other belligerents either by holding the civilian population hostage or by effectively laying siege to the targeted population in an effort to induce them to flee from a given territory. The latter practice is one form of what is often referred to as "ethnic cleansing."

The other type of humanitarian intervention involves the use of military forces to carve out areas within a state designated as "safe havens" or "no-fly zones." In these areas, civilians are promised protection by an international force against efforts by either government or rebel forces to target these civilians for political gain.

Of course, these distinct forms or subcategories of humanitarian intervention should not be understood as mutually exclusive in practice. Some missions, such as the UN Protection Force (UNPROFOR) in Bosnia, contained elements of both.[19] In that instance, the UN force was concerned with protecting the delivery of supplies to the civilian victims of the Bosnian war. As part of the effort to facilitate this, as well as to prevent the sorts of atrocities associated with "ethnic cleansing" by Bosnian Serbs, the UN established so-called "safe havens." Among these was the notoriously failed example of Srebrenica.

Despite the existence of some missions which consist of both types of humanitarian intervention, the distinction is a useful one both as a way to highlight the primary purpose of specific operations and as a way to understand the impact of a mission upon the state-building process. Thus, for example, one can distinguish the two phases of the UN Operation in Somalia (UNOSOM I and UNOSOM II) from other missions such as Operation Provide Comfort in northern Iraq (which will be discussed in greater detail in *Part III*) or Operation Tourquoise in Rwanda. The Somalia missions had as their *primary* goal the provision of security for the delivery of supplies to civilians, who were deprived of food and other necessary items as part of a deliberate strategy on the part of Somali warlords. In contrast to this, the operations in Rwanda and Iraq were designed to provide safe havens for Iraqi Kurds and Rwandan Tutsis respectively so as to prevent "ethnic cleansing."

In terms of the focus of this study upon the issue of how to create stable states, one of the corollaries to the notion that an inverse relationship exists between successful intervention and successful state-building is the proposition that the more successful the humanitarian operation is in terms of satisfying its primary goal, the more likely it is to impede the state-building process and, therefore, the less likely it is that the conflict will be resolved and a stable state will emerge. The expectation is that this would be especially true in the case of operations designed to provide safe havens precisely because they interfere with the essential primordial process of consolidation of state authority, which normally occurs through the removal of members of rival ethnic groups. By the very nature of their ethnicity, these rival groups would be unlikely to identify with, and be loyal to, the emerging ethnic state. It is this very claim which will be tested subsequently in the case study dealing with Iraq in the immediate aftermath of the 1991 Persian Gulf War.

Another type of intervention for which there are some precedents during the Cold War but which has become more common in the post-Cold War era is referred to as peace enforcement. In terms of the issue of state-building, peace enforcement operations also can be subdivided into two different categories. One category involves efforts by some state or group of states outside of the conflict to forcibly impose a solution upon the belligerents. Examples of this approach to peace enforcement would include: India's intervention in support of the independence of Bangladesh in 1971, Israel's effort to install in Lebanon a friendly government under Bashir Gemayel in the early 1980s, the United Task Force (UNITAF) effort to disarm the various Somali clan-based militias as a prelude to peace talks aimed at national reconciliation, and the pursuit by UNOSOM II of the Somali warlord, Mohammed Farah Aideed.

A different kind of operation involves international military support for one of the belligerents to a conflict. This assistance is intended to help that party impose its own solution upon the other parties to the dispute. Although the term had not yet come into existence, the case of the UN Operation in the Congo (ONUC) in the early 1960s is perhaps the earliest example of this form of peace enforcement.

Despite the fact that the situation in the Congo pre-dated by several decades the end of the Cold War, it nevertheless foreshadowed many similar events which would become commonplace in later years across much of the globe. As a post-colonial state, the new country immediately faced the challenge of ethnic and regional separatism. Furthermore, the failure of the Belgians to prepare the people of the Congo for eventual self-government resulted in the virtual collapse of the central government as the country became mired in a struggle for power between opposing factions at the moment of its transition to independence. Finally, this was the most ambitious and intrusive intervention by the UN within a state prior to the end of the Cold War. Consequently, it deserves to be looked at briefly as a prototype for the kind of mission that would come to be known as peace enforcement.

Following the independence of the Congo from Belgium in 1960, the country found itself faced with a secessionist movement in Katanga Province instigated by the Belgians and a constitutional crisis between President Kasavubu and Prime Minister Lumumba. In an attempt to preserve the territorial integrity of the new country and to prevent the collapse of the central government, which would have created a political vacuum in the heart of Africa and made the Congo a target for superpower competition and perhaps confrontation, a large UN force was dispatched to assist the president of the new country. Although the fighting was prolonged and bloody (lasting four years), the mission did succeed in preventing the dismemberment of the Congo and preserving the central government under the authority of President Kasavubu—who later would be replaced by Mobutu.

A somewhat less successful early example of this form of peace enforcement mission was the non-UN sponsored Multinational Force (MNF) dispatched to Lebanon during that country's civil war. Intended both to facilitate the departure of the Palestine Liberation Organization following the 1982 Israeli invasion and to assist the Lebanese government in the country's multi-sided civil war, the MNF eventually came to be seen not as a neutral force attempting to restore order to Lebanon but as just one more faction in the fighting. Following the bombing of the US Marine barracks in 1983 and the killing of more than two hundred marines, the US and the other members of the force withdrew without completing their assignment.

The failure of the MNF to install a stable government in Lebanon, combined with similar failures by the Arab League-sponsored Syrian intervention during the Lebanese civil war and the unilateral initiative by the Israelis to install Bashir Gemayel as a pro-Israeli leader in Beirut following the 1982 invasion of the country, suggest that forcible intervention of the peace enforcement variety by itself will not result in the creation of a stable governing authority.

It would be a mistake, however, to conclude from these cases that peace enforcement can play no role in the establishment of a self-governing state. Any such conclusion bumps up against the case of ONUC cited above. A more reasonable conclusion, therefore, would seem to be that in those situations in which intervention does occur, the key consideration lies in the *execution* of the operation. The question is not *whether* force should be used but *how* it should be used.

In terms of the issue of state-building, the puzzle would seem to be to explain why it is that the results of peace enforcement have been mixed. The examples alluded to above, as well as the dubious results of more recent initiatives in Afghanistan and Iraq, would seem to suggest that a variation of the thesis developed by Richard K. Betts is in order. He suggested that if intervention is to take place, the conventional wisdom that such intervention should be impartial is misguided. Rather, those engaging in intervention should be prepared to take sides in order to tilt the balance in favor of one of the belligerents. The alternative of impartial intervention leads to unending conflict, in which neither party wins and neither party has any incentive to yield.[20]

This argument is fine as far as it goes, but it does not go far enough. By itself, it does not explain why intervention by ONUC on behalf of Kasavubu succeeded in consolidating power while similar acts of intervention by the MNF or the Israelis did not. The available evidence suggests that intervention should not only reject the doctrine of neutrality or impartiality; *it also should be rooted in the Realist notion of power politics. As such, it should be based upon the best available intelligence assessment as to the military capabilities of the rival contenders. An operation which ignores the issue of the relative capabilities of the contending forces and focuses instead upon promoting the strategic interests or agendas of those engaging in the intervention is more likely to fail than one which seeks to work with whomever is most able to (re)establish order.* Thus, for example, a major reason why American interventions on behalf of Chiang kai-shek in China or Diem in South Vietnam failed (and, parenthetically, why the post-Saddam operation in Iraq will in all likelihood fail as well) was because they confused a set of shared interests between the outside party and the local factional leader with the far more important consideration of the capacity to restore order. The same could be said for the Israeli attempt to install Gemayel and then sign a peace treaty with him in 1983. Utilizing statistical analysis of the results of conflict situations, Roy Licklider comes to a similar conclusion.[21]

Another case in point of the misuse of impartial intervention would be the case of Somalia. A dispassionate reading of the political reality of the situation requires that one acknowledge that the pursuit of Aideed by UN forces (despite the fact that he controlled arguably the most powerful militia and the one perhaps best able to restore order within the country following the collapse of the Somali state) may have made sense from a moral or even a legalistic perspective, but it was counterproductive from the political standpoint. It undermined his effort to restore order to the country through the removal of rival clan militias. These militias were collectively responsible for reducing a large portion of the country to a condition of anarchy and lawlessness. Since, as Hobbes recognized long ago, it is first necessary to restore order before one can even speak of the rule of law, it would seem to be axiomatic that any action which reverses these priorities (as the pursuit of Aideed did) is ultimately self-defeating in terms of the early stages of the state-building process.

Finally, another type of intervention by the UN in the post-Cold War era has been the idea of post-conflict peace-building. Sometimes mislabeled as "nation-building"[22] (a related term which, however, refers to the creation of a *political community* rather than a *political entity* or *set of institutions*), this form of intervention is in some respects reminiscent of the League of Nations Mandate system and the UN Trusteeship system. Much as those systems were designed, at least in theory, to assist colonies with the preparation necessary to function as viable independent states through the building of institutions associated with modern statehood, post-conflict peace-building operations are intended to perform essentially the same types of functions in war-torn or failed states. In addition to re-building the physical infrastructure of a country (roads, bridges, schools, hospitals, etc.), disarming warring factions, and removing weapons such as land mines from the countryside, these missions are also designed to administer the country temporarily while the institutions of government (such as the police force, the military, the judiciary, and democratic political organs) are developed. Towards the end of their missions of national reconciliation, post-conflict peace-building operations often act as neutral observers of nationwide elections. Their function is to ensure the fairness of both the voting process and the tabulation of election returns. Some early examples of post-conflict peace-building would include the UN Observer Mission in El Salvador (ONUSAL), the UN Angola Verification Mission (UNAVEM), and the UN Transitional Authority in Cambodia (UNTAC). More recent examples would include the UN Interim Administration Mission in Kosovo (UNMIK)[23] and the UN Transitional Administration in East Timor (UNTAET).[24]

On its face, post-conflict peace-building would seem to offer a non-violent alternative to the bloody state-building process described in this study. By assisting war-torn countries in the process of developing their economic infrastructure and by providing confidence-building measures, such as disarmament of rival militias and neutral election monitoring, this form of non-violent international intervention seemingly offers the best hope for state-building without the terrible human costs associated with the removal or destruction of entire ethnic communities. For these reasons, this approach to international intervention is worthy of consideration in a study such as this one, which seeks to understand the relationship between ethnic violence and the state-building process. After all, what better way to understand this relationship than to try to understand whether violence is indeed necessary as a way to build viable states?

Given the promise of a non-violent path to state-building, the important question which needs to be considered is whether this approach in fact has been successful in those cases in which it has been tried. A brief discussion of UNTAC is instructive as it represents one of the most extensive cases of post-conflict peace-building yet attempted. In effect, Cambodia was placed under UN trusteeship during the period of the mandate.

Most accounts of UNTAC suggest that initially the mission appeared to be the very model of successful state-building. The early success of this mission offered hope that states could adopt stable, functioning, democratic political systems without having to undergo the sort of bloody process described in these pages. Cambodia, a country already torn apart by years of cross-border aggression and internal warfare, was slowly being re-built. Rival factions were disarmed and elections were held under international supervision. Up to this point, there is little disagreement that UNTAC was successful.

The problem, however, came about *after* the elections were held. Despite the apparent successes of UNTAC, the Khmer Rouge faction refused to accept the outcome of the elections and made the decision to return to armed struggle. This refusal indicated that the political system put in place was actually considerably more fragile than one might have thought at first. It also suggested that democratization is a considerably more complex process than the architects of the Cambodian system seemed to think.

Before reaching even a tentative conclusion as to the success or failure of UNTAC, it is important to first ask whether the refusal of the Khmer Rouge to accept the outcome of democratic elections represents an aberration in an otherwise remarkable success story of a country being rebuilt under the watchful eye of an international peace-building operation or whether it represents evidence of failure by UNTAC to address one of the more fundamental issues associated with state- and nation-building. As indicated elsewhere in this study, this fundamental issue involves the creation of a homogeneous population with a clear sense of national identity *prior to* the establishment of a democratic political system. A related question is whether such an outcome could only be achieved violently—in this case, through either the success of the Khmer Rouge on the battlefield or their violent removal as rival state makers.

Although it is beyond the scope of this study to conduct an in-depth analysis of the Cambodian situation, it would seem that, despite apparent signs of success in the beginning, UNTAC represents a failure. This is not so much a failure of *implementation* (in which case a different approach such as perhaps including more election monitors, for example, may have been more successful) on the part of those on the ground as it is a failure of *operational design* on the part of those responsible for the creation of UNTAC. The attempt to circumvent the violent nature of the state- and nation-building processes assumed that the outcome of free and fair elections would be universally accepted by all factions that participated in the civil war. The literature on state-building suggests, however, that this sort of democratization requires a prior homogenization of the population. Without this, the results of elections are not likely to be accepted and may even serve as catalysts for either the start of, or a return to, factional fighting. This claim regarding elections is further borne out by the experience of Iraq following its elections in 2005.

Albeit in a much different context, it should not be forgotten that it was the *election* of Abraham Lincoln (an election whose procedural fairness was not in question) which served as the catalyst for Southern secession and eventual civil war precisely because it occurred under conditions in which any prior sense of national cohesion had all but evaporated. It would seem that the elections held in Cambodia had a similar effect. The response of the Khmer Rouge was not to the *process* but to the *result* in the absence of any underlying sense of national unity.

If this interpretation is correct, then the problem with the UNTAC mission was not that it was attempted, but that it was attempted *too soon*. None of the rival factions had been able to consolidate its position during the civil war by defeating the other rival contenders and accumulating power at the center. In other words, efforts at disarmament may have been counterproductive in that they prevented anyone from establishing the necessary position of dominance as a precondition for the homogenization of the population and the creation of national unity through the elimination of rival state makers. According to Cohen, Brown, and Organski, this consolidation of state power is usually a bloody process. Once completed, however, it generally leads to a significant decline in the level of internal violence since the violence is part of the state-building process itself.

Although the complexity of the Cambodian situation is well beyond the scope of this particular study, there would seem to be a prima facie case that UNTAC would have been more successful in rebuilding the political institutions of the country and monitoring elections if it had waited until there had been a decisive military victory for one of the parties to the conflict. The effort to hold elections prematurely in a country without a democratic political tradition, which was still at the stage of trying to sort out the basic issue of centralized accumulation of power, appears to have been built upon a very shaky foundation. It should be stated, however, at this point that this conclusion is necessarily only tentative. In this instance, there is simply no way to prove a counterfactual hypothesis that elections would have been successful if they had been held after the emergence of a military victor. The best that can be said is that such an outcome would appear to be more consistent with the literature on the subject of state-building.

Of particular value in this regard are the theoretical insights of Barrington Moore and Bruce D. Porter into the relationship between war and democratization as described in *Chapter Two*. Moore stresses the need to *remove impediments* to the creation of a democratic political system, and Porter is interested in the ways in which wars stimulate political mobilization and create pressures from below for widening the circle of political participation. Taken together, these concepts help to explain the paradox that central accumulation of power during the early stages of the state-building process can actually be a prelude to the later creation of a viable democratic state based upon wider participation. Implicitly, these arguments call into question the effectiveness of well-intentioned efforts to find short-cuts to democracy, which seek to circumvent this violent process, by demonstrating the role that war plays in democratization. They also offer a cautionary tale for similar attempts to install democracy in Iraq, which will be considered later in this study.

CONCLUSION

The preceding discussion has laid the foundations for an examination of the claim that UN or other external intervention in ethnic conflicts undermines the state-building process in post-colonial states. Beginning from the premise that, at least in its earliest stages, state-building is an inherently violent process, logic would seem to dictate that efforts to interfere with this violence through outside intervention of the sorts described in this chapter are unlikely to result in the creation of viable states capable of effective self-government.

The statement above represents a generalization concerning the state-building process based upon historical experience. As this chapter has demonstrated, the post-Cold War era has been one in which the sort of violence which might have been tolerated in earlier periods has come to be seen as unacceptable. Consequently, international organizations and ad hoc groupings of states have become less tolerant of the argument that external intervention in internal conflicts violates the sovereignty of the state in question. One result of this intolerance has been a greater willingness to engage in increasingly intrusive forms of intervention *with or without the consent of the host government.*

It is at this point that the issue is joined. The question is whether it is possible to, in effect, have it both ways. *Can the United Nations continue to adhere to a Charter which enshrines the state-centric idea that state sovereignty is the central principle of international relations while at the same time undertaking intrusive forms of intervention in ethnic conflicts within post-colonial states even if such intervention has the effect of weakening these states and thereby compromising the fundamental principle upon which the UN is based?* After all, the state-centric idea of international relations presupposes the existence of *viable* states. This, in turn, assumes that governments are capable of exercising sovereign control over their own territories. If, therefore, the preceding statements regarding the harmful effects for the state-building process of international intervention in internal conflicts were correct, the policy implications would be profound. Either the state-centric model would have to be abandoned, which would require that some as yet unspecified form of political organization would have to take its place, or it would be necessary to reconsider the entire notion that intervention should give priority to short-term humanitarian considerations over longer-term state-building concerns.

The first step in trying to address this rather complex issue is to inquire as to whether, in fact, the relationship between violence and state-building alleged in this study represents merely one of many possible paths to state-building, which happens to have been the method used in the past but is not necessarily relevant to contemporary efforts, or whether it represents something close to an iron law in politics, which applies across political eras.[25]

It is at this point that the issue moves from the theoretical to the empirical. The focus in the remaining chapters will shift from broad generalizations to a closer look at the issue of state-building in a part of the world which has been the subject of an unusually high degree of external intervention. Beginning with a general discussion of the Middle East as a region and the role that intervention (both in the form of imperialism since the end of the Ottoman empire and in the form of more recent attempts to deal with conflicts in the successor states) has played historically, attention will then shift to the case of Iraq specifically.

The choice of Iraq is no accident. It reflects the fact that this country is an early example of a post-colonial state. Although Iraq came into existence following the First World War, it nevertheless possesses many of the same characteristics found in newer post-colonial states, which were the product of the decolonization process after the Second World War. As a result of having boundaries which were determined by outsiders, the state is an amalgam of different ethnic and sectarian groups. In the absence of any well-developed sense of national identity, the relationship of these groups to one another has been traditionally one of uneasy coexistence punctuated by intermittent periods of outright violence.

At the dawn of the post-Cold War era, this country found itself in the midst of both ethnic and sectarian conflicts between Sunni Arabs and Sunni Kurds, on the one hand, and Sunni Arabs and Shi'a Arabs on the other. As was the case with its comparatively early independence relative to other post-colonial states, Iraq again has found itself to be ahead of the curve. It was one of the first countries to experience some of the sorts of intrusive intervention described in this chapter—forms of intervention which would become more commonplace as the divisions of the Cold War international system receded into memory. As such, it provides as close to an ideal laboratory as one is likely to find in political science for the study of the impact of external intervention upon the relationship between ethnic conflict and the state-building process.

Before proceeding to an in-depth examination of this case study, however, one word of caution is in order. This point is in the nature of a general caveat with regard to all scientific inquiry. As Karl Popper has observed, even the most rigorous of scientific tests cannot *verify* a hypothesis. The most one can hope for is that the theory will not be falsified.[26] In terms of this study, the significance of Popper's contention is that it is not possible to prove definitively the generally harmful impact of UN intervention upon the state-building process in post-Cold War societies experiencing ethnic conflict. The most that can be established in this, or any other, empirical case study is that the hypothesis represents a logically coherent and plausible explanation of events. The standard of proof, then, is whether the case study chosen contradicts in any significant way the expected relationships between the three sets of phenomena being examined. If there is no significant contradiction,[27] then the theory has met Popper's test of falsification.

At first glance, this caveat might appear to be a disclaimer against the entire study. That is most assuredly not the purpose it is intended to serve. The purpose is rather to acknowledge candidly the limitations inherent in an endeavor such as this in order to sharpen the focus of this research and to develop a set of reasonable expectations as to what can and cannot be accomplished. To place limits upon expectations is not to deny the value of the research but rather to clarify its contribution to the existing literature.

It is to a detailed examination of the Middle East, generally, and the case of Iraq, more specifically, that this study now turns.

Part III
Case Study

Chapter Eight

Patterns of State Formation in the Middle East and Western Europe

A Comparison

STATE FORMATION IN THE MIDDLE EAST: SOME GENERAL CHARACTERISTICS

As is the case with most of the countries in the non-European, post-colonial world, a central theme in the politics of the Middle East[1] has been the struggle surrounding the formation of modern states.[2] In one way or another, the problems of state formation have touched, and continue to touch, almost every other issue confronting the peoples of this region. For this reason, it is useful to discuss this issue as a prelude to the discussion of the particular situation in Iraq and especially the events following the Persian Gulf War in 1991. Without such a prior discussion, any attempt to test the theory developed in this study in terms of its relationship to the circumstances in Iraq would be largely unintelligible.

Although in some respects the general outlines of state-building in the Middle East have resembled those found in Western Europe beginning during the Middle Ages,[3] there also have been important differences.[4] The principal difference is that in Western Europe, the formation of states was an internally generated process free from interference by those outside the region. As Charles Tilly explained, state boundaries were frequently the result of territorial conquest rather than the product of largely arbitrary designations by colonial powers. Those contenders for statehood which were defeated in this neo-Darwinian struggle simply disappeared as separate entities and were absorbed by the victorious state makers as part of a process which led to the expansion of territorial boundaries and the consolidation of the number of states.[5]

As previously mentioned, this process of consolidating the number of states stands in marked contrast to the fate of contemporary states. The argument by Jackson and Rosberg that juridical sovereignty is responsible for the continued existence of many post-colonial states in Africa despite the absence of empirical sovereignty could just as easily be applied to the experience of state formation in the Middle East. This distinction between juridical and empirical sovereignty, and the consequences which follow from it in terms of the survival of states, would seem to fit the experiences of certain states in the Middle East—particularly Lebanon[6] and, quite possibly, Iraq as well.

As will be seen, the roots of many of the political pathologies in Iraq (most notably the absence of a shared sense of national identity,[7] the problem of establishing governing capacity, and the difficulties experienced on the path to democratization) and elsewhere in the Middle East can be traced back to broader trends throughout the region—specifically, the manner in which state formation occurred.

Of particular concern in terms of this study, is the legacy of imperial intervention and control, whose roots date back to events following World War I. In a very real sense, the states system in the Middle East, with all of its defects, is the product of this intervention. Thus, it would not be an exaggeration to modify Tilly's famous dictum by suggesting that in this context, *intervention* by imperial powers (not war) made the state.[8] And yet, ironically, it was this same imperialist intervention which has produced many of the infirmities of the contemporary Middle Eastern state.

STATE FORMATION IN THE MIDDLE EAST: THE ROLE OF FOREIGN IMPERIALISM

It is beyond the scope of this particular chapter to engage in a detailed discussion of the history of European colonialism in the Middle East. Suffice it to say that throughout the nineteenth century, Great Britain had a strategic interest in preventing the expansion of first Napoleonic France and later tsarist Russia into the Middle East. Among the many reasons was its concern about maintaining access to India. This strategic interest was served through indirect intervention by Great Britain aimed at preserving the territorial integrity of the Ottoman Empire[9] (sometimes referred to as the "Sick Man of Europe") against both internal and external threats.

Britain's strategic calculations regarding the preservation of the Ottoman Empire, however, were altered in the late nineteenth and early twentieth centuries. This change was precipitated by its perception of Imperial Germany as a growing menace combined with the increasingly close ties which developed between the Ottomans and the Germans as a result of Germany's interest in the building of a railway to Baghdad, which, at the time, was part of the Ottoman Empire. From the perspective of the British, German access to the Middle Eastern territories of the Ottoman Empire would pose the same sort of threat to British interests in the area as that traditionally posed by Russia.

In the end, the growing relationship between Germany and the Ottoman sultan would cause a rupture in relations between Great Britain and the Ottomans. The final break came about as a result of the decision by the Ottomans to support Germany in the First World War. In so doing, the Ottoman Empire was transformed from a British client to a British adversary. This turn of events, coupled with the defeat of the Central Powers in the First World War, would result in the Islamic empire's demise[10] and its reconfiguration as the modern state of Turkey.[11]

Following the end of World War I and the collapse of the Ottoman Empire, the victorious European powers sought to implement the terms of the Sykes-Picot agreement of 1916.[12] Under the terms of this secret[13] wartime agreement, the British and French planned to carve up the region into colonial possessions. In deference to the Wilsonian ideal of national self-determination and to certain conflicting wartime promises made by the British to the Sharif Husayn of Mecca and to Zionist leaders in Great Britain,[14] the newly created League of Nations referred to these de facto territorial possessions as "mandates"[15] rather than "colonies."

The notion of mandates was a departure from previous European experience. It was intended to convey the impression that the European presence was only temporary. The suggestion was that this presence was for the sole purpose of providing assistance to the peoples of the region as they made the transition from being former members of the Ottoman Empire to the achievement of full-fledged self-determination. The underlying assumption was that this transition would require some indeterminate period of tutelage before the peoples of the area would be capable of exercising full sovereignty.

In reality, however, the creation of British and French mandates masked a de facto policy of colonial domination virtually indistinguishable from that found elsewhere in the British or French empires at the time.[16] This policy involved the division of the former Ottoman territories in the Middle East amongst themselves with little or no regard for the interests or demographic characteristics of the peoples who lived there.[17] As events unfolded, the territorial demarcations of these mandates,[18] eventually would become the boundaries of nominally independent states.[19]

Despite the eventual exercise of self-determination, the states that came into being and their boundaries were tainted from the very beginning by the perception held by many in the area that they lacked authenticity and, therefore, legitimacy.[20] This widely held perception grew out of the fact that the idea of the nation-state was imported from Europe rather than being rooted in the political thought of Islam or the history of the region.[21] In addition, the so-called "nation-states" created during the middle of the twentieth century did not bear any discernible relationship either to indigenous processes of state formation and political development or to demographic patterns of settlement in the region. Consequently, many residents of the area viewed the boundaries established in the area as artificial, and therefore, illegitimate. Similarly, the claims that those living within those boundaries constituted distinct nations were likewise viewed as illegitimate or inauthentic.[22]

The creation of so-called national distinctions imposed *from the outside* posed a challenge to the prevailing Islamic ideas about the foundations upon which the political community traditionally had been deemed to be legitimate. The concept of the nation-state and claims that those living within these newly created states constituted distinct nations, i.e. Syrians, Lebanese, Jordanians, Iraqis, etc., shattered the ideal of unity within the Arab/Islamic worlds. This was a direct consequence of the attempt to forge new political communities out of disparate, sometimes antagonistic, ethnic or religious sub-national groups. These groups had little or no history of cooperation; their only common characteristic was that of shared territory as opposed to a common set of beliefs.[23]

Further compounding the sense that these newly created political communities were illegitimate was the introduction of *secularism* and its attachment to the idea of nationalism. By its very nature, this secular nationalism posed a threat to traditional Islamic political thought by seeking to elevate dhimmis[24] to a position of equality with Muslims. The unstable nature of this situation would fuel the development of both transnational[25] and sub-national ideologies.[26] In the decades following independence from European control, these ideologies would compete for the identities and loyalties of peoples across the region with the state-based national ideologies developed by state leaders and secular political thinkers.

As an aside, it is worth noting that the imposition of so-called "artificial" state boundaries upon the peoples of the region and the resulting reaction in the form of transnational and sub-national ideologies raises an interesting question regarding the proper way in which to conceptualize the area commonly referred to as the Middle East: assuming that one accepts the notion of "the Middle East" as a region (neither the designation itself nor its parameters are by any means self-evident), should this region be seen as constituting a single cultural homeland (whether Arab or Islamic) currently comprising many different states (analogous to the idea of one Germany made up of two states during the Cold War) or should it be viewed instead as a multicultural region consisting of a number of individual states—each of which comprises many different communities and, therefore, sources of allegiance? As will be seen, the failure to resolve this question has had important implications for the state-building process in Iraq and throughout the Middle East.

At this point in the discussion, however, the key point is that the experience of state-building in the Middle East does not exactly parallel that of Western Europe.[27] Middle Eastern state makers have been burdened with certain problems which their Western European counterparts did not have to confront at a similar stage in their political development. One of these is the need for state makers in the Middle East to attempt to consolidate their power through the development of political institutions while simultaneously attempting to justify the existence of their various states[28] and regimes to populations for whom the *very idea* of the territorial nation-state, the specific boundaries of existing states, and the concept of secular authority lack legitimacy.

This situation is decidedly different from the state-building experience in Western Europe. In that case, the state developed coterminously with the states system. As a result, there was no external intervention to impose boundaries upon the region.

This is not to suggest that the process of state formation was a smooth one in Western Europe. All of the literature suggests otherwise. Among the many issues confronted was that of the struggle between transnational and more particularistic sources of authority. Although the issue of transnational identity and sources of authority was confronted by Western Europeans in the form of the rivalry between the hierarchy of the universal Catholic Church and reigning monarchs within specific territories, who were emerging as state leaders, an important difference from the Middle East was that this issue was sorted out without outside interference. Also important is the fact that it was addressed over a considerably longer period of time. Among the many developments included in this process were: the challenge by Martin Luther to papal authority and the resulting Protestant Reformation in central Europe, the challenge by Henry VIII to the authority of the Pope, which resulted in the creation of a *national* Anglican Church, and the Thirty Years' War, which effectively shattered the unity of the Holy Roman Empire and gave rise to the existence of separate states and the modern notion of state sovereignty. Along with the formalization of the division of Europe into separate states, the Treaty of Westphalia at the end of the Thirty Years' War codified the notion of secular (princely) authority as sovereign over religious authority.

Two very important differences between the Western European and Middle Eastern experiences with state-building were the fact that the states in Western Europe came into existence as a result of indigenous processes rather than outside colonial intervention and the fact that they came into existence prior to the technological changes responsible for the development of mass politics. As a result, it was possible for emerging state makers in Western Europe to avoid the problem of having to legitimize their states and their regimes to their respective populations in the face of opposition from religious rivals during the earliest stages of the state-building process involving the consolidation of state authority.

While there certainly were differences in the two sets of experiences, this study takes issue with what would appear to be the conventional wisdom on one particular point. To say that the situations in Western Europe and the Middle East are different in important respects is difficult to deny. It does not necessarily follow, however, that one must draw the conclusion from these differences that the earlier Western European experience is of little or no value for an understanding of state-building in this part of the world. Whereas Tilly, along with a line of scholars going back to Otto Hintze, at times seem to take the position that differences in the historical and systemic conditions[29] under which contemporary state-building occurs render the earlier experience to be of little or no value as a model for the present, this study takes a different approach. Recognizing that the Western European path to state formation seems to have produced the most successful states in the world to date in terms of their stability and capacity for governance, the suggestion is that this path can be viewed as a *model* or *ideal type* against which other historic paths might be compared. The purpose of such a comparison is to see how the results of other factors, such as external intervention, have impacted this state-building process.

The discussion of the differences between Western European and Middle Eastern patterns of state formation, then, provides a context within which it will be possible in the next chapter to test the theory regarding the relationship between intervention, ethnic conflict, and state-building with specific reference to the process of Iraqi state-building. This examination will look at the overall role of British imperial intervention in terms of the initial stages of state/boundary formation in Iraq and then will focus special attention upon the subsequent efforts by external powers to interfere with the violence associated with ethnic conflict in Iraq following the Persian Gulf War. The question to be answered is whether the intervention which occurred inside Iraq, particularly after the Gulf War, altered the *trajectory* of Iraqi state-building away from the results one could reasonably have expected had Iraq been permitted to emulate the Western European path of unencumbered violence. If intervention did alter the path of state formation in Iraq, then it is important to understand the effect that intervention in its various forms has had upon the development of Middle Eastern states generally, and Iraq in particular, because this difference between the European and Middle Eastern experiences played a crucial role in undermining the capacity of Iraq to develop the means to effectively govern its own territory as a necessary stage in the state-building process.

Thus, contrary to those who would contend that the Western European experience with state-building is irrelevant to the issues confronting post-colonial states, such as Iraq, in the post-Cold War era, it is ironically enough the very fact that these experiences *are different* which renders the earlier experience of special relevance to an understanding of the state-building process. It is precisely the absence of intervention during the Western European experience with state-building which enables it to be used as a model or frame of reference against which the impact of intervention upon the state-building process in Iraq can be studied.

Thus, the fact that the process of building states in the Middle East has been subject to different social forces does not invalidate the usefulness of the Western European model as a way to understand how these forces, and particularly external intervention, have altered the experience with state-building and impacted positively or negatively the governing capacity of states in this part of the world. Viewed in this manner, the history of state-building in Western Europe identified by Tilly can be understood not in terms of its historical uniqueness but rather as a general model or universal constant, ceteris paribus, used to understand the impact of other forces upon the state-building process elsewhere in the world.

Returning to the issue of the relationship between imperialist intervention and state formation in the Middle East, the legacy of European intervention through the drawing of colonial boundaries has had a profound and demonstrable effect upon the politics of the region with important implications for the state-building process in this part of the world. Among the consequences for the politics of the Middle East has been a history of regional instability as a direct result of the way states were formed. This can be observed in the sizable number of disputes between states over boundaries.[30] In addition to border disputes rooted largely in economics (such as the specific issues which led to the invasion of Kuwait by Iraq in 1990)[31] or struggles over strategic waterways (as in the longstanding dispute between Iran and Iraq over the Shatt al-Arab waterway),[32] boundary disputes in the Middle East frequently involve questions of identity[33] and the problem of nation-building.[34] The following are all examples of border conflicts in the region driven *primarily* by issues of identity and questions of the authenticity of the political community rather than economic considerations: the competing claims of Palestinians and Israelis to the same territory;[35] the Syrian view that Lebanon, Jordan, and Israel were all carved out of Greater Syria;[36] the Iraqi claim that Kuwait was historically an integral part of the territory which comprises modern day Iraq;[37] and the ongoing Kurdish struggle against the governments of Turkey, Iran, and Iraq[38] in order to realize the dream of an independent Kurdistan, the establishment of which was called for by the Treaty of Sèvres at the end of World War I and later thwarted by the Lausanne Conference.[39]

Of course, this is not to suggest that identity and economic issues are, or need be, mutually exclusive. Indeed, rarely is a conflict reducible to a single dimension. One need only look at the dispute between Iraq and the Kurds involving rival claims to the oilfields of Kirkuk in the northern part of Iraq, and the efforts by various Iraqi regimes to consolidate control over this area through a policy of ethnic cleansing[40] known as "Arabization"[41] to see the ways in which the two issues can become intermingled. The point, however, is to emphasize the issue of political identity and to suggest that identity-based conflicts over borders are largely the product of a state-building process in which the states themselves have been burdened by the perception that they are artificial creations, whose boundaries were imposed externally upon the peoples of the Middle East.[42]

In addition to border disputes between countries or between countries and sub-national groups, such as the Kurds or the Palestinians, the challenge of state-building in the Middle East has been complicated further by the existence of transnational ideologies such as pan-Arabism and pan-Islamism. These ideologies seek to undermine the legitimacy of existing states.[43]

Although perhaps rooted in Islamic teachings, the efforts by advocates of transnational ideologies to undermine the states system in the Middle East are not merely an abstract philosophical or religious exercise. Given the history of European imperialism in the region, these alternatives to state-based claims upon the loyalties of the people frequently have been used to challenge perceived inequities in the distribution of global power. In this regard, it often has been suggested that the existing states system in the Middle East, rather than representing the triumph of self-determination over colonialism, is actually itself a legacy of the earlier colonial system. The argument is that during the colonial era, external powers attempted to divide a single people, whether defined in Arabic or Islamic terms, into different, and potentially antagonistic, peoples so as to perpetuate the weakness of the region.

If one starts from the premise that the territorial divisions, which occurred following the First World War, were the product of European colonial efforts to render the region vulnerable to outside penetration and domination, it does not require much of a logical leap to conclude that the perpetuation of these territorial divisions into the post-colonial era only serves the interests of outside powers. For those traumatized by the history of Western colonialism, it is not difficult to view the post-colonial legacy of territorial divisions as part of a grand design by those outside the region, who are eager to maintain this weakness so that the area will continue to be vulnerable to external interference and neo-colonial forms of economic and political domination.

It is, therefore, one of the ironic aspects of transnationalism in this part of the world that those who advocate one or another form of these transnational ideologies are able to make the argument that loyalty to one's own particular state is not really patriotism but treason to the larger (Arab? Islamic?) community in the service of outside powers. One need only look at the criticisms leveled against the decisions by King Abdullah of Transjordan to annex the West Bank following the first Arab-Israeli war, by Sadat to make peace with Israel, and by the Saudi royal family to accept the presence of American forces within Saudi Arabia before, during, and after the 1991 Persian Gulf War. Employing the distinction in Arabic between the terms "al-qawmiyyah" (non-territorial cultural or communal forms of nationalism, e.g. pan-Arabism or pan-Islamism) and "al-wataniyyah" (territorial, or state-based, nationalism or patriotism, e.g. Syrian, Iraqi, or Egyptian nationalism), pan-Arab and/or pan-Islamic critics of these decisions (each of which can be justified in state-based terms with reference to the idea of raison d'état) have argued that they represented a betrayal of the wider community in the service of either self-interest or some foreign interest rather than acts of patriotism in defense of the national interest. Interestingly, even the defenders of these decisions have felt it necessary to justify their actions in such transnational or communal terms rather than by explicit reference to the national interest of the country in question.

At various times and in various ways, leaders have attempted to champion the pan-Arab or pan-Islamic cause against foreign domination. Men such as Gamal Abdel Nasser, Ayatollah Ruhollah Khomeini, and Saddam Hussein have claimed to speak on behalf of the Arab or Islamic worlds in their respective struggles against alleged neo-colonial forms domination. In each instance, the goal was to utilize a transnational appeal for the purpose of undermining the existing states system in the region. Not coincidentally, it was also a way to legitimize their own particular claims to hegemonic power based on the suggestion that they were the opponents of outside forces, who were seeking to maintain a system of external domination through a policy of divide and rule. Thus, in contrast to subnational ideologies, transnational ideologies seek not merely to re-define the boundaries between particular states so as to allow for the creation of new states (e.g. the creation of an independent Kurdistan) or to call into question the existence of specific states within the region (e.g. Palestinian national opposition to the existence of Israel); the function of transnational ideologies is far more radical. They seek to challenge the *very existence* of the states system in the Middle East preferring instead the idea of a single, undifferentiated political community.

This last point concerning the uses of transnational ideologies as ways to legitimize a ruler's authority introduces another of the many ironies of Middle Eastern politics. Due to the fact that the states system in the region was imposed from the outside, the challenge of establishing legitimacy extends not only to the existence of the states themselves but also to the rulers of those states: if the state is *il*legitimate, then how can the ruler of that state claim to be legitimate? Given the alien nature of the Western-style territorial nation-state in this part of the world, it would seem that, paradoxically, one way to legitimize one's own rule is to de-legitimize one's own state[44] while claiming to be the leader of a community which more closely approximates some theoretical ideal. In this respect, the dynamic is somewhat akin to the phenomenon of an incumbent who runs *for* an institution by running *against* it.

The challenge to the legitimacy of the existing states system also has implications for the issue of democratization. Since democracy involves the notion of popular sovereignty, there can be no democracy until the question of the identity of the people who claim this right is settled. The appeal of transnational ideologies greatly complicates this process. For one thing, the ideological challenge of transnationalism to the existing states system means that the definition of the political community remains contested (communal versus state-based) and, therefore, uncertain: is the goal democracy for some unified concept of the *Arab world* under a set of common political institutions (rather like the European Union or perhaps the United States) or is it a league of democratic *Arab states* each with its own set of democratic institutions responsible to its particular national constituency?

As if this were not already problematic enough, *the nature* of transnationalism itself in the Middle East only adds to the complexity of the issue. The fact that ideologies overlap but do not coincide means that there is competition between rival ideologies each seeking to define the community in its own terms. Thus, for example, one can be an Arab without being a Muslim or vice versa. Thus, an "Arab democracy" presumably would have to include Arab non-Muslims but not necessarily non-Arab Muslims living in the Arab world; on the other hand, an "Islamic democracy" most likely would have to include non-Arab Muslims while excluding certain Arabs from the political community.

Until these issues are resolved, it is difficult to see how democratization can take place. After all, the democratic notion of the will of the people cannot be implemented if it remains unclear precisely which individuals constitute "the people" who are entitled to participate in decision making.

Thus, a good case can be made that the failure to sort out these issues related to state- and nation-building is an important reason for the absence of democratization in the region. If, for example, one takes a case such as Iraq, it is possible to argue that the concept of democracy could not be applied there until the question of political identity is resolved. Do the people in that state constitute a distinct nation known as Iraqis or are they part of some larger community of Arabs or Muslims? Alternatively, are they perhaps several smaller communities consisting of Shi'is, Sunnis, Kurds, Turkomans, etc.? If Iraqis constitute a distinct nation, then they are entitled to determine their own future independently of outside interference according to the will of the people *of that state*. On the other hand, if the population of Iraq is merely a subdivision of some larger community, then decisions made by Iraqis which contradict those of the larger Arab or Muslim communities would be contrary to the democratic notion of the will of the people. This point is similar to the idea that decisions made in accordance with the will of the people of a particular state in the US may not contradict those which reflect the will of the people of the United States as a whole. By the same token, if the people of Iraq constitute several communities rather than one, which were arbitrarily thrown together, then there is no Iraqi people capable of expressing its will.

Closely related to the issue of democracy is the issue of national self-determination. It can be argued that if Iraqis constitute a separate political community, as defined by the boundaries of the Iraqi state, then efforts by other states in the region to intervene in Iraq's internal affairs in the name of pan-Arabism or pan-Islamism would constitute an illegitimate infringement upon the sovereignty of its people. If, on the other hand, Iraqis are considered to be part of a larger (Arab? Islamic?) community, due to the artificial nature of the Iraqi state, then efforts by others in the region (for example Iranian Shi'a militias) to conduct operations on Iraqi soil in order to either negate the existence of Iraq or to provide assistance to groups within Iraq who may be at odds with the Iraqi government would not constitute "outside" interference in the internal affairs of a state. Instead, such activities would be an internal matter because Iraq would be part of a wider "Arab" or, in this case, "Islamic" homeland.

In point of fact, the Iraqi invasion of Kuwait in August, 1990 was justified by Saddam Hussein in a similar fashion. By defining the border between Iraq and Kuwait as an artificial boundary, he claimed that the military operation was not an act of external interference in the affairs of a neighboring state but rather an internal matter involving an attempt to reclaim Iraqi territory, which the British had severed illegitimately from the rest of the country in the first place. By this definition, Kuwaitis were really renegade Iraqis similar in some respects to the way that the People's Republic of China views Taiwan.

This last point raises one final area which needs to be considered with reference to the relationship between transnational ideologies in the region and the state-building process. Thus far, the discussion concerning intervention has focused upon the role of *external* powers in the region. The existence of transnational ideologies within the region makes the problem more complicated than this, however. In addition to intervention by Western powers, various state leaders within the Middle East have aspired to regional hegemony through intervention in the affairs of other states. Some notable examples of this would include: Nasser's intervention in Yemen during its civil war in the 1960s and Syrian and Iranian intervention in Lebanon during the Lebanese civil war in the 1970s and 1980s.

Such acts of intervention undermine the capacity of state leaders in these countries to exercise effective governance understood in terms of Max Weber's famous definition of the state as a compulsory organization possessing a monopoly of the legitimate use of force within a given territory. As long as either outside forces are present within a state or rival militias challenging the authority of the government receive outside military and/or economic assistance, it is difficult to see how regimes can consolidate their power within the existing state boundaries.

The presence of outsiders also complicates the process of democratization by making it necessary for state leaders to maintain a strong attachment to their own military[45] and other security apparatuses in order to fend off external efforts to exert control. Attachments to military or security forces are seldom conducive to the development of democracy as these forces tend to be used to stifle dissent—a necessary component of democracy.

CONCLUSION

The discussion above dealing with several of the issues associated with state formation has laid out in general terms some of the many ways in which the state-building process in the Middle East deviated from the earlier Western European model. Despite the importance of the military in this region[46] and the existence of frequent clashes between states, a key difference has been that war generally did not play as decisive a role in the building of states in the Middle East. Whereas the creation of states was the product of a lengthy process of wars involving conquest, absorption, and territorial expansion and consolidation in Western Europe, prefabricated states were transplanted into the Middle East through colonial intervention. The net effect of this difference upon the state-building process has been that state makers in the region confronted as a given a set of circumstances which involved an extended period of struggle in the case of Western Europe.[47]

Building upon Tilly's neo-Darwinian notion of state-building, it has been argued throughout this study that attempts to circumvent this process come at a significant price in terms of state capacity. This circumvention may occur through a variety of means. One is the creation of pre-fabricated states, as happened in the period after World War I. Another is in the form of external intervention to prevent the use of war making for state making purposes, as occurred both during and after the 1991 Persian Gulf War. Differences between the two varieties notwithstanding, both forms of outside involvement will have the same net effect. By altering the state-building trajectory away from the Western European model, which has a proven track record of producing strong states capable of exercising effective governance, the efforts of post-colonial states-in-the-making to achieve "empirical sovereignty" will be hobbled.

Viewed in this fashion, Middle Eastern border wars and struggles to repress or expel those internal opponents who reject either the state or the regime[48] may be seen as the somewhat belated efforts by would-be state makers to engage in state-building wars analogous to their Western European counterparts. Their function is to reverse the negative consequences which are a direct result of the short-cut to statehood which occurred in this part of the world.

Implicit in the preceding discussion is the notion that the path to the building of effective states is a bloody one. The goal of this chapter and the next is to examine what happens to this path when war is foreclosed as an option to state-building through the activities of external actors, who, for a variety of reasons ranging from humanitarian considerations to self-interest, choose to intervene in order to stop the violence. This question will be dealt with in the next chapter in greater detail with particular reference to the 1991 Kurdish uprising in Iraq and its aftermath. The events surrounding this situation provide a good test for the suggestion that external intervention in the form of missions such as Operation Provide Comfort interfered with the building of a strong Iraqi state.

As a prelude to this examination of the events in Iraq in 1991, it is useful to look at the interaction between the specific history of Iraqi state formation and the wider issue of the search for state and regime legitimacy in the Middle East generally. In this way, it will be possible to relate the manner in which the Iraqi state came into being to general trends in Middle Eastern state formation, which include the many problems of states in this part of the world.[49] At the same time, a better appreciation of the origins of the Iraqi state and the challenges it has faced will facilitate an understanding of the issues which arose during the 1991 uprisings particularly in the Kurdish northern part of the country. Taken together, the discussion of general trends in the region and the specific case of Iraq will make it possible to see the consequences for the state-building process in that country of the decision to intervene on behalf of the Kurds in that bloody civil war. It also will be possible to better appreciate the constraints upon the state-building process, which are a consequence of other regional considerations such as the competing/complementary efforts by Turkey to resolve its Kurdish problem in the context of its own state-building process.

Chapter Nine

W(h)ither Iraq?

The Impact of Intervention in Ethnic Conflicts Upon the State-Building Process

STATE FORMATION IN THE MIDDLE EAST: THE CASE OF IRAQ

As the preceding discussion makes clear, the process of state formation in the Middle East took a different path from that of Western Europe. The principal difference lay in the fact that in most Middle Eastern countries, including Iraq, the creation of states was inextricably linked with colonial intervention. This difference was particularly crucial as it related to the matter of establishing boundaries and the impact that these newly created boundaries had upon the development of a sense of national identity and on the legitimacy of regimes.

An important byproduct of the interaction between external intervention and state formation within the Middle East has been the use of ethnic and/or religious symbols by regimes seeking to consolidate their control within the state. This, in turn, has generated a similar process on the part of those groups within the state whose own self-definition does not coincide with the official ideology. They have been forced to rely upon ethnicity as a way to challenge either existing regimes[1] or the boundaries of many of the newer states in the Middle East.

In order to appreciate the significance of this general pattern of intervention and state formation for the case of Iraq, and more specifically the Kurdish uprising which occurred in 1991, it is necessary to have some familiarity with the historical background surrounding the creation of the modern state of Iraq and the process by which the Kurdish region of Mosul came to be incorporated within the new country.[2] This background helps to explain the Kurdish desire for independence and also the reasons why the uprising occurred in 1991–at a moment when the regime of Saddam

Hussein appeared to be seriously weakened following his defeat by coalition forces during the Gulf War.

While it is impossible to lay out a detailed description of this complex relationship in the relatively limited space available here, some of the key issues which would come to the forefront during the 1991 uprising will be identified. Of these, perhaps the most important concerns the impact of safe havens and humanitarian assistance upon the course of events in northern Iraq. A related matter of importance for this analysis is the relationship between this form of intervention and the question of state-building in Iraq.

The relationship between colonial intervention and state formation in Iraq in the years after World War I parallels rather closely the history of state formation in the Middle East overall. Unlike the post-Cold War era, the focus was not upon humanitarian assistance or peacekeeping but rather upon the desire by colonial powers to advance their own interests in the region following the defeat of the Ottoman Empire. In the specific case of Iraq, little attention was paid to the wishes of the diverse peoples living in the area. As a result, the new country of Iraq was a contrived entity created by the victorious British, in concert with their French allies, after the First World War.

As part of their effort to dismember the defeated Ottoman Empire and expand their own imperial holdings, the British and French literally invented the modern state of Iraq at a meeting held in Cairo in 1921.[3] The territory which, at the time, became known as the Kingdom of Iraq eventually consisted of three former Ottoman vilayets (provinces), each of which possessed its own distinct ethnic and/or sectarian character: Basra (primarily Shi'a Arab) in the south, Baghdad (having a mixed but primarily Sunni Arab population) in the center, and Mosul (primarily Sunni Kurd although with a small population of Turkomans and Assyrian Christians among others) in the north.

Originally, Mosul was not designated to be part of the new state/mandate of Iraq. According to Section 3 of the Treaty of Sèvres (1920)[4] negotiated between the Allied governments and the new state of Turkey (itself a rump state consisting of the Turkish portions of the former Ottoman Empire still under the control of the Ottoman sultan), the creation of an independent state known as Kurdistan, which would include Mosul, was envisioned. The boundaries of this proposed Kurdistan were supposed to consist of various mountainous regions in the ethnically Kurdish parts of the modern states of Turkey, Syria, Iraq, and Iran. Despite the promise of independence for the Kurds, however, this state never came into existence.

The failure of the Allies to honor their original commitments to the Kurds would leave a lingering sense of betrayal and bitterness that would sow the seeds of discontent for generations to come within the Kurdish community. The result would be repeated attempts by the Kurds to achieve their dream of independence through periodic uprisings against the British and later against the Iraqi, Turkish, and Iranian authorities. Prior to the creation of the autonomous Kurdish Regional Government in northern Iraq following the Persian Gulf War, the closest the Kurds had come to self-rule was the rather short-lived Mahabad Republic in Iran in the immediate aftermath of the Second World War. It is worth noting, therefore, that the uprising in 1991 was not a unique event but rather one in a long series of similar events dating back to the creation of Iraq in the 1920s and, in a very real sense, of the states system itself in the Middle East.

Since the repercussions of the failure to create an independent Kurdistan would be felt for generations, it is worthwhile to take a moment to explain the failure of the Kurds to achieve independence following the First World War. Briefly stated, the key reason for the failure to implement the Treaty of Sèvres involved changes within the Turkish portion of the former Ottoman Empire. Although the Ottoman sultan, Muhammad VI, had agreed to the terms of the treaty, the secular nationalist government of Mustafa Kemal rejected these terms because they amounted to the virtual dissolution of the remaining portion of the Ottoman Empire, which had been reconstituted as the new national state of Turkey. Following the overthrow of the sultan and the new Turkish regime's military successes against the Greeks, Turkey found itself in a position to demand that the Treaty of Sèvres be renegotiated. As a result of a rather complex series of events beyond the scope of this analysis, the Treaty of Sèvres eventually would be superseded by the terms agreed to during the Lausanne Conference in 1923.[5]

Of particular interest in terms of this study was the question of the final determination of the status of the predominantly Kurdish former Ottoman vilayet (province) known as Mosul. Although initially slated for inclusion within the larger state of Kurdistan, the invalidation of the Treaty of Sèvres by the Lausanne Conference dashed the hopes of Kurds for their own independent state and meant that the decision as to their fate would need to be revisited. While the Kurds at the time were divided between those who favored Turkish rule and those who favored British rule, the Arbitration Commission of the League of Nations meeting between January and March of 1925 made a final determination in 1926 that Mosul should be included within the British mandate of Iraq.[6] Thus, from the very beginning of its history, colonial intervention played a crucial role in the issue of state formation for both Iraq and the aborted state of Kurdistan.

It is worth mentioning that the decision to make Mosul part of Iraq served several important British strategic interests. One of these involved the presence of oil in the region, especially in the area around Kirkuk.[7] These oil reserves were considered important to the overall economic viability of the Iraqi mandate.[8] In addition, V. H. Rothwell points out that another reason for Britain's interest in this oil supply dates back to the First World War and involved the need for a secure source of oil for the British navy.[9]

Perhaps just as important in terms of the British reasons for the inclusion of Mosul within Iraq as these economic considerations was a political calculation which grew out of concern for the stability of the newly established Sunni Arab, Hashemite monarch, Faisal ibn Hussein. Given the fact that the majority of the population within the newly created country were *Shi'a* Arabs while Faisal was a *Sunni* Arab from the Arabian Peninsula, who had been installed on the throne by the British,[10] the legitimacy of his regime was suspect from the start. Recognizing this,[11] the British utilized various approaches in order to strengthen the support of the people of Iraq for this pro-British monarch. One was to use religious appeals designed to highlight the new king's descent from the Prophet Muhammad.[12] Another was to bolster support for this Sunni monarch by offsetting the numerical superiority of the Shi'a population. In order to achieve this objective, the number of Sunni Muslims within the mandate would be augmented through the incorporation of the former Ottoman province of Mosul, with its largely *Sunni* Kurdish population, within Iraq.[13]

The British insistence upon the inclusion of Mosul within Iraq is noteworthy for its ironic consequences. In their determination to address the numerical imbalance between *sectarian* groups within the new country, it appears that they either failed to notice, or perhaps were not concerned about, another line of cleavage which they themselves had created within Iraq: the *ethnic* division between an Arabic majority and a Kurdish minority.[14] Although both are primarily Sunni Muslims,[15] the Kurds represent a culturally distinct community from that of the Arabs. The former are an Indo-European ethno-linguistic group whose dialects, not all of which are mutually intelligible,[16] are more closely related to Persian than to Arabic.[17]

Given the British concern at the time for the stability of the Hashemite monarchy, it is fair to say that the decision to focus upon the issue of *sectarian* parity to the apparent exclusion of the issue of *ethnic* imbalance within Iraq represented a monumental miscalculation. Instead of creating a more stable regime through sectarian balance between Sunnis and Shi'is in Iraq, as the British apparently had hoped, their efforts appear to have succeeded only in adding another layer to Iraq's identity crisis. In the process, they sowed the seeds for future turmoil in the country.

By forcibly including an ethnically Kurdish region within the boundaries of a predominantly Arab state, the British, as was so often the case with colonial powers, unwittingly laid the foundations for the territorialization of ethnicity once Iraq became independent. The reason is that Iraq, as presently constituted, is a country which has lacked a defining national character[18] owing to the manner in which its boundaries were drawn. Instead of either allowing each of the former Ottoman provinces to develop into an independent state with its own cohesive population sharing both sectarian and ethnic affinities or simply uniting the two predominantly Arab provinces of Basra and Baghdad into a single state (albeit one with a Shi'a majority, which might have provided greater cohesion[19] but would not have served British imperial interests), the incorporation of Mosul within Iraq virtually guaranteed that any effort to devise a plan for a single Iraqi national identity would result in failure. This dilemma is captured perhaps most succinctly by Sandra Mackey: "Like so many other postcolonial countries, Iraq, in the pursuit of a national identity, has been required to constantly struggle against the complications of its own internal divisions."[20]

In the absence of a national identity, it is perhaps to be expected that leaders would attempt to utilize ethnicity as the glue which could bind the population of the state together. Whenever, as was true in the case of the identification of Iraq with its Arab inhabitants,[21] ethnicity becomes associated with the state-building process in an ethnically heterogeneous society (especially one in which there is a relatively neat territorial demarcation between ethnic groups), this association becomes a recipe for ethnic mobilization, counter-mobilization, and the resulting conflict between groups. Such has been the case between Arabs and Kurds within Iraq from the very beginning. At best, the Kurdish population within Iraq have felt only a rather tenuous sense of identification with the state itself while continuing to nurture the dream of an independent Kurdistan. Early signs of this desire for independence and of the disruption caused by British intervention in the area can be seen in the Kurdish uprisings of the 1920s and again in 1930 under the leadership of Sheikh Mahmud, a religious and tribal leader among the Kurds of northern Iraq.[22]

Left unresolved, the issue of Iraqi state-building in an ethnically heterogeneous environment would continue to confront the challenge of ethnic conflict between Arabs and Kurds within the country over the next several decades. During this time, the policies pursued by various Iraqi regimes, both under the monarchy until 1958 and then under various republican regimes, would alternate between periods of reconciliation and repression. Thus, for example, after the overthrow of the monarchy in Iraq in 1958, the new ruler, 'Abdelkarim Qassem, attempted to coopt the Kurds in order to widen the base of support for his regime. Whereas the monarchy had been responsible for expelling the leader of the Kurdish Democratic Party (KDP), Mustapha Barzani, to Iran,[23] Qassem initially would assume a much more conciliatory posture by permitting Barzani to return to Iraq. In addition, until his power was consolidated, Qassem encouraged Kurdish participation within his regime.[24] Relations quickly deteriorated, however, as Barzani began to agitate for autonomy beginning in 1961.[25] In place of earlier attempts to gain the allegiance of the Kurds, the regime now pursued a policy of repression, which resulted in a new round of fighting.

This repression would continue following the ouster of Qassem in 1963 by the Ba'athists. During this initial Ba'athist period, a form of ethnic cleansing known as "Arabization" was utilized against the Kurds. The aim was to consolidate Iraqi control over the oil-rich region of Kirkuk by replacing its Kurdish residents with Arabs from the south and center of the country,[26] who presumably would be more loyal to the regime in Baghdad. Consistent with the theory outlined in this study regarding the role of ethnic conflict in facilitating population transfer or elimination as a way to consolidate the control of a regime over territory, this policy of Arabization is precisely what one would expect from the regime as part of the state-building process.

Although the Kurdish resistance would continue intermittently until its military defeat in 1975, it is worth pointing out that the Ba'athists did not always rely upon a policy of repression. There were efforts made during this time, albeit disingenuous ones, towards reconciliation. In the midst of the conflict, the Ba'athists, who, after an initial period of instability, would rule Iraq from 1968 onwards, extended an offer of autonomy to the Kurds in 1970. In addition to proposing certain cultural rights, the "March Manifesto," as it came to be known, offered the Kurds autonomy over three of the five northern governorates (provinces): Irbil, Suleymania, and Dohuk.[27] By 1975, however, the Ba'athists, like Qassem before them, had reversed course and resorted to military means to crush the Kurdish insurrection without ever honoring the pledge of autonomy.

The Sunni Arab dilemma briefly outlined here of attempting to build an Iraqi state under the leadership of a minority sect in a country which is also ethnically bifurcated between Arabs and Kurds would be complicated further by the entanglement of the state-building issue with both regional and global international relations—each of which involved external intervention of one type or another. In this context, the Kurdish issue would become a pawn in the interactions between states, who would intervene selectively in order to utilize this issue as a means to gain leverage over the Iraqi regime.

At the regional level, perhaps the most significant instance of external intervention was the support offered by the Shah of Iran for the Kurdish uprising during the early 1970s. This support would eventually include the use of Iranian military intervention in Iraq. Both the decision to assist the Kurds and the later decision to withdraw this support would have an impact upon the course of events involving the Kurdish question inside Iraq as well as upon the relationship between Iraq and its neighbor Iran.

Seeking to promote Iranian interests, the Shah wanted to revise the border between Iraq and Iran so that it would run through the thalweg (midpoint) in the Shatt al-Arab waterway. This would facilitate Iran's access to its oil refinery at the port city of Abadan.[28] In pursuit of this goal, the Shah, who had little intrinsic interest in promoting Kurdish independence given the presence of a fairly sizable Kurdish population in Iran as well,[29] nevertheless provided assistance to the Iraqi Kurds in their struggle against the regime in Baghdad. The purpose was to put pressure on the Ba'athists to renegotiate the disputed Iran-Iraq border along lines more favorable to Iran.[30] In January 1975, this pressure went so far as to include the deployment on behalf of the Kurds of two regiments of the Iranian army *inside* Iraqi territory.[31] The use of this strategy by the Shah was apparently successful as it resulted in the negotiation of the Algiers Agreement in March 1975.[32] Under the terms of this agreement, the revisions to the border demanded by the Iranians were accepted by Iraq in return for a pledge by the Shah to abandon his support for the Kurdish rebellion.[33] Since Iranian support for this rebellion had enabled it to continue, the withdrawal of that support in 1975 resulted in the collapse of the insurgency shortly thereafter.

In addition to regional considerations, the Kurdish issue also was intertwined with global issues relating to the wider Cold War.[34] The decision by Saddam Hussein to issue the so-called "March Manifesto" in 1970 was heavily influenced by Iraqi efforts to curry favor with the Soviet Union at the time.[35] The Ba'athists were concerned about their security in the aftermath of the decision to nationalize the Iraqi Petroleum Company (IPC). In addition, they were concerned about the possibility of external aggression by the pro-American, Iranian regime owing to the border dispute between the two countries, as well as the continuing internal conflict over Kurdish autonomy. In the context of the times, it is not surprising that the Iraqi regime viewed the Soviet Union as a natural ally. Since the IPC was, in effect, a consortium of the world's largest oil companies, all of which came from Western countries,[36] and since Iran was already aligned with the United States in the Cold War struggle, it was natural for the Ba'athists to look to the Soviet Union for support.

Iraq's efforts to enter into a patron-client relationship with the Soviet Union were complicated, however, by the fact that the Ba'athists had persecuted members of the Iraqi Communist Party. In much the same way that the Shah had utilized the Iraqi Kurdish issue to extract concessions from the regime in Baghdad, the Soviet Union, disturbed by the treatment of Iraqi communists, was providing support for the leader of the Kurdish Democratic Party, Mustapha Barzani, as a way to exert pressure upon the Iraqi regime aimed at obtaining concessions on the communist issue.

Hoping to end Soviet support for the Kurds, Saddam Hussein visited Moscow in January of 1970. The meeting was a success. One of the conditions imposed by the Soviets, however, was that, in exchange for agreeing to withdraw their support for the Kurds, a reluctant Hussein (whose own preference at the time was to deal with the Kurdish issue through military means) would pledge that there would be no massacre of the Kurds. Pursuant to the agreement reached with Moscow, Hussein issued the so-called "March Manifesto," which contained an autonomy plan for the Kurds.

Despite the fact that this autonomy plan was never implemented, and it appears that Hussein never had any intention of doing so, it would be a mistake to conclude that the application of external pressure upon the Iraqis by the Soviet Union was of no significance. It was important in terms of the role that this sort of outside intervention played in influencing the course of events related to the Kurdish question in Iraq. While it is fair to say that the actions of the Soviet Union were driven by considerations having nothing to do with sympathy for the plight of the Kurds, this, however, is quite beside the point. The pressure placed upon Iraq effectively foreclosed certain options to the Iraqi regime in dealing with the Kurdish question. In so doing, this form of intervention by a global superpower in the conduct of the internal affairs of Iraq had a direct impact upon the state-building process within that country. By eliminating the option of the use of force by the Iraqi regime against the Kurds in order to complete the process of Arabization, the Soviet Union effectively prevented a resolution of the issue of Iraqi national identity in this ethnically divided state.

From what has been said thus far about Iraq, it would appear that a wider pattern can be discerned. The examples of the impact of intervention upon Iraqi state formation dating back to the founding of the state and continuing throughout its history would seem to confirm a general observation made in the previous chapter regarding the relationship between intervention and state formation in the Middle East. It appears that various forms of outside intervention have been responsible for *both* the existence of most of the states in the Middle East, including Iraq, and, paradoxically, the inability of these states to develop effective control over their territories (what Jackson and Rosberg refer to as empirical sovereignty) through military conquest and population homogenization in a manner resembling that in which the United States and the states of Western Europe were able to do.

Following a line of argument developed by those such as Mohamedou and Ian Lustick, which builds upon the work of earlier scholars such as Charles Tilly, it is small wonder that Middle Eastern regimes, such as that of Saddam Hussein, have attempted to utilize the same sort of brute force as that exercised by Western state makers during their formative periods. In the case of later state makers, such as the various Iraqi regimes including that of Saddam Hussein, this use of force is best understood not in terms of the idiosyncrasies of the individual leader but rather as a way to escape the limitations imposed upon the state-building process from the outside.[37] These limitations involve external efforts to determine arbitrarily the territorial limits of the state and the populations to be included within it as members of the national community without regard to the lessons learned from history. These lessons point to the fact that historically the state- and nation-building processes associated with the successful formation of states have generally involved a considerable degree of brutality in the short-term in order to resolve issues of control, legitimacy, and community. If, however, these issues are left unresolved because of attempts to circumvent the brutality in the short-term, they continue to exact a heavy (perhaps even more brutal) toll in the long-term.

As the above examples illustrate, this problem is compounded by the efforts of regional or global powers to interfere with the internal politics of the state through the manipulation of various groups within the target state in order to serve the interests of those external powers. This type of intervention in pursuit of one's own interests has much in common with the original colonial intervention responsible for creating states such as Iraq. The result of these various forms of intervention in the internal politics of Iraq leading to external manipulation of the Kurdish issue by powers such as the U.S., the Soviet Union, and Iran has been to complicate the efforts by Iraqi state makers to establish the sort of national cohesion which is so important to the consolidation of control within the state. This consolidation of control, in turn, is indispensable if the state is to develop the capacity for self-governance necessary to no longer be a weak or quasi-state.

It remains to be considered whether the past is prologue. Has the pattern of intervention in Iraq observed in the preceding examples continued into the post-Cold War era? Perhaps even more importantly, if this pattern has continued through assistance to the Kurds, has it interfered with the state-building process in Iraq? In other words, has it prevented the consolidation of regime control over the territory of the Iraqi state as a prerequisite for its further development along lines similar to those observed in the West? These are the questions which need to be addressed when looking at the impact of the behavior of external powers upon the state-building process in Iraq in the aftermath of the 1991 Persian Gulf War.

In pursuit of this objective, the remainder of the chapter will be devoted to an examination of the post-Gulf War uprisings in 1991 and the resulting Allied intervention in the north. This examination will seek to understand the impact of this external intervention upon the state-building activities of the Iraqi regime. In so doing, the argument that intervention in the form of safe havens, no-fly zones, and the provision of humanitarian assistance, all of which occurred in the spring of 1991 in northern Iraq, interfered with the development of a viable Iraqi state by preserving the territorial integrity and ethnic heterogeneity of the state while preventing the consolidation of regime control and the creation of a cohesive national identity will be tested.

INTERNAL WAR AND EXTERNAL INTERVENTION: THE CASE OF IRAQ

At 9:00 PM (EST) on February 27, 1991, President Bush announced in a televised speech to the nation that the Allied coalition had met all of its objectives in the Persian Gulf War, and that a cease-fire would take effect the following day.[38] Within hours of this speech, the Iraqi government announced that it too had accepted in principle a cease-fire. The cease-fire brought to a conclusion the Persian Gulf War—a military conflict whose origins went back to the Iraqi invasion of Kuwait on August 2, 1990.

A few days later, on March 3, General Norman Schwarzkopf and General Khalid Ibn Sultan of Saudi Arabia met with Lieutenant-General Sultan Hashim Ahmad al-Jabburi, Iraq's Vice-Chief-of-Staff, and ten senior Iraqi military officers at Safwan air base in Iraq to outline the specific terms of the cease-fire.[39] Under the terms laid out at this meeting, the occupation of Kuwait was terminated, military operations were suspended by both sides, and Iraq was prohibited from flying fixed-wing aircraft.[40]

While Iraqi use of fixed-wing aircraft was banned, the use of rotary-wing helicopters was permitted. The decision to permit Iraqis to fly helicopters within their own territory represented a concession by the coalition to the Iraqis. Ostensibly, the reason for this concession was that the weeks of Allied bombing prior to the beginning of the ground war on February 24 had destroyed a significant portion of Iraq's transportation infrastructure of roads and bridges thereby making air travel a necessity.[41] What had seemed at the time to be an innocuous decision by the military leaders of the coalition eventually would have unintended consequences for the struggle within Iraq, which was already beginning and which would intensify in the weeks to come.[42]

Quite literally on the heels of the just concluded Gulf War, Iraq found itself in the midst of a civil war,[43] which, to borrow a famous phase from Chapter XIII of Thomas Hobbes' *Leviathan*, was " . . . nasty, brutish, and short."[44] For a brief, but extremely bloody, period during March and April of 1991, the country was on the verge of complete anarchy and possible dismemberment as Shi'a Arabs in the south and Kurdish rebels in the north heeded what they understood to be the call of President Bush for the Iraqi people to rise up and overthrow the minority Sunni Arab-dominated Ba'athist regime of Saddam Hussein.[45]

Although the primary focus of this chapter is the situation in northern Iraq, it is impossible to discuss events in the north without also understanding what happened in the southern part of the country because it was the apparent initial success of the Shi'a uprising in the south which encouraged the Kurds in the north to pursue their own objectives against the regime of Saddam Hussein. In addition, the southern situation provides a useful counterpoint to events in the north in that the former was relatively free of external intervention of the humanitarian, peacekeeping, or peace enforcement variety.

Whereas the response from the outside to events in the north occurred within weeks of the initial uprising, there was no similar attempt to intervene in the south until August 1992–almost a year and a half later. At that time, pursuant to the provisions of UN Security Council Resolution 688,[46] which had been adopted on April 5, 1991, the US, Britain, and France imposed a no-fly zone in the southern part of the country below the 32nd parallel.[47] This would later be extended upward to the 33rd parallel.[48] By the time the Allies intervened in the south, however, the Shi'a rebellion had long since been crushed, and Baghdad had already reestablished control over the area.

Since intervention in the south occurred long *after* the conclusion of actual hostilities, it is, for all practical purposes, beyond the scope of this inquiry and is mentioned here in order to highlight certain points. One is that the political gains, in terms of consolidation of authority, achieved militarily by Hussein in the south were ultimately undone through outside intervention. The other point is that the difference in the treatment of the two regions had less to do with humanitarian considerations (since the situation was at least as bad in the south) as it had to do with concerns about regional politics and the possible de-stabilizing effects of Hussein's campaign against the Kurds in the north.

The Allied decision *not* to intervene during the uprising in the south is precisely the reason why it is useful to take a brief look at the situation there. Although there are significant differences between the two uprisings in Iraq, the failure to intervene in the conflict in the south does provide some points of comparison with the situation in the north in terms of the theoretical inquiry into the impact of such interventions in internal conflicts upon the state-building process. Accordingly, before discussing the Kurdish uprising, this Shi'a revolt will be examined.

THE SHI'A UPRISING: THE IMPACT OF NONINTERVENTION

Accounts vary somewhat as to the immediate catalyst for what would become a much wider revolt by the Shi'a Arabs in the south of Iraq. Dilip Hiro suggests that the uprisings began on March 2 in the southern city of Nasiriyeh when a group of Iraqi army deserters fought, and successfully defeated, Iraqi government forces.[49] Faleh Abd al-Jabbar identifies the first sparks of the uprising as occurring on February 28 in the Sunni towns of Abu'l Khasib and Zubair, which are located about 60–70 kilometers south of Basra.[50] Sandra Mackey makes no mention of these incidents but claims that the uprisings began when an Iraqi tank commander, withdrawing from Kuwait at the conclusion of the Persian Gulf War, expressed his anger at Saddam Hussein by firing his gun turret at a portrait of the Iraqi leader in the southern city of Basra.[51]

It would appear that most accounts of the uprising agree with Mackey's identification of the events in Basra as the starting point.[52] This, however, is not to deny the veracity of these other claims. It is entirely possible that what began as a series of isolated localized events in various parts of southern Iraq eventually fed into a coordinated rebellion. In that case, the question of when and how the uprising began would be less of a factual than an analytical question having to do with the *significance* of the events identified by various analysts. It is rather like trying to decide whether the Cold War ended with the collapse of communist regimes in Eastern Europe in 1989 or the collapse of the Soviet Union in 1991. Both events are factually correct; the central question is the importance one attaches to these events.

Despite differing accounts as to the specific origins of the conflict, the one thing that is clear is that during the first week of March, acts of defiance by Iraqis in the south, such as those described above, turned into a spontaneous rebellion. This rebellion, in turn, would end up posing a far more serious threat to the survival of the Hussein regime than had the Gulf War itself.[53] The reason is that, while spontaneous, the rebellion was not confined to a few isolated incidents. Sparked by events such as those described in Basra, the uprising would quickly spread to engulf much of southern Iraq including Suq al-Suyukh (March 2); Nasiriyeh, Najaf and Kufa (March 4); Karbala (March 7); and then on to Amara, Hilla, and Kut.[54]

As the uprising spread in the south, Shi'a soldiers returning from Kuwait deserted units under Sunni command to join the insurgents. In the days to come, the rebels swept north and west. In the process, they went from one government installation to another confiscating weapons, which had been stored in various warehouses. During the rampage which followed, the activities of the rebels resembled those of a mob more than an organized force. As the rebellion gathered momentum, the insurgents engaged in the seizure and brutal execution of numerous individuals associated with the Ba'athist regime. Among those caught up in the turmoil were civilian government officials as well as Sunni army officers and members of the Iraqi security services.[55]

In order to understand this outpouring of rage, it needs to be remembered that the Shi'a, who constitute a majority of the population of Iraq, have long resented their second-class status within a state dominated by Sunni Arabs—a resentment which, as stated previously, dates back to the founding of the country under the British-imposed rule of a Sunni Arab monarch.[56] Indeed, as an indication of the depth and longevity of their opposition to Sunni domination, Shi'a leaders repeatedly during the 1920s (the period when the Iraqi mandate had been formed prior to formal independence in 1932) had gone as far as to propose that a permanent British presence remain stationed in Iraq as an alternative to living under Sunni rule![57]

This resentment, however, was not merely a thing of the distant past. As recently as the 1980s, the harsh treatment of Iraqi Shi'a clergy by Saddam Hussein, who feared the potential of a Shi'a-sponsored Iranian-style revolution in Iraq,[58] had served to aggravate further the already bitter relationship between the Shi'a in the south and the regime in Baghdad.

The litany of historical grievances was exacerbated by a more immediate sense of anger at the current regime on the part of the Shi'a. This was a result of a series of costly military misadventures. In a little over a decade, Iraq, under the leadership of Saddam Hussein, had engaged in a war with Iran, which had lasted eight years and cost about one million lives on each side.[59] In addition to the loss of life, the war itself ended essentially in a stalemate thereby highlighting the futility of the conflict and magnifying the bitterness over the sacrifices made. Furthermore, the economic costs of the war for Iraq[60] were a major reason for its decision to invade Kuwait in 1990.

Almost immediately after this costly and futile war against Iran in the 1980s, from which the country had yet to recover, Saddam Hussein launched the country on another conflict. This time, the struggle was with the Allied coalition led by the United States following the invasion of Kuwait. In many ways, this struggle would prove to be even more costly for Iraq. The Persian Gulf War, as it came to be known, resulted in the taking of 58,000 Iraqi prisoners, the occupation of fifteen percent of Iraq's territory, and the destruction of all but seven of the original forty-three Iraqi divisions.[61]

Built upon a deep-seated sense of frustration and resentment at their treatment historically, the anger at the regime over these military blunders was felt perhaps most keenly by the Shi'a in the south. They believed that they had borne a disproportionate share of the burden and had been used as cannon fodder by the regime in Baghdad in these two military campaigns.[62] In the end, despite the enormous sacrifices made by Iraqis generally, and the Shi'a in particular, Iraq had nothing to show for these military (mis)adventures except for a country left largely in ruins.

It would appear that the timing of the spontaneous outpouring of rage by the Shi'a was brought on by the convergence of several factors. In addition to the longstanding grievances against the Sunni Arabs and the anger at the results of the two most recent conflicts involving Iraq, one cannot dismiss the importance of another factor: the demonstration of vulnerability by the Ba'athist regime. The clearly lopsided nature of the rout of Iraqi forces at the hands of the coalition during the Gulf War may well have indicated to the Shi'a that this would be an opportune moment to revolt.

Another factor, which may have contributed to the timing of the uprising were statements by the leader of the victorious coalition, President Bush. In various remarks made, he had offered what certainly seemed to many to be encouragement to the Iraqis by suggesting that they should take matters into their own hands and depose Saddam Hussein.[63]

Despite the existence of such outside encouragement, however, it appears that, at least in the case of the Shi'a, when the uprising occurred, it was seen by its participants as essentially an internal matter aimed at overthrowing Hussein and transforming Iraq from a dictatorship into a democratic state.

This perception, however, would undergo a significant change as a result of certain outside events which took place on March 7. On that day, President Hashemi Rafsanjani of the Islamic Republic of Iran, whose country had fought a bloody, costly, and ultimately inconclusive eight year war against Iraq following an act of aggression by Hussein in September 1980, chose to insert himself into the events unfolding in southern Iraq. In a public statement, he called upon Hussein to resign.[64] This request, combined with persistent reports that "tens of thousands" of armed Iranians had crossed into Iraq[65] to support the Shi'a uprising and statements from various leaders of the Tehran-based Supreme Assembly of Islamic Revolution in Iraq (SAIRI) emphasizing the Islamic nature of the struggle,[66] suggested that the uprising was not merely an internal matter and had implications beyond the politics of Iraq.

At the same time, it is ironic that such efforts to broaden the struggle by infusing it with Islamic themes seriously weakened the chances for success of the rebellion.[67] One reason is that the injection of Islamic ideology into the uprising by a relatively small number of individuals associated with the Badr Brigade, trained and armed by Iran and operating under the leadership of the cleric Muhammad Bakr al-Hakim,[68] introduced an element which only served to divide the insurgents themselves. Many Shi'is in Iraq had fought on the side of *Iraq* in its recent war against Iran. For them, as for most Shi'a Arabs in Iraq, the appeal of secular Iraqi nationalism was far stronger than the appeal of Islamic revolution. They viewed the Iranians as *Persian* outsiders rather than as fellow Shi'is, and did not wish to see an Islamic state in Iraq modeled after that in Iran.

To those familiar with Iraqi politics, this should not have come as a surprise. As Pierre-Jean Luizard and Joe Stork point out, it is the Shi'a in Iraq who traditionally have favored an Iraq-centered approach. This is in marked contrast to the Sunni Arabs, who, as a minority within the boundaries of Iraq, have tended to emphasize the pan-Arab themes associated with the Ba'ath party as opposed to a distinctly Iraqi orientation.[69]

From what has been said, it is clear that most Shi'is viewed the rebellion as a struggle against the regime.[70] Their aims were both social and political and were focused on the creation of a democratic Iraqi political system[71] and a more equitable Iraqi society. Consequently, this was not a struggle to create an Islamic state in Iraq nor was it an attempt by the Shi'a Arabs to secede from the country. Indeed, Sandra Mackey points out that the Shi'a desire to remain within Iraq is one of the key differences between this uprising and the Kurdish uprising, which unfolded concurrently in the north.[72]

Unfortunately for the insurgents, however, this was not the way the revolt was perceived within the Iraqi Sunni Arab community. Despite the opposition of the vast majority of Iraqi Shi'a to the creation of a theocracy or any form of Iranian hegemony, the intervention by Rafsanjani and by Islamist elements within Iran probably did more harm than good to the cause of the insurgents. Hussein's exploitation of the widespread fear of Iranian hegemony played into longstanding Sunni doubts about the loyalty of the Shi'a within Iraq. As such, it served to unite the Sunni Arabs behind Saddam Hussein as perhaps nothing else could have at the time.

Whereas Sunni Arab regular forces had borne more of the brunt of the Allied campaign in Kuwait than had the Republican Guards and, therefore, might have been expected to oppose the regime in Baghdad, Saddam Hussein skillfully manipulated the Sunni Arab fear of Iranian hegemony as a way to raise doubts about the loyalty of the Shi'a community. Utilizing organs of the media, such as *al-Thawra*, to wage a propaganda campaign suggesting that the Shi'a Arabs, despite their protestations to the contrary, were actually agents of a foreign conspiracy involving Iran,[73] he was able to rally the Sunni Arab troops to his support against the Shi'a in the south.

Facing the prospect of losing their privileged position within Iraqi society as well as the possibility of danger to their physical survival if the Shi'a uprising should spread to the capital city of Baghdad, with its mixed population of Sunnis and Shi'is, the uprising quickly came to be seen by the Sunni Arabs as a sectarian war. Under the circumstances, many Sunni Arabs, who otherwise might have seen Hussein as a brutal dictator, looked upon him instead as a national savior.[74] In this political climate, they were prepared to fight for the regime in what turned out to be a savage campaign to crush the Shi'a uprising.[75] At the heart of the counteroffensive against the Shi'a were the elite Republican Guards.

During the Gulf War, Hussein had decided wisely to hold some units of this elite fighting force in reserve in Baghdad while recalling some others during the struggle with the Allies over Kuwait.[76] Hussein apparently believed, correctly as it turned out, that these forces might be needed to quell internal resistance once the war was over.[77] For these Saddam loyalists, especially the Republican Guards, the insurrection in the south provided them with an opportunity to redeem themselves after the humiliating defeat against the coalition. If this were not reason enough to remain loyal to the regime and to do its bidding, Hussein made sure that their morale was lifted through the institution of a pay increase.[78] Consequently, when the time came to put down the rebellion, the Iraqi armed forces, and especially the Republican Guards, fought fiercely in defense of the regime.

The outcome of the struggle also was influenced by factors beyond the internal situation in Iraq. Perhaps just as damaging for the insurgency as the ability of Saddam Hussein to regroup after the Gulf War was the unwillingness of outsiders, particularly the Arab states in the Gulf region, to come to the assistance of the Shi'a rebels. Their reluctance grew out of the fear, similar to that expressed by Hussein, that helping the insurgents would only work to the advantage of Iran. The prospect of the sort of Iranian intervention described above or the possibility that Iraq might fragment with an Iranian-style regime in the southern part of the country unnerved the regimes of the Gulf region.

Given their own dislike for Saddam Hussein, which grew out of his invasion of Kuwait and his use of Scud missiles against Saudi Arabia during the Gulf War, one might ordinarily have expected these countries to offer their assistance to the Shi'a rebels especially if their goals had been limited to the ouster of Hussein. Once, however, Islamic ideology was injected into the revolt and it appeared that the objective of the uprising was to spread revolutionary Islam, these already fragile monarchies saw no reason to support the Shi'a. From their perspective, a sort of Islamic version of the Cold War era "domino theory" developed. The fear was that a successful Iranian-style revolt within Iraq would mean that they would be the next targets of similar calls for the creation of revolutionary Islamic regimes of the Iranian variety. Consequently, the type of regional assistance which might have strengthened the resistance to Hussein in the south was not forthcoming.[79]

Just as regional assistance did not materialize, neither did assistance come from beyond the region. During the spring of 1991, the Soviet Union was beset by internal challenges and on the verge of collapse.[80] Under the circumstances, just as it had avoided involvement during the Gulf War itself, the situation inside the Soviet Union was such that it was hardly in a position to become enmeshed in a crisis inside Iraq—especially since, in the waning days of the Cold War, Iraq's utility as a client state had ceased to exist.

For its part, the US was similarly reluctant to become engaged in this conflict on the side of the Shi'is. In no small measure, this reluctance was a result of the general perception of Shi'a Islam in the US. This perception was influenced largely by events dating back to the toppling of the Shah and the assault on the American embassy in Tehran in 1979. These negative images of Shi'ism in the United States were reinforced by the taking of American hostages by Shi'a militias in southern Lebanon, who were widely believed to have ties to Iran. The seeming convergence of a number of facts caused many in the policy making establishment in the US to be wary of the events unfolding in Iraq following the Gulf War. It should be remembered that the religious leaders in Iran were *Shi'is*, who had expressed a general desire to spread Islamic revolution throughout the Middle East and had expressed specific support for the Iraqi Shi'a revolt, those who had held Americans hostage in Lebanon were *Shi'is*, and the Iraqi insurgents in the southern part of the country were also *Shi'is*. Under the circumstances, policy makers in the US perhaps could be forgiven for sharing the concern (apparently rooted in oversimplification and guilt by association) of many of the regimes in the region about the possibility of creating more "Irans" in the Middle East.

It also should be recalled that, beginning during the Iran-Iraq war in the 1980s, the US had pursued a policy rooted in the strategic logic of balance of power politics. According to this view, Iraq should properly be seen as a potential counterweight to the spread of Iranian-style revolution throughout the Middle East.[81]

Although the uprising in the south appears to have had little to do with the creation of a base for Iranian hegemony, the context within which it occurred was such that the US could hardly be expected to provide the sort of assistance or protection for the Shi'a akin to that which eventually would be provided to the Kurds in the north of the country.[82]

Indeed, the United States government's fear of possible Iranian expansionism was so great that American troops actually went out of their way to interfere with the insurgency. Thus, for example, in one such incident during the uprising, American soldiers prevented the Shi'a rebels from seizing desperately needed weapons from an army barracks in Nasiriyeh. In other instances, the Americans actually destroyed weapons which they had seized rather than turn them over to the insurgents.[83] In other words, while officially neutral during the insurgency, it appears that the Americans actually intervened in a manner which undermined the chances that the rebellion would succeed. In so doing, they demonstrated a preference for a weakened, albeit brutal, Hussein, who would be unable to threaten his neighbors, rather than the prospect of an Islamic regime in southern Iraq.

It is noteworthy that external intervention on behalf of the Shi'a in Iraq did not occur until August 1992–nearly a year and a half after the uprising and its brutal suppression by Hussein. The fact that this intervention came long *after* the uprising was defeated suggests that the primary purpose behind the imposition of a no-fly zone in the south was not to assist the Iraqi Shi'a. According to Con Coughlin, it was actually linked to an earlier finding signed by President Bush in May 1991 authorizing the CIA to "create the conditions for the removal of Saddam Hussein from power."[84] For a whole series of reasons, the US and its allies were unable to devise a plan which could satisfy this objective. Instead, a no-fly zone, which applied to both fixed- and rotary-wing aircraft, was established below the 32nd parallel by the US, Britain, and France.

While the imposition of this restriction on Iraqi airspace may have provided some protection to the Shi'a in the south (exactly how much is unclear because of Hussein's propensity for challenging this infringement upon Iraqi sovereignty),[85] it appears that this was not the primary reason for its imposition. Rather, the southern no-fly zone, which was placed initially at the 32nd parallel and later pushed further north to the 33rd parallel, in conjunction with the one established earlier in northern Iraq above the 36th parallel, was designed to increase the pressure on Hussein by giving the Allies effective control over one-third of Iraq's airspace.[86]

When one considers the relative lack of external assistance to the rebels *during the uprising*, however, the apparent hostility of the Americans to the potential for the uprising to benefit Iran,[87] the lack of consensus within the Iraqi Shi'a community over the purposes of the revolt, and the absence of any organizational structure in terms of either a unified leadership or a coherent strategy behind these spontaneous uprisings,[88] the speed with which forces loyal to Hussein were able to crush the insurgency in the south is hardly surprising.

Making use of some 700 tanks and 1400 armored personnel carriers, which had been withdrawn from the Kuwaiti theater of operations prior to the Gulf War cease-fire, Hussein loyalists launched a brutal assault against the Shi'a rebels on March 9.[89] Beginning with the recapture of Basra, the pro-Saddam forces moved on to take the Shi'a holy city of Karbala under the protection of helicopter gunships,[90] which, as was stated previously, the Iraqis had been permitted to fly according to the terms of the Gulf War cease-fire. By the middle of March, the rebellion had been crushed, and Hussein had regained control of the southern part of the country. It is estimated that 200,000 people died in the south between March and September 1991 while somewhere between 40,000–100,000 Shi'is fled to Iran and another 37,000 ended up in Saudi Arabia.[91]

This brief look at the Shi'a uprising in the south and the brutal response to it by Saddam Hussein serves as a prelude to an examination of events in the northern part of the country. From the evidence, it would seem that the events described here are consistent with the overall thesis that ethnic (or, in this case, sectarian) conflict represents one of the early stages in the state-building process in divided post-colonial societies. In this case, the sort of uninterrupted violence utilized by Hussein in the south of the country appears to have provided a mechanism for the establishment of effective territorial control by the central government in the face of resistance to centralization by those at the periphery. Clearly, resistance to the regime's control in the south was repressed forcibly and Hussein did regain, if only temporarily, control over the region.[92] Indeed, the only reason that this control was temporary was because of Allied intervention in the summer of 1992 as part of a concerted strategy to deny the Ba'athist regime the fruits of military victory in the southern part of the country. Nevertheless, the initial Ba'athist operation in the south would appear to be a near-perfect textbook case of the correlation between uninterrupted internal violence and state-building. Likewise, the subsequent Allied intervention, ostensibly for the benefit of the Shi'a, supports the contention that such intervention undermines the state-building process as it clearly reversed the process of regime consolidation, which appears to have been underway in the country.

Continuing along this line of reasoning, with the exception of some Iranian assistance to the insurgents during the Shi'a uprising (the value of which remains dubious and which perhaps inadvertently played directly into the hands of Saddam Hussein), the civil war in this part of the country unfolded without the sort of outside intervention—particularly intervention aimed at interfering with the bloodshed—which would characterize the concurrent situation in the north of the country.

On its face, the events in the south offer an interesting point of departure for an examination of the events which unfolded in the northern part of Iraq at the same time. Since the conflict in the north was prevented from running its course by the intervention of humanitarian workers and later the creation of safe havens followed by a no-fly zone, the question is whether intervention in this case prevented the regime in Baghdad from consolidating control over this part of the country in the way it had done in the south. If so, it would provide further evidence consistent with the expectation of the theory that intervention aimed at preventing internal conflict also interrupts the state-building process in divided societies.

If, therefore, the political outcomes in the north and south of Iraq in the aftermath of the uprisings were different (despite the fact that neither uprising against Hussein ultimately was successful), any conclusions drawn from this would be strengthened by the fact that both sets of events occurred *concurrently* within the *same* country. As a result, it is possible to hold constant certain other variables (such as spatial, temporal, or political differences), which otherwise might account for the differing outcomes. Thus, for example, it would be impossible to explain the different results with reference to the existence of different political systems or regimes or to the existence of different international systems, such as Cold War bipolarity versus the post-Cold War international system. In order to subject this expectation to a more rigorous test, however, it is necessary to compare the outcome of the situation in the south with the effects of the Allied intervention in the north of Iraq.

Before doing so, however, a note of caution is in order. It is important to remember that while theories are designed to be elegant, facts are usually more complex. For this reason, although the events in the south do tend to confirm the general thesis of this study, one should be careful not to read *too much* into the fact that the conflict in the south was allowed to run its course. While certain variables can be held constant, this is not to suggest that there may not be other mitigating factors which enter into the attempt to apply this theory to the factual situation in Iraq. In making the comparison between events in the south and the north, one difficulty which arises is that the situations bear only a surface similarity to one another. The similarities extend to the fact that both occurred at the same time and both involved attacks upon forces loyal to Saddam Hussein.

Beneath the surface, however, there are important differences between the two situations, which must be acknowledged in order for the situation in Iraq to serve as a useful test of the theory. This poses the problem, frequently associated with the case study method when the number of cases is as limited as it is in this study, of isolating the impact of the variable in question by holding constant all of the other potential variables except the one which is to be tested. In this case, the variable in question is the impact upon the state-building process of either the presence or absence of external intervention designed to interfere with ethnic conflict. Without a wider database, the best that this study can hope to accomplish is to identify some of the relevant variables worthy of further examination, attempt to focus upon the one variable which is of particular interest, determine whether the case in question is consistent with the theoretical relationship between the variables established earlier, and finally raise questions for future research.

Admittedly, this is an imprecise technique, but it does represent a useful first step in the study of the role of intervention in the state-building process. Hopefully, this will lead to further research in this area. Before turning to the case of the Kurdish uprising in northern Iraq, therefore, some of the relevant variables will be identified.

One variable which needs to be identified is the underlying reason for the violence: is the goal control of the central government or secession? The Shi'a uprising appears to have been motivated by an attempt to redress inequities *within* Iraqi society with apparently no serious thought given to secession from Iraq. On the other hand, the Kurdish uprising in the north appears to have been an attempt to achieve the goal of either full independence or, at a minimum, greater autonomy for the Kurds.[93] This suggests that while the two situations occurred concurrently, they represented different threats to the Iraqi state and the Ba'athist regime, which could be dealt with in distinct ways.

From the standpoint of the Hussein regime, the Shi'a threat would appear to have been the more dangerous of the two. While, arguably, it posed no threat to the territorial integrity of Iraq (assuming, of course, that Iranian involvement did not lead to the secession of the Shi'a portions of southern Iraq or some sort of Iranian irredentist attempt to acquire these territories), the violence in the south did present a direct threat to the regime itself. Any attempt to redress the grievances of the Shi'a community would almost certainly involve movement towards democratization. This sort of transformation of the Iraqi political system would mean that the Shi'a *majority* would necessarily have a greater role in the governance of the country than it ever has had before. Of course, this expanded role would come at the expense of the Sunni Arab Ba'athist minority regime of Saddam Hussein.

On the other hand, the Kurdish challenge was precisely the opposite threat from that of the Shi'a. The desire to create an independent Kurdish state represented a threat to *the territorial integrity of the Iraqi state* and to the continued control by Iraq of the disputed oil fields in Kirkuk. At the same time, however, the Kurdish goal of separation from Iraq posed no direct threat to the continuation of the Iraqi *regime*. To the extent that this uprising might pose any threat to the regime at all, it was only in the sense that, if successful, the absence of the largely *Sunni* Kurdish north of the country would widen the sectarian gap between the Shi'a and Sunni populations in Iraq. This, in turn, arguably would make the regime's grip on power all the more tenuous. It might even place greater pressure upon it to pursue a strategy of union with other Arab states in the region so as to create the sort of sectarian balance within the country which would be reminiscent of British efforts earlier in the century to incorporate Mosul within the Iraqi mandate.

While the issue of sectarian balance and the threat posed by Kurdish secession may be *important* for the Iraqi regime, it clearly does not represent a threat of the same order of magnitude. Both Iraq and the Hussein regime could survive a successful uprising by the Kurds. Indeed, it could be argued that in terms of the relationship between Sunni Arabs and Kurds, the issue of ethnicity always has been more salient than the issue of sectarianism. Consequently, it is not at all clear that the presence of the

Kurdish north has been a stabilizing force in the politics of the country. If anything, the history of the country would suggest otherwise.

The challenge posed by the Shi'a, however, goes to the very heart of the Ba'athist regime. If the Shi'a were to be successful, Iraq would survive but not the Ba'athist regime. For this reason, Saddam Hussein chose to concentrate first on dealing with the Shi'a revolt[94] while initially allowing the Kurds to pursue their agenda without impediment. Only later did he deal with the Kurdish issue.

Another variable, which needs to be identified, involves the impact of organizational structure upon the two uprisings. The important question involves the degree to which each was orchestrated by a clearly defined and identifiable leadership. As discussed above, the Shi'a uprising was essentially a spontaneous rebellion lacking any sort of formal organization[95] despite the efforts of the Iranian-trained Badr Brigade to assume the leadership of this struggle.[96] The inability to identify a clearly defined leadership in this instance combined with the claim by Mackey that the Shi'a were not interested in secession but redress of grievances *within the Iraqi state* raises the question of whether this situation represents a case involving potential rival (Shi'a) state makers comparable to that which existed in the north.

In the absence of a leadership capable of speaking for the rebels, it is entirely possible that the insurgents themselves were motivated by different objectives, as seen in the case of the split between secularists and revolutionary Islamists. To the extent, therefore, that these uprisings represented spontaneous outbursts of Shi'a rage lacking focus or direction except in their fury against all things Ba'athist, one should be cautious in speaking of the forcible elimination of *rival state makers* by the Hussein regime as it went about the business of reestablishing control in the south. It, therefore, remains an open question as to whether the Shi'a uprising in the south offers a useful counterpoint to events in the north with regard to the issue of state-building. If the cases do not constitute like samples, the value of any comparison is extremely limited.

On the other hand, it is clear that for a period of days or weeks, the central government in Baghdad *had* lost control over the southern portion of the country. In the context of these rather amorphous conditions, in which southern Iraq was closer to anarchy than to the establishment of a rival government, the rather technical question of whether one can identify specific rival state makers would seem to be a rather small issue to quibble about. Arguably, the important point is that the regime had lost control over this area. Indeed, many of its own troops had deserted from the military in order to join the insurrection! Under these circumstances, the need to rely upon force to establish central government control over this area and the fact that Hussein was successful in meeting his objective in the absence of external intervention would seem to follow the outlines of the theory rather closely.

In contrast to the situation in the south, the Kurdish uprising occurred under conditions in which a well-established political organization already existed. Once the uprising in the north was underway, a clearly identifiable Kurdish leadership was able to quickly orchestrate the activities associated with the rebellion: "Unlike the Shi'ites, the Kurds had a recognized political leadership—Jalal Talabani's Patriotic Union of Kurdistan and Masood Barzani's Kurdistan Democratic Party (KDP)– quickly asserted control over the North."[97] Peter Galbraith suggests that one consequence of this difference was that the uprising in the north was far less violent than in the south.[98]

Another consequence of the differing levels of organizational structure was that the existence of Kurdish factionalism would lead to sustained intra-ethnic conflict between rival Kurdish organizations in 1994 following the intervention of outside powers and the creation of the Kurdish Regional Government (KRG) in 1992. Interestingly, in contrast to this situation in the north, the largely unorganized and leaderless violence in the south would dissipate almost as quickly as it had begun in no small measure because of the absence of intra-ethnic factionalism capable of sustaining the conflict over a protracted period of time.

The introduction of the issue of *intra*-ethnic violence raises an additional question as to whether ethnicity itself is a useful social category for an understanding of the processes involved in state-building. The premise of the theory in this study has been that *ethnic* conflict is the result of the reliance upon ethnicity by both regimes and rebels, acting as rival state makers, seeking to mobilize their respective communities in a struggle for control over territory as the first step toward the creation of viable states. The question of whether there might be rival elites competing *within* the ethnic community while it is challenging the central government (and the impact that this phenomenon may have upon the entire effort to wrest control of territory in order to create a new state or, alternatively, to undermine such an attempt) suggests a possible level of complexity beyond the scope of the theory used in this study.

Having identified some of the possible factors other than intervention, which may have affected the outcomes of each of the twin uprisings in the spring of 1991, the remainder of this chapter will concentrate on the events which unfolded in the northern part of Iraq in the months immediately following the Gulf War. Cognizant of the potential impact of these mitigating circumstances and of the limits they impose upon any conclusions reached in this study, the focus nevertheless will be on the question of the extent to which outside military intervention either influenced or determined the outcome of the 1991 Kurdish revolt and its aftermath. Accordingly, utilizing the example of the successful reestablishment of central authority in the south by military means as an experimental control, particular attention will be devoted to the degree to which outside intervention either facilitated or hindered the state-building process in Iraq. Towards that end, the situation in the north will be compared with what has already been said regarding the events in the south during the Shi'a uprising.

While it is important to identify these variables as potentially mitigating factors in terms of any conclusions reached in this study, the demands of parsimonious elegance require that they be held constant for the purposes of theory-building. This is not to suggest that they are insignificant but rather that they are beyond the scope of this particular study.

THE KURDISH UPRISING: THE IMPACT OF INTERVENTION

On March 4, 1991, within days of the start of the uprising in the south of Iraq, Kurdish rebels, known as "pesh mergas"(a term meaning "those who face death"),[99] took control of the town of Rania near Erbil. Although the timing of the uprising in the north was clearly influenced by the circumstances at the time, including the initial successes of the southern rebels, these events differed from the Shi'a uprising in that they were not the result of some spontaneous outburst on the part of the Kurds. During the Allied military buildup in Saudi Arabia following the invasion of Kuwait by Iraq, the usually contentious Kurdish factions had engaged in a remarkable degree of coordination and planning. Supporters of Massoud Barzani's KDP and Jalal Talabani's PUK crossed over from Iran into northern Iraq and infiltrated the so-called "jash" (a derisive term meaning "donkeys," which was used to describe those Kurds who worked in the service of the government in Baghdad) in preparation for just such an uprising in the event that the Hussein regime were to collapse in the face of the Allied offensive during the Gulf War.[100]

By March 20, a little more than two weeks after it had begun, the Kurdish insurrection in the north of the country was largely completed and had resulted in de facto Kurdish control of all of the major cities in Iraqi Kurdistan including: Erbil, Sulaimaniyah, Jalula, Duhok, Zakho, and, Kirkuk.[101] Of these, the oil rich city of Kirkuk was perhaps most important as any potential Kurdish state would not have been economically viable without it. The relative ease and speed with which the Kurds accomplished their objectives in the north can be attributed to two factors: prewar planning and coordination among the usually rival Kurdish factions and the relative absence of government resistance during the early phases of this campaign due to the fact that the elite Republican Guards were directing their fire power towards the uprising in the south.

Towards the end of March, however, within a week of the capture of Kirkuk by the Kurds, the tide of the civil war in the north began to turn. The Republican Guards, which had successfully crushed the uprising in the south, were sent north by Hussein to address this challenge to Iraq's territorial integrity. Utilizing helicopter gunships, Iraqi forces pounded Kurdish positions near Mosul.[102] Heavily outgunned, the Kurdish pesh mergas made a brave but futile effort at resistance.

The experience of Mosul would be repeated across northern Iraq, most notably in Kirkuk. On March 28, Iraqi armored and infantry divisions mounted an all-out assault upon that economically crucial city. During this assault, government forces utilized heavy artillery, multiple rocket launchers, and helicopter gunships.[103] These gunships, which Iraq had been permitted to fly under the terms of the Gulf War cease-fire agreement, were used to conduct missile attacks and to drop napalm.[104] By the end of the day, Kirkuk was once again under the control of the Iraqi government. On April 6, a little more than a week later, the Revolutionary Command Council in Iraq declared that the Kurdish uprising had been crushed.[105]

On the same day that Kirkuk fell, a mass exodus of Kurdish refugees heading towards both the Turkish and Iranian borders began. As events in places such as Mosul and Kirkuk made it increasingly evident that the rebellion was collapsing, it is estimated that between 400,000 and 500,000 Kurds fled to the Turkish border and between 1 million and 1.5 million Kurds started fleeing towards the Iranian border.[106]

The reason for this widespread panic, which resulted in a massive flow of refugees, can be traced back to Kurdish memories of the devastating "Anfal campaign" during the recently concluded Iran-Iraq war and the understandable fear that this experience would be repeated following the collapse of the uprising. The "Anfal campaign" was part of a wider history of so-called "Arabization." In this particular case, it consisted of efforts by the Iraqi military to eliminate most, if not all, of the Kurdish population in the north. This brutal campaign had been the result of concerns by the Hussein regime that the Kurds constituted a disloyal element within Iraq and still harbored separatist ambitions. It was feared, therefore, that the Kurds living in the north might be willing to join forces with Iraq's foe, Iran, during the war between those two countries.

Although, as discussed earlier, Iraqi regimes had periodically engaged in what has been termed "Arabization" as part of a campaign to consoli-date the control of the regime over certain parts of northern Iraq (most notably the oil-rich city of Kirkuk) by seeking to replace the Kurdish popu-lation with Arabs from elsewhere in Iraq, the campaign undertaken during the 1980s was different both in terms of the catalyst for it and the severity of it. The Anfal was a direct response by the regime in Baghdad to Iranian efforts at the time to exploit the Kurdish issue.

Sensing an opportunity to open another front in its war with Iraq, Iran worked to create a fifth column within Iraq during the Iran-Iraq war. In this regard, the actions by the Islamic Republic of Iran hearkened back to similar efforts by the Shah, who had exploited the Kurdish issue within Iraq as a tactic in order to place pressure upon the Ba'athists to revise the border between Iran and Iraq.

In the case of the Anfal, however, the Iraqi response was particularly brutal. Unlike Iraq's suppression of the Kurdish uprising in 1975, following the Algiers Agreement and the withdrawal of support for the Iraqi Kurds by the Shah, this campaign took the struggle to an entirely different level through the introduction of chemical weapons.[107] Furthermore, the aim was not merely to suppress Kurdish resistance but to eliminate the root causes by depopulating the Kurdish areas. This practice of eliminating an entire population from a given territory within a state so as to consolidate one's hold over that territory later would come to be known by the term "ethnic cleansing."[108]

Perhaps the most notorious incident during this campaign (Mackey describes it as "the most notorious poison gas attack since World War I")[109] involved the Iraqi Kurdish village of Halabja in March 1988. Located a mere fifteen miles from the border with Iran, Kurdish pesh mergas joined forces with elements of the Iranian army to push the Iraqi army out of an area near the strategic dam of Darbandikan.[110] A few days later a sin-gle Iraqi warplane approaching from the west dropped several canisters containing various chemical agents including mustard gas, nerve gas, and possibly hydrogen cyanide. The unleashing of these weapons resulted in the deaths of an estimated 5,000 Kurdish villagers while countless others experienced the horrific effects associated with exposure to these chemi-cal agents.[111] Overall, the "Anfal campaign" resulted in the massacre of between 50,000 and 200,000 Kurds, the forcible displacement of more than 800,000 people, and the destruction of all but 1,000 of what had been 4,000 Kurdish villages.[112]

Returning to the current situation, the devastating blow against Kirkuk in March 1991 and the emerging refugee crisis prompted by the fear of another Anfal in the wake of the collapsing rebellion[113] caused the leader of the KDP, Massoud Barzani, to make an urgent appeal on April 1, 1991. He requested that the US, Great Britain, and France act immediately through the UN to save the Kurds from "genocide and torture"[114] at the hands of Saddam loyalists. For a variety of reasons, which will be discussed shortly, there was a failure to act immediately. The delayed response of these countries caused the refugee crisis to grow worse and enabled the Baghdad regime to move beyond Kirkuk and to retake control of the predominantly Kurdish cities of Erbil, Dohuk and Zakho.

The request for action by the United Nations to protect the Kurds initially met with only limited support. One of the earliest to support the idea of providing assistance were the French. Despite their efforts to persuade the Security Council to adopt a resolution to this effect on April 2, however, the idea faced opposition from three of the five Permanent Members of the Security (China, the Soviet Union, and the United States), any one of which had the power to veto such a resolution. A principal reason for the opposition of these countries was their concern that, once enacted, such a resolution would set a dangerous precedent for the future. The establishment of this precedent might lead to the involvement of the Security Council in the internal affairs of states[115]–something expressly prohibited by the Charter of the United Nations.

Beyond this issue, the US had its own additional reasons for opposing UN action. One of these involved concern about the prospect of expanding the original UN mandate for action in the Persian Gulf. Security Council Resolution 660,[116] which had authorized action against Iraq, had called solely for the expulsion of Iraq from Kuwait. It said nothing about involvement in the internal affairs of Iraq once this more limited mission was accomplished. On this basis, the US had been able to assemble a wide coalition of countries willing to oppose the invasion of Kuwait. The coalition assembled against Iraq was remarkable in that it included a number of Arab states, which share membership with Iraq in the Arab League. The significance of this fact cannot be overstated because it contravened the ideology of pan-Arab solidarity and the tendency to be suspicious of Western intentions in the region. It seems more than likely that the only reason that Arab states were willing to support a foreign power against a fellow Arab state was because that Arab state had violated the cardinal rule of respect for the sovereignty of another Arab state. To have acted otherwise would have placed their own states and regimes in jeopardy.

At the same time, however, it is almost certain that this support did not represent the granting of carte blanche to the Allied coalition. Agreement by the Arab states with coalition objectives was limited to the restoration of the Iraq-Kuwait border. Any effort to expand the original mandate in such a manner as to include involvement in the internal politics of Iraq by deposing the Hussein regime unquestionably would have been viewed as beyond the bounds of the UN mandate and as a dangerously destabilizing action, which placed other regimes in the region in jeopardy as well. The one notable exception to this general rule among Arab states was Syria, which had its own reasons for wanting to see Hussein removed from power having to do with a longstanding rivalry between Syrian and Iraqi wings of the Ba'athist party.

Another reason for reluctance by the US to countenance Security Council support for action within Iraq was the fear of a Vietnam-style quagmire.[117] Key American policy makers, among them National Security Advisor Colin Powell and Allied commander during Operation Desert Storm H. Norman Schwarzkopf, had come of age in the military during that conflict. Understandably, they were concerned about the possibility that such a revision of the UN mandate would place the lives of American soldiers at risk by involving them in what had been already at the time a longstanding conflict, punctuated by periods of civil war, between Iraqi Arabs and Kurds.[118] From the standpoint of these members of the so-called "Vietnam generation," this was a conflict in which the US had no clear interest and no exit strategy.

Despite the argument by those such as Sandra Mackey that Vietnam and Iraq were entirely different situations,[119] the prevalence of the so-called "Vietnam syndrome" can be seen in the comments by then-Secretary of Defense (and later Vice President in the second Bush administration) Dick Cheney. In what arguably would prove to be prescient comments, given the course of events in Iraq in 2003, Cheney articulated the concerns of those in policy making circles at the time who opposed involvement in the internal politics of Iraq following the Gulf War: "If we'd gone to Baghdad and got rid of Saddam Hussein—assuming we could have found him—we'd have had to put a lot of forces in and run him to ground some place. He would not have been easy to capture. *Then you've got to put a new government in his place and then you're faced with the question of what kind of government are you going to establish in Iraq? Is it going to be a Kurdish government or a Shia government or a Sunni government? How many forces are you going to have to leave there to keep it propped up, how many casualties are you going to take through the course of this operation* [italics added]?"[120] Indeed, the first President Bush recognized that this fear of entanglements in unwinnable wars or quagmires, sometimes called the "Vietnam syndrome," affected not only the political elites in the country but also the American public.

Consequently, when he ultimately made the decision to authorize human-itarian assistance and establish safe havens within northern Iraq, Bush felt the need to justify this decision by reassuring the public that it would not lead to a situation similar to that which occurred in Vietnam: "All along, I have said that the United States is not going to intervene militar-ily in Iraq's internal affairs and *risk being drawn into a Vietnam-style quagmire* [italics added]. This remains the case."[121]

It is interesting to note that this reluctance on the part of the United States to support the provision of international assistance to the Kurds is in some ways eerily reminiscent of events leading up to the Hungarian upris-ing in 1956. While the contexts were different in the two situations (the Iraq situation in 1991 did not pose the threat for the US of a confrontation with the Soviet Union), the American role in the Kurdish uprising and its aftermath was nevertheless ironically similar. As in the case of Hungary, statements coming out of Washington, in this case from President Bush, seemed to lend encouragement to the idea of a popular uprising.[122] Such statements no doubt were influenced by the assessment shared by many Western leaders at the time that the recent military defeat by Iraq meant that Hussein would be gone within a year.[123] Nevertheless, when the time came to back up these words with actions, the US chose not to come to the aid of the rebels.[124] As indicated, however, there was one very important difference between this situation and the 1956 uprising in Hungary. While the US failure to intervene in the Hungarian situation might be understood in terms of the fear of superpower escalation, no such danger existed in this post-Cold War scenario in Iraq.

To be sure, it would be simplistic, and ultimately entirely speculative, to suggest that the Kurdish uprising would not have occurred but for the encouragement of the US. The above discussion, therefore, is not meant to suggest that all of the responsibility for the uprising can be placed at the feet of the United States. Con Coughlin points out, for example, that the severity of the defeat suffered by Hussein's military during the 100 hour air war in February also served to convince many Kurds that the time was ripe for them to pursue their long awaited goal of independence.[125]

At the same time, however, President Bush's own words, while not expressly declaring the willingness of the US to provide military assistance, leave the seemingly clear *impression* that the US favored the removal of Hussein and would support the efforts of the people of Iraq to move in that direction: "But there's another way for the bloodshed to stop, and that is for the Iraqi military and the *Iraqi people* [italics added] to take matters into their own hand (sic.) and to force Saddam Hussein the dicta-tor to step aside and to comply with the UN and then rejoin the family of peace-loving nations."[126] The unmistakable impression left by these words makes it difficult for the US, therefore, to absolve itself entirely of any responsibility for the uprisings or their aftermath.

Having initially raised the issue of revolt, it would seem that a fair interpretation of these remarks would have to conclude that the President had provided, at the very least, encouragement to the Kurds (and the Shi'a for that matter) to rise up against Hussein—a fact acknowledged by Con Coughlin.[127] Consistent with this reading of events, the reluctance of the United States to provide assistance to the Kurds, even as they were facing defeat and the prospect of another Anfal campaign at the hands of the surprisingly still viable Republican Guards, was arguably an abdication of its responsibility to "the Iraqi people" and, therefore, requires some explanation.

Despite the belief on the part of the Kurds that they would receive external assistance against Baghdad from President Bush, it appears that the rebels misread the intentions of the Bush administration. Although his ambiguous rhetoric understandably may have appeared to the Kurds to indicate support and encouragement for their efforts and a willingness to provide assistance if needed, it would seem that Bush actually anticipated something quite different from what ultimately occurred. Instead of the *popular* uprisings which took place in the days and weeks after the Gulf War, it later became apparent that Bush preferred some sort of *military* coup by Hussein's Sunni officer corps.[128] Indeed, given the strategic calculus at the time, it would appear that one reason for the failure of the US to provide assistance to the Kurdish uprising was that, from the American point of view, the failure of the Kurdish uprising, in the form in which it had unfolded, would actually be preferable to its success. This last point requires some elaboration.

Despite Bush's apparent rhetorical clumsiness, the American perspective was that a popular revolt by the Iraqi people was not the preferred option. Such a revolt was thought to pose a grave threat to the territorial integrity of Iraq (with the possibility that the country might fragment into two or perhaps three separate states corresponding rather closely to the original Ottoman provinces which constitute the modern state of Iraq) as well as to the stability of the wider region and beyond. Whatever his crimes, Saddam Hussein was widely perceived to be a stabilizing factor both internally and regionally. Although his means were brutal, there was no denying that he had held the country together. Evidence for this sentiment can be seen in the remarks by former US Assistant Secretary of State for Near Eastern Affairs, Richard Murphy: "If he survives, and is defanged, so what, why worry about it? He can make all the speeches he wants. A weakened Saddam with a weakened army and a weakened political reputation is maybe better for us if he is in power than if he is martyred. I don't think we want to get anywhere near Baghdad."[129]

In order to understand this comment and similar sentiments expressed by others at the time, it is necessary to understand the strategic assessment of the US in the Persian Gulf and beyond. In what amounted to an updated form of the old "domino theory" of the Cold War era, which had held that communist expansion was to be opposed anywhere anytime because of the potential for each success to lead to additional successes, the strategic assessment in the early 1990s was heavily influenced by the notion that the removal of Hussein by a truly popular uprising would likely lead to the splintering of Iraq along ethnic and sectarian lines. This, in turn, would undermine the country's role as a counterweight to the expansionist aims of Iran.[130] Accordingly, the security of the Gulf region and the wider Middle East required the containment of Iran in much the same way that it was once believed that the security of Europe and the Free World required the containment of communism. It follows that any weakening of Iraq would pose a serious danger to the region and beyond.

From a strategic vantage point, therefore, the order of the day was balance of power politics, which dictated that the preservation of the territorial integrity of Iraq was essential as a counterweight to the hegemonic ambitions of neighboring Islamist Iran. In this context, the absence of an Iraqi bulwark against what were perceived to be the expansionist designs of an Iranian regime still under the influence of the revolutionary Islamist ideology of Ayatollah Khomeini (despite his death two years earlier) represented a series of political, military, and economic threats to the United States and its allies. Thus, it was generally assumed that a popular uprising would weaken Iraq and provide numerous opportunities for Iran to expand its influence.

The most obvious opportunity that the dismemberment of Iraq would open up was the possibility of Iranian hegemony in the oil-rich Persian Gulf. As a hostile power, Iranian dominance could endanger Western access to the region's oil supply. The interruption of this access would threaten to cripple the economies of Western Europe and Japan[131] as well as play havoc with world oil prices. Indeed, this assessment had been the principal reason for the American tendency, despite official neutrality, to lean towards Iraq during the long Iran-Iraq war in the 1980s. At the time, the perception of Iran as a threat to the region's oil supply outweighed concerns about evidence of Hussein's brutal human rights record, which, among other things, had included the use of chemical weapons against the Kurds in the north.

Another concern was the danger that Iranian-style revolutionary Islam might spread throughout the entire region in the absence of an Iraqi buffer state to act as a physical barrier to its expansion. The possible spread of this ideology represented a threat to the stability of a number of friendly governments in the region including Egypt, Saudi Arabia, and Jordan. The overthrow of the Saudi monarchy and its replacement by a revolutionary Islamic regime, for instance, almost certainly would interfere with the flow of oil to the West and to Japan. If such an outcome were to materialize, the prospect that the world's largest oil supplier was ruled by a regime hostile to the industrialized countries could lead to an energy crisis reminiscent of similar shocks to the world economy during the 1970s.

Furthermore, the possibility that the pro-Western, i.e. pro-American, regime in Egypt might be toppled and replaced by an Islamist government would pose serious security challenges for the US and its allies. In this regard, it needs to be considered that the implacable hostility of the ideology of revolutionary Islam to the idea of Zionism almost certainly would mean that a pro-Iranian regime in Egypt would abrogate the Egyptian-Israeli peace treaty.[132] Although this treaty (the first of its kind between an Arab state and Israel) has not been all that either of the signatories would have liked, it arguably has provided a modicum of stability in an otherwise turbulent Middle East.[133] For this reason, the preservation of this agreement has been a cornerstone of American foreign policy in the region. The removal of Egypt from the so-called "rejectionist camp" of states hostile to the existence of Israel has been essential to efforts to prevent the prospect of another Arab(Islamic?)-Israeli war in accordance with the oft-stated theory that one cannot make war without Egypt, and one cannot make peace without Syria.

The correlation between a pro-Western Egyptian government receiving two billion dollars annually from the US and the maintenance of the Egyptian-Israeli peace treaty is one which is not lost upon pro-Iranian Islamic militants in the region. Thus, what is often perceived in the West as a courageous act by Sadat to bring peace to the region is perceived very differently among Islamists throughout the Middle East, particularly in Iran. For them, the peace treaty is not about peace but about surrender to American and Israeli hegemony in the region. Consequently, it is not much of a leap to suggest that an Islamist, pro-Iranian government in Egypt would negate this treaty just as the Islamist government in Iran completely reoriented the foreign policy of that country away from the West following the overthrow of the Shah.

Thus, in addition to threatening friendly regimes in Egypt, Jordan, and Saudi Arabia, the prospect of Iranian hegemony in the region raised the specter that this would threaten the security or continued existence of Israel. As the only stable, democratic, pro-Western regime in the region, which also possesses a sizable reservoir of domestic political support in the US among Jews, evangelical Christians, and others, a threat to the existence of Israel would pose serious political problems for the United States both in terms of its regional policies and its own domestic politics.

As if all of these considerations were not enough, another reason that the US had to be concerned about possible threats to the territorial integrity of Iraq involved the destabilizing effect that an independent Kurdistan in northern Iraq might have upon the Kurdish situation in its neighbor Turkey.[134]

Given the sizable Kurdish population on both sides of the Turkish border with Iraq, Turkey, a NATO ally of the United States which had been engaged in a long internal struggle against the separatist Kurdish Workers Party (PKK), was deeply concerned about the implications of events in northern Iraq for its own Kurdish situation. For the Turkish government, the fear was that, if Iraq should fragment, the prospect of the creation of an independent Kurdish state might provide encouragement to the PKK to pursue either the creation of a second independent Kurdish state or perhaps the creation of a Greater Kurdistan[135] together with its Kurdish compatriots on the Iraqi side of the border.

In addition to the possibility that events in neighboring Iraq might galvanize Kurdish ethnic consciousness in Turkey (something which the Turks had worked very hard to discourage even to the point of denying the existence of the Kurds as a distinct ethnic group),[136] the concern for the Turks was that an independent or autonomous Kurdish territory in northern Iraq might provide a base of operations for the PKK from which it could either launch attacks against Turkey and/or facilitate infiltration by hostile Iraqi Kurds into Turkey.[137]

Turkish concern about the prospect that the March 1991 uprising might lead to an independent Kurdish state in northern Iraq, with possible spillover effects on the Turkish side of the border, was first expressed by Turkish President Turgut Ozal during a meeting with President Bush at Camp David on March 24, 1991.[138] Initially, this concern took the form of opposition to American or Allied intervention in the Kurdish uprising. Turkey's preference was to let the Iraqis sort this issue out for themselves. The danger from the Turkish standpoint was that intervention might undermine the territorial integrity of Iraq. Viewed from Turkey, the preservation of the territorial integrity of Iraq played an important role in the preservation of the territorial integrity of Turkey since, as indicated above, the alternative of a Kurdish state would provide encouragement to like-minded Kurdish separatists in Turkey and might even provide them with a base of operations from which to launch military or paramilitary campaigns against Turkey.

As the crisis in the north of Iraq unfolded, however, the Turkish position underwent something of a transformation. Turkey's security concerns about the possibility of a Kurdish entity in northern Iraq emerging from Allied intervention were somewhat offset by the growing pressure created by the mass exodus of hundreds of thousands of Kurdish refugees heading for the Turkish border. As international pressure mounted on Turkey to help these refugees, the Turkish government concluded that resettlement within Iraq with Allied guarantees of protection (in effect the creation of an autonomous Kurdish region within Iraq), while still generating concern, was preferable to allowing these refugees to cross the border into Turkey.[139] At the same time, however, Turkey was careful to stress that any autonomous Kurdish region within Iraq not be recognized as an independent state.

American sensitivity to Turkish concerns on this issue grew out of two sets of concerns. One was the desire to avoid a schism with an important NATO ally. It should be remembered that, at the time, the Soviet Union still existed and the shape of the post-Cold War world was anything but clear. Under the circumstances, it made no sense to risk alienating a member of the pro-Western alliance by taking actions in northern Iraq, which the Turkish government would deem as hostile or threatening to its vital security interests.

Furthermore, the possibility that Allied intervention in northern Iraq might invite aggression by Turkey across the border into northern Iraq as a way to suppress Kurdish resistance inside Turkey would only serve to undermine the stability of this vital region. Since American policy was premised upon the need for stability in the area, such a needless provocation of Turkey understandably might be seen as counterproductive to American interests in the Middle East.

Given the serious potential implications of the Kurdish situation in northern Iraq and the delicate nature of the question of intervention, it is not surprising that several members of the Security Council, including the United States, were slow to react to events. Eventually, however, after several days of inaction, this initial reluctance to respond to events in northern Iraq would be overcome as a result of a variety of pressures. One such pressure was the heightened sensitivity of public opinion in the Western democracies due to the coverage by the media of the unfolding humanitarian crisis. Also important was the gradual shift in the Turkish position on the Kurdish question in Iraq from one of opposing intervention to one of supporting it as the lesser of two evils. As a result, the UN Security Council adopted Resolution 688 on April 5.[140] Among other things, this resolution, which was rejected by Iraq, demanded that Iraq end the repression of its own people and allow access by international humanitarian organizations.

At first, Resolution 688 had little effect upon the situation on the ground. As the refugee crisis continued unabated in the aftermath of the Kurdish defeat, international debate continued as to how to implement the mandate from the Security Council. European leaders attending a summit of the EC (formerly European Community now known as the EU or European Union) in Luxembourg on April 8 endorsed, in principle, the idea of creating UN "safe havens" in northern Iraq backed by military force to protect the Kurds from further Iraqi attacks. This idea was based upon a proposal put forward by the British for creating "enclaves" under the supervision of the UN on the Iraqi side of the Turkish and Iranian borders.[141]

Although initially not willing to commit to the idea of Kurdish "safe havens," the United States became increasingly concerned about reports that it was at odds with its European allies over this issue. As a result, on April 10, the US supported the creation of a safe haven above the 36th parallel. Iraq was required to cease all military activity beyond a line which stretched from the Turkish border to a line south of Mosul but which did not include Kirkuk. In addition, the Americans warned Iraq that force would be used if the Iraqis attempted to interfere militarily with humanitarian relief efforts for the Kurds.[142] This was followed by the decision of President Bush and the leaders of France, Great Britain, and Turkey to begin the implementation of Operation Provide Comfort in northern Iraq on April 16.

Two days later, the Special Representative of the Secretary-General of the United Nations, Prince Sadruddin Aga Kahn, negotiated a Memorandum of Understanding with the Iraqi government, which, among other things, allowed UN humanitarian agencies to operate throughout the country.

In order to gain a fuller understanding of events at the time, this explication of the diplomatic maneuvering which was taking place in world capitals and at the UN needs to be supplemented by a discussion of events on the ground having to do with the emerging crisis and the Allied response. The operational aspects of the response to the crisis in northern Iraq consisted of two interrelated components. The first was humanitarian assistance to the Kurdish refugees. The objective was to address the immediate humanitarian disaster, which had unfolded as a result of the Kurdish flight to the mountains along the border with Turkey following the collapse of the uprising. The unwillingness of the Turkish government to allow the Kurds to enter the country, for reasons having to do with both the unmanageable size of the refugee flow as well as its own internal struggle with the PKK, had left this population homeless and facing desperate conditions. On the one hand, the Kurds were confronted with severe winter conditions along the mountainous border region. These resulted in " . . . hypothermia, exposure, exhaustion, and bacteria-ridden drinking water, which led to pneumonia, diarrhea, and cholera"[143] and contributed to a death rate of between 400–1,000 per day.[144] This problem was complicated further by human rights abuses perpetrated by Turkish border guards. On the other hand, the refugees faced the prospect of another Anfal campaign by the Iraqi Republican Guards should they attempt to return to their homes within Iraq. More fearful of the latter, the Kurds refused to come down from the mountains despite the humanitarian catastrophe which was unfolding.

Due in large part to the pressure of public opinion generated by media accounts of the suffering along the Turkish border[145] shortly after the start of the refugee crisis, the US, Britain, Italy, Germany, and France began Operation Express Care designed to airdrop supplies to the Kurdish refugees. By the end of the first week of operations, this mission had dropped 1,727,200 pounds of supplies including food, water, clothing, tents, and blankets to the refugees.[146] Although the humanitarian benefits of the airdrops were limited by certain logistical problems, Thomas Weiss notes that one important side effect of the airdrops was the need to protect the aircraft being used against attack by the Iraqis. This, in turn, introduced the concept of a no-fly zone into the mission.[147]

While humanitarian assistance did provide some relief, the logistical difficulties associated with providing assistance to remote mountain areas quickly became apparent.[148] In addition, a crucial factor in the transformation of the original humanitarian mission was the growing pressure from Turkish President Ozal for Allied intervention to stem the tide of refugees: "The logic of the longer-term response to the refugee crisis was largely dictated by Turkey. It wanted the Kurds off Turkish soil as soon as possible—but *not* into a separate Kurdish state. The only alternative was some guarantee of safety for the Kurds within Iraqi borders, as President Ozal quickly pointed out. 'We have to get [the Kurds] better land under UN control,' he said on 7 April, 'and to put those people in the Iraqi territory and take care of them.'"[149]

As a consequence of these factors, and particularly Turkish ambivalence towards the crisis unfolding on its border with Iraq, the emphasis began to shift from merely providing assistance to the Kurds to attempting to repatriate them to areas within northern Iraq. The problem, however, was to convince the Kurdish refugees, still fearful for their safety within Iraq, to come down from the mountains. It is at this point that the interface between the two components of the Allied response to the crisis occurred. The humanitarian component under Operation Express Care, which had already been augmented by the presence of military security for the overflights, would now interact with the military component of the response in the form of the creation of a safe haven for the Kurds in northern Iraq. In this way, Operation Provide Comfort, which lasted three months from April 1991 until July 1991 and was intended to be a temporary measure designed to lay the foundations for a hand-off to the UN and various NGOs, was born.

During the brief period in which Operation Provide Comfort was in place, the mission was successful in greatly alleviating the suffering of the Kurdish population. Among the successes, the mortality rate dropped precipitously. By the end of April, the number of deaths per day had fallen from an initial figure of between 400–1,000 down to 50.[150] This rate continued to fall throughout May. Similarly impressive was the rapid repatriation rate of Kurds returning from the mountains along the border with Turkey to that part of Iraqi Kurdistan under the protection of the Allies.[151] In addition, the nutritional status of the Kurdish population returned to prewar levels within only a matter of weeks from the start of the operation.[152]

It must be acknowledged, however, that the consequences of this intervention have not been uniformly positive. In order to understand why this is so, it is necessary to look beyond the initial period of humanitarian intervention to the longer-term *political consequences*. In so doing, it is necessary to acknowledge the fact that the original humanitarian crisis in the north, as was the case in the south as well, was not the product of some natural disaster but rather of political decisions made by various parties. Indeed, in situations such as that which occurred in northern Iraq, in which this sort of population displacement leading to a humanitarian catastrophe is a political objective of one of the belligerents (in this case the regime in Baghdad), it would seem to be nearly impossible to compartmentalize the humanitarian crisis from its political roots and implications. Consequently, it is not surprising that what began as a specifically *humanitarian* mission aimed at providing essential relief to a refugee population evolved gradually and seemingly seamlessly into a *political* mission.

As Operation Provide Comfort and the creation of a no-fly zone above the 36th parallel were implemented, they necessarily involved the Allies in the politics of the area through the provision of protection for a de facto Kurdish autonomous region. Inevitably, whatever the official claims regarding the preservation of Iraqi territorial integrity or the unwillingness to recognize a separate Kurdish state, de facto autonomy for the Kurds also meant the inability of Baghdad to exercise effective sovereignty over the northern part of the country. What emerges from this tale is a muddled picture in which the Allies, as a matter of official policy, insisted upon preserving the territorial integrity of Iraq while simultaneously preventing the Iraqi government from controlling a significant portion of its own territory. The convergence of Kurdish demands for self-government, Turkish resistance to the idea of an independent Iraqi Kurdistan, Allied insistence upon the preservation of the territorial integrity of a weakened Iraq as a bulwark against Iran, while at the same time, supporting the overthrow of the Baghdad regime, and the attempt to balance all of these objectives somehow would result in a peculiar situation from the standpoint of Iraqi state-building. While Iraq would retain its formal or *juridical* statehood as a single entity at the insistence of outside powers, its *empirical* capacity to exercise the sort of sovereignty associated with that statehood would be severely curtailed by the actions of these same outside powers.

In order to understand the impact upon the state-building process in Iraq of this Allied intervention, it is necessary to look more closely at the political consequences which arose in the aftermath of the initial intervention within Iraq.

ALLIED INTERVENTION IN THE NORTH: THE AFTERMATH

From the beginning of Operation Provide Comfort, it had been anticipated that eventually the Allied military presence would be replaced by the UN and NGOs.[153] Indeed, between July and October of 1991, coalition ground troops were removed at the urging of the United States leaving in place: " . . . a small military liaison office staffed by US, UK, French and German personnel and an 'air exclusion zone' covering those parts of the three predominantly Kurdish governorates of Dohuk, Erbil and Sulaimaniyya which lie above the 36th parallel. The zone is policed by coalition warplanes stationed at Incirlik air base in Turkey."[154]

The removal of coalition ground forces combined with the failure of autonomy negotiations between Baghdad and the Kurdistan Front, which consisted of Barzani's KDP and Talabani's PUK, resulted in a renewal of fighting between the Iraqi government and Kurdish pesh mergas in October and November of 1991. Unable to use its aircraft above the 36th parallel in order to defeat the Kurdish forces, Iraq decided to remove its troops from the three governorates under Kurdish control. As a result, a de facto, but not de jure, border was established between the territory under the control of the Iraqi government and the territory in the north controlled by the Kurds.

On May 19, 1992, an election was held in northern Iraq for the 105 seats in the newly created Kurdish National Assembly (KNA) of the autonomous Kurdish Regional Government (KRG). The election ended in a virtual tie between the KDP and the PUK with each winning approximately 42 percent of the votes.[155] The result was a power-sharing agreement between the two parties in which each would receive fifty seats and the remaining five seats would be allocated to members of the minority Assyrian-Chaldean Christian community.[156]

On the surface, despite the refusal of the Allies to recognize the Kurdish entity as a separate state,[157] it appeared as if the KRG was well on its way to establishing itself as an independent state of Kurdistan. The protection offered by the coalition against Iraqi air attacks made possible the establishment of self-governing institutions by the Kurds—an essential prerequisite for independence. Thus, although the Kurds were careful to avoid the use of the term independence out of deference for the concerns of Turkey and Iran[158] (and the possibility that a declaration of independence might result in an invasion by one or both of these neighbors and/or perhaps the withdrawal of coalition protection), there were signs which seemed to point in the direction of evolving statehood. Had this been the case, it might be possible to argue that while intervention impeded *Iraqi* state-building, it also facilitated *Kurdish* state-building. In fact, however, the signs pointing to the evolution of Kurdish statehood were largely illusory and concealed a growing rift between the KDP and the PUK. In the end, this internecine conflict would undermine Kurdish efforts at self-government. The autonomous KRG would be divided between these two factions—each of which would look to outside forces for support against its rival. Ironically, one of those outside forces would turn out to be the government of Iraq!

In order to understand this factional conflict, it is necessary to appreciate the impact upon the Kurds of the creation of safe havens. Although the Allies appeared to be offering protection to the Kurds against Iraq, closer examination reveals a more complicated picture. Ronald Ofteringer and Ralf Backer suggest that the protection afforded to the Iraqi Kurds after the 1991 uprising has been ineffectual. They go on to charge that, in fact, the economic situation of the Kurds actually worsened while the so-called protection was little more than a way to keep the Kurdish population in a kind of international legal limbo. As such, the safe havens have preserved the Kurds as a stateless community similar to the status of Native Americans living on reservations.[159]

This rather pessimistic view of external intervention ostensibly on behalf of the Kurds is shared by Sarah Graham-Brown: "The view of Iraqi Kurdistan as a democratic enclave under Western protection has gradually given way to a recognition of the untenable conditions under which this 'experiment' is taking place."[160]

The criticisms leveled against the creation of safe havens, particularly with respect to the worsening economic impact upon the Kurds, need to be understood against the wider backdrop of what was happening in Iraq in the early 1990s. During this time, Iraq was experiencing the effects of UN-authorized economic sanctions designed to ensure compliance with UN resolutions demanding the elimination of all weapons of mass destruction. In addition, the US had made the removal of Saddam Hussein from power a condition for the lifting of the sanctions regime.

While the entire country felt the effects of this policy, the situation in Iraqi Kurdistan was particularly acute. The decision by Saddam Hussein to impose an additional set of punishing internal sanctions upon this region following the withdrawal of Iraqi troops and the creation of the Kurdish entity in the fall of 1991 compounded an already bad situation.[161]

For their part, the US and the UK were unwilling to distinguish between the autonomous Kurdish entity in the north and the remainder of Iraq when it came to the observance and enforcement of international sanctions. In part, they were motivated by the fear that any exemption for the Kurdish areas might open the door to smuggling by providing a conduit through which supplies intended for the Kurdish entity in the north would end up instead reaching areas controlled by Baghdad. In addition, the British and Americans also were concerned that any distinction made in the sanctions regime between the north and the rest of the country would constitute official recognition of the independent statehood[162] of Iraqi Kurdistan.[163] The refusal to recognize Kurdish independence goes back to the regional issues discussed earlier—especially the implacable opposition of Turkey to the existence of an independent Kurdistan.

The double sanctions experienced by Iraqi Kurdistan, which included both those imposed upon all of Iraq as well as those imposed by the Iraqi government upon the Kurdish autonomous entity, had a devastating effect.[164] In addition to the dire economic consequences for Iraqi Kurds, these sanctions also exacerbated tensions between the KDP and the PUK. This, in turn, was a major reason for the collapse of the Kurdish Regional Government in 1994[165] and the eventual partition of Iraqi Kurdistan between the two factions. On top of the difficulties associated with paying the salaries of government workers, the shrinking economic pie in the area under Kurdish control helped to ignite old resentments between the two rival Kurdish organizations headed by Barzani and Talabani.

In what became a politically poisonous atmosphere, fighting broke out in December 1994. What amounted to a Kurdish civil war followed accusations by Talabani's PUK against the KDP, which only controlled one-third of the total Kurdish territory but which included the area along the lucrative Iraqi-Turkish border, that the KDP was withholding funds from the Kurdish Regional Government. For its part, the KDP leveled countercharges against the PUK accusing it of similar acts of withholding funds.[166]

Ultimately, the tensions between the two factions would result in outside intervention. In August 1996, the PUK attacked the KDP with the help of Iranian artillery. In response, Barzani made "a deal with the devil" and accepted aid from Saddam Hussein. While the no-fly zone remained in effect at the time, this did not prevent Iraqi ground forces from using artillery pieces as well as 350 tanks and as many as thirty to forty thousand troops, principally Republican Guards, to push Talabani's forces back towards the Iranian border.[167]

By the time the fighting between rival factions, each of which was assisted from the outside, was finished, the PUK had regained most of what it had lost in the way of territory. Despite the Allied enforcement of the no-fly zone throughout the period of hostilities, the result of this Kurdish civil war was the destruction of the Kurdistan Regional Government. Instead of a single Kurdish entity exercising self-rule under the protection of the Allies, the idea of an autonomous Iraqi Kurdistan would cease to exist and would be replaced by the de facto partition of the area between the KDP and the PUK. In addition, as demonstrated during the 1996 hostilities, the idea of a no-fly zone above the 36th parallel did nothing to prevent Iraqi forces from entering the Kurdish north of the country using ground troops.

From this discussion, it would appear that the long-term *political* and *economic* results of Allied intervention and its aftermath (in contrast to whatever humanitarian effects the intervention may have had initially) have been disastrous for the Iraqi regime, the Kurds, and, perhaps most importantly in terms of this study, for the process of state-building. In sum, the picture that emerges is one of economic deterioration combined with fratricidal warfare. The results included the destruction of both the hope and the reality of Kurdish self-government and the de facto division of northern Iraq between rival Kurdish factions. These factions were little more than organized criminals or militias. All of these developments occurred against the backdrop of a porous system of limited protection for the Kurds by Allied forces in a region recognized internationally (including by the Allies!) as within the territorial confines of Iraq but nevertheless beyond the reach of the Iraqi government in a strange kind of international no-man's land or black hole.

Part IV
Conclusion

Chapter Ten
Conclusion

This study began with an examination of three discrete bodies of literature dealing with the issue areas of ethnicity/ethnic conflict, state-building, and UN peacekeeping. It quickly became apparent that while it may have been possible to compartmentalize these subject matters during the Cold War, the interaction between the three sets of phenomena in the post-Cold War era had rendered this approach obsolete. Increasing ethnic identification and conflict was linked to both the collapse of states and the creation of new states. In addition, these developments were occurring at a moment when the role of the UN was undergoing significant change. As a result of the changed dynamics within the Security Council following the conclusion of the Cold War, the organization was either engaging in, or authorizing, the use of more muscular and intrusive forms of intervention to stop internal conflicts than generally had been the case in the past. Under the circumstances, it was argued that a new paradigm designed to integrate these heretofore disparate occurrences would be necessary. Accordingly, the primary goal has been to fill this gap in the literature. As a result, a theoretical framework was developed to explain how these three sets of phenomena fit together. This, in turn, was tested against a case study which incorporated all of the elements described above—that of Iraq in the aftermath of the 1991 Persian Gulf War.

Beginning with the premise of a state-centric world, it is impossible to ignore the fact that many of these supposedly sovereign states continue to experience difficulty establishing effective governance over some or all of their respective territories. In many instances, these difficulties are a direct consequence of the experience of colonialism. The history of colonial domination and then decolonization resulted in the creation of artificial states, whose boundaries bore no discernible relation to the demographics of the area. As was seen, the crippling effects of this legacy upon post-colonial states were exacerbated by developments corresponding to the end of the Cold War and increasing globalization. The result has been a disconnect between the *principle* of state sovereignty and the *experience* of failing or collapsing states. This gap between the ideal and the reality gives to the question of how states consolidate their control over territory a degree of urgency which did not exist just a few short years ago when the energies of the world were consumed by other questions involving issues of bipolarity and/or economic development. At that time, many states were able to conceal their weakness as a result of the patron-client relationships developed during the Cold War.

Faced with a new and more complex international reality, in which the number of ethnic conflicts within states has been on the rise and the UN and other international bodies have engaged in more intrusive forms of intervention, while continuing to espouse the principle of state sovereignty as the cornerstone of international relations, this study took up the challenge of attempting to develop a parsimonious model of the impact of both ethnic conflict and external intervention upon the state-building process in post-colonial states.

Building upon a vast body of scholarly literature, the first step was to suggest that violent ethnic conflict within states should be understood not merely as a destructive force, in the way that Zartman argued in his book, *Collapsed States*, but also as a constructive force. As an *initial* stage in the state-building process, uninterrupted violent ethnic conflict represents a struggle for control of territory by ethnic entrepreneurs purporting to represent different communities within the same post-colonial state. The model suggests that, in the absence of outside intervention, the result of this struggle will be military victory by one of the belligerents. This also will entail the subjugation or removal of other contenders for statehood and their ethnic compatriots. In addition, the military capabilities of the various would-be state makers will determine the amount of territory that each is able to control and, therefore, whether the original boundaries of the post-colonial state will expand, contract, or remain the same.

In other words, at this stage in the political development of newer states, the twin processes of determining the territorial limits of the state and creating a more homogeneous population within those limits are accomplished by force of arms. These two occurrences represent a very early, but necessary, stage in the state-building process analogous to that which occurred in Western Europe centuries ago.[1]

Of course, since history never repeats itself exactly, no analogy is perfect. One very important difference lies in the fact that contemporary state makers are using violence not only to create states but also to *undo* the burdensome legacy of imposed colonial boundaries. Much of the political instability within post-colonial states associated with the rising number of failed/collapsing states, therefore, can be traced to this legacy of an earlier era. Thus, properly understood, ethnic violence represents a mechanism by which the political map is redrawn. Simultaneously, the ethnic divisions which exist within states as a result of the earlier creation of artificial territorial units are eradicated.

As the in-depth discussion of the literature in *Chapter Two* demonstrated, there is nothing new about this attempt to link violence with various stages in the state-building process. A number of scholars have argued for quite some time that everything from the initial formation of states to their subsequent democratization can be traced to the consequences of violent struggle.

Up to this point, the model is fairly straightforward in its suggestion of a direct relationship between ethnic conflict and the development of a viable state capable of exercising control over its territory. Such a model relies rather heavily upon the earlier experience of Western Europe but also includes more contemporary examples such as that of Palestine/Israel from 1947–49 or the 1991 Shi'a uprising in southern Iraq. Although arguably every bit as brutal as contemporary cases of state formation, the Western European prototype occurred during a time period when there was no external body analogous to the UN capable of interfering with this violent process. The correlation between uninterrupted violence and state formation in this case and the others mentioned would seem to present a prima facie case for a causal relationship.

Solely on the strength of these examples, however, it is impossible to say whether the violence associated with the creation of particular states was an *integral* part of the process or was merely *incidental* to it. The mere fact that violence coincided with specific cases of state formation does not, by itself, establish a causal relationship. In order to test the claim that a relationship of cause and effect exists between violence (in this case, ethnic conflict) and the building of states, it is necessary to alter the value of the independent variable of military success in internal conflict. This can be accomplished by examining a case or cases of state formation in which either there was no internal violence at all or the violence was interrupted as a result of outside intervention. Since the concern is with the question of how external intervention in ethnic conflicts affects the state-building process, it would seem to be appropriate to focus upon cases involving external intervention.

The experience of certain post-colonial states, especially after the Cold War, is instructive because the more intrusive forms of intervention witnessed during this time period offer an unprecedented opportunity to alter the value of the independent variable by comparing cases of interrupted and uninterrupted violence. Consequently, those cases in which the use of outside intervention successfully interfered with internal ethnic conflict *before* any party had achieved a decisive military victory are of particular interest. By comparing the consequences for the state-building process of cases involving interrupted and uninterrupted violence, it should be possible to draw certain general conclusions concerning the role of violence as either a *necessary* or a *contingent* element in the creation of states capable of effective self-governance. Briefly stated, the question raised by the successful use of external intervention in order to curb violent ethnic conflicts, and/or reverse their homogenizing effects, is: what impact does external interference with internal violence have upon the state's ability to develop the capacity for effective governance?

In an attempt to answer this question, *it was suggested that intervention in ethnic conflicts which succeeds in halting the violence will have a negative impact upon the state-building process.* For the sake of theoretical elegance, this proposition does not distinguish between the many different types of intervention which have emerged in the post-Cold War environment. It makes no distinction, for example, between impartial intervention of the traditional peacekeeping variety designed to separate belligerents with the consent of the parties and more intrusive forms of intervention, such as peace enforcement, which may be designed to determine the outcome of a conflict by helping one of the belligerents to achieve a military victory.

To be sure, the contrast between more muscular cases of peace enforcement, such as ONUC in the Congo in the early 1960s, and more traditional cases, such as UNFICYP in Cyprus, suggest that the *type* of intervention may be crucial to a determination of the outcome. Indeed, there is some reason to believe that peace enforcement missions which support a particular belligerent would be more effective in promoting state-building *precisely because they facilitate the violent consolidation of authority rather than interfere with the violence.* It was beyond the scope of this particular work, however, to test this hypothesis. Any such attempt to investigate the many different forms of intervention which have emerged in recent years and then develop a theory which assigns a value to each in terms of its impact upon the state-building process would violate the first rule of theory-building: parsimony. It also would interfere with the primary mission of this study, which was to begin the process of understanding the impact of external intervention in ethnic conflicts upon the state-building process. Accordingly, while a further examination of the differential impacts of various forms of intervention would represent a useful refinement of any conclusions reached here, such an exercise is quite simply beyond the scope of this particular analysis.

In order to test the theory developed in this study, the experience of Iraq was used as a case study. Iraq was chosen because it embodies many of the aspects of the experience of post-colonial states generally. These include the existence of artificial boundaries drawn by a colonial power interested in furthering its own interests with little or no regard for the needs of the indigenous population. The result, as in so many other cases, is a society divided along ethnic and sectarian lines lacking a clear sense of an overarching, in this case Iraqi, national identity.

Another feature which makes Iraq a useful case study is the fact that Iraqi regimes repeatedly have responded to challenges from groups within the state by resorting to violence as a way to assert control over the territory bequeathed to them by the British. Long before the term "ethnic cleansing" had come into vogue in relation to events in the Balkans in the early 1990s, Iraqi regimes were practicing a form of this known as "Arabization" in order to gain control over the predominantly Kurdish areas in the north of the country, and especially the all-important oil-rich region of Kirkuk.

In addition to efforts to use violence in order to homogenize the population of Iraq, Lustick pointed out that it also had been used by the Iraqi regime of Saddam Hussein in order to redraw the map of the Persian Gulf. According to Lustick, this use of violence was part of an effort to convert Iraq into a regional hegemon in much the same way that early Western European state makers had expanded their territorial possessions in the pursuit of great power status—all the while engaging in the process of state consolidation by reducing through absorption into larger states the number of states in the system overall. Here, too, the case of Iraq fits rather nicely with the attempts of this study to draw certain parallels between the experience of contemporary state makers and that of their counterparts in Western Europe.

At the same time, however, as indicated above, the analogy to Western Europe is not exact. While useful as a point of departure for understanding contemporary events, there are important differences between the two situations. The restoration of Kuwaiti sovereignty through the use of force from the outside and the continued preservation of Saudi sovereignty through the stationing of troops belonging to external powers on Saudi soil as a hedge against possible Iraqi adventurism highlight a key difference between the experiences in Western Europe and the Middle East. As Lustick points out, this difference is responsible for the failure of a regional great power to emerge in the Middle East. Whereas the consolidation of the number of states through the disappearance of failed states in Western Europe was a frequent occurrence resulting in the increased power of the remaining states at a similar early stage in the development of states in that region, external enforcement of juridical sovereignty resulting in the preservation of otherwise weak or failed states has interfered with the efforts by regional state makers in the Middle East to achieve the same sort of success in the area of state-building.

Although the issue of building a great power was not one which specifically was addressed by this study, the finding that outside intervention prevented state makers in this part of the world from determining the boundaries of the state by force is consistent with the argument that intervention, in this case to enforce artificial boundaries by upholding the norm of juridical sovereignty, interferes with the state-building process.

Thus, Iraq was chosen as a case study because it represents one of a relatively small but growing number of cases of post-Cold War intervention designed to interfere with the uses of violence described above. Iraq offers a useful laboratory for testing the claim that efforts to interfere with the use of force by the regime undermined the state-building process within that country because intervention has played a prominent role in recent Iraqi politics and has taken a variety of different forms. One form was the use of what amounted to collective security by the UN Security Council during the Persian Gulf War (the first time since the extraordinary circumstances surrounding the Korean operation in the early 1950s) in order to reverse the effects of Iraqi efforts at regional great power status through the forcible expulsion of Iraq from Kuwait. Another form of intervention has been the use of economic sanctions designed to ensure compliance with UN resolutions requiring the removal of all weapons of mass destruction from Iraq. A third form that intervention has taken has involved the creation of a no-fly zone and humanitarian assistance in the north of the country designed to protect the Kurdish population. This was followed by the imposition of a no-fly zone in the southern part of Iraq for the purpose of applying pressure as part of a strategy intended to encourage regime change.

In order to better understand the relationship between intervention in ethnic conflicts and the state-building process, this study has focused upon the events which occurred inside Iraq in the spring of 1991. As such, only some of the types of intervention mentioned above have been examined. Specifically, the use of intervention in the predominantly Kurdish north has been compared with the period of uninterrupted violence in the mostly Shi'a south.

From this comparison, some rather interesting results emerged. In part, they are consistent with the expectations of the theory. Just as is true with any theory, however, the findings in the case of Iraq also suggest that reality is by its very nature more complex. Consequently, further refinement and study is needed in order to continually improve the understanding of this rather complicated relationship between intervention and state-building in the post-Cold War era.

The events described in the case study present a rather muddled picture of the situation in northern Iraq. While Baghdad retained *de jure* sovereignty over the region, Allied intervention in the form of humanitarian assistance and the imposition of a no-fly zone above the 36th parallel effectively prevented the Iraqi regime from exercising control in the north. The deliberate and successful campaign to reverse the Iraqi effort to ethnically cleanse the area of Kurds undermined the efforts of the regime to consolidate its control over the region—especially the disputed oil-rich city of Kirkuk.

At the same time, the refusal of the Allies to allow the Kurds to declare an independent state of Kurdistan coupled with the imposition of dual sanctions upon this region created both a long-term humanitarian disaster and a situation characterized by political uncertainty and instability in northern Iraq. The reason for this instability can be traced directly to the intervention of outside powers and their insistence that the Kurdish regions in the north remain part of Iraq while refusing to allow either the regime in Baghdad or the autonomous Kurdish Regional Government to exercise full sovereignty over this area.

In this regard, the attempt by outside powers to preserve the territorial integrity of Iraq while simultaneously reversing the Iraqi regime's policy of ethnic homogenization within its borders is similar to the policy adopted by the European Community and the United States towards Bosnia in the early 1990s. In that case, the goal was the preservation of both the territorial integrity *and* the ethnically mixed population of that newly created country. As Susan Woodward points out in her book, *Balkan Tragedy*, that policy in Bosnia created a recipe for instability and civil war.[2]

Likewise, in the case of Iraq, external intervention preserved a volatile political situation characterized by periodic episodes involving confrontations either between the Iraqi regime and certain Kurdish factions (specifically the PUK in 1996) or between the regime and the Allied forces enforcing the no-fly zones.

From the standpoint of the theory developed in this study, the difference between the relatively uninterrupted violence in the south and the Allied intervention in the north would seem to provide partial support for the claim that uninterrupted violence contributes to the early stages of the state-building process. In contrast to the rather muddled picture in the north, the success of the Republican Guards in the south enabled Hussein to re-establish de facto, as well as de jure, control over this part of the country. To be sure, the success in the south was conditioned by the eventual imposition of a no-fly zone below the 32nd parallel, which was later moved north to the 33rd parallel. The fact that this later policy reversed somewhat the gains of the regime's war in the south, however, only seems to lend further support to the claim that external intervention interferes with the state-building process.

Applying the theory to the situation in the north, however, does pose a problem because the intervention by the Allies was incomplete. Whereas the expected result of intervention which interrupts the use of violence is interference with the state-building process in cases of ethnic conflict, the facts surrounding the Allied intervention in this case are not a perfect fit with conditions outlined in the theory. In fact, outside forces *did not* entirely prevent the use of force by the Iraqi regime. The events in 1996, during which the Baghdad regime assisted Barzani's KDP in its struggle against Talabani's PUK (which was receiving assistance from Iran), demonstrate that the restriction on the use of Iraqi air power did not prevent the regime from engaging in fighting on the ground in the north.

On the other hand, the use of the Turkish facilities at Incirlik air base to enforce the no-fly zone did interfere with the capacity of the Iraqi regime to use its air superiority in order to deal a decisive blow against Kurdish resistance and autonomy. From this, it can be concluded that the *partial* interruption of violence in this case appears to have been an important reason why the conflict between the Iraqi government and the Kurdish pesh mergas remained unresolved and why, at least until it fragmented into warring factions, a Kurdish autonomous region continued to exist *within* an Iraqi state but *beyond the control* of that state.

The failure to allow the Baghdad regime to consolidate its position in the north while simultaneously preventing the Kurds from doing the same introduces an element into the equation which was not dealt with in the original theory. This concerns the importance of maintaining regional stability as a competing logic to that of state-building. Since it played an important role in the Iraqi situation, it is worthy of further discussion here. At the heart of the matter is the following question: *what happens if the turbulent nature of the violent pursuit of state-building has adverse consequences for the preservation of stability within the wider region?* In other words, is it more important to allow a violent state-building process to proceed or is it more important to intervene so as to preserve regional stability?

Viewed in isolation, the first steps toward the building of a success-ful state within Iraq according to the model developed in this study would have involved the expulsion of the Kurdish population from the north. In addition to humanitarian concerns, however, another problem with this approach is that it would have undermined the ability of Turkey to con-solidate its own control over territory by effectively dumping Iraq's Kurd-ish population onto the Turkish side of the border alongside Turkey's own sizable Kurdish population. Thus, the state-building process left to its own devices would appear to become a zero-sum game, in which the suc-cess of violent state-building in one state oftentimes comes at the price of interfering with the same process in a neighboring state facing the same challenges.

Although this would oftentimes seem to be the case, one exception to this general rule might be cases in which there is an exchange of popula-tions between two states such that ethnic minorities in each state cross over the border into a neighboring state in which they would become part of the ethnic majority. The case which comes most readily to mind would be that of India and Pakistan immediately following independence. Although the transfer of populations did involve considerable bloodshed, it arguably contributed to the homogeneity of each state and thereby solidified the international borders in the east[3] and the west with the notable exception of Kashmir, which continued to have a predominantly Muslim population and a Hindu ruler.

Even the instability associated with Kashmir, however, would seem to support the claim that the failure of ethnic (and/or sectarian) homogeni-zation contributes to political instability and, therefore, interferes with the state-building process. For the moment, this conclusion must remain tenta-tive. Further research would be needed in order to determine whether the sort of population exchanges described here actually produced more stable states in the cases of India and Pakistan.

Returning to the larger point regarding the zero-sum nature of the state-building process, it would appear that in many, if not most cases, the sort of state-building process described in these pages creates problems for the stability of the region as a whole. One such problem is that post-colonial states generally begin from a condition of weakness. Each state, therefore, has an interest in becoming stronger by consolidating its control over the territory within its borders through the forcible removal of ethnic minorities while at the same time attempting to re-define its borders by force. Unfortunately, however, the removal of these groups from one state also means that they likely will end up in a neighboring state. As a result, the state on the receiving end will face the same problem of being unable to consolidate its own control within its borders. From what has been said, it would appear that, leaving aside cases of population transfer of the sort which took place in the 1920s between Greece and Turkey or in the 1940s between India and Pakistan, in which the populations in the region are somehow sorted out such that each ends up residing within a state in which it would be a part of the majority, there would seem to be only four possible outcomes to the violent state-building process outlined in this study.

The first outcome would be the success of some states at the expense of others. In this scenario, those states which are able to homogenize would continue on the path to building effective states. On the other hand, those states which are the recipients of refugees from their neighbors and are unable to consolidate control within their borders through the removal of minority ethnic groups would remain weak or perhaps become failed states. State failure, in turn, offers the prospect that paramilitary organizations will take advantage of the existing power vacuum within the juridical state to establish what amount to de facto states within the state. There is also a greater likelihood of outside intervention by other states designed to establish what amount to spheres of influence on the theory that politics, as with nature, abhors a vacuum.

To a certain extent, this was the situation in Lebanon in the aftermath of the civil war in Jordan in September 1970. That war resulted in the movement of the Palestine Liberation Organization (PLO) from Jordan to Lebanon. The weakness of Lebanon both before and during its long civil war provided a situation in which rival militias operated *de facto* states within the juridical state of Lebanon. In addition, outside powers, particularly Syria and Israel, intervened militarily in Lebanon and occupied sizable portions of that country.

A second possible outcome to the violence associated with state-building is that the movement of populations across borders may become a casus belli between states as each competes to rid itself of unwanted ethnic minorities. This sort of competitive state-building increases the likelihood of acts of aggression across international borders as states attempt to prevent refugees from one state from moving into another especially if, in so doing, they would be joining an ethnic minority on the other side of the border and thereby augmenting its numbers within the new host society. An example of this scenario would be the border between Turkey and Iraq and the efforts of each to deal with their respective Kurdish minorities.

According to this scenario, there is a tension between two competing logics. One of these involves the steps required to create strong states through the violent consolidation of control over territory. The other is the need to preserve regional stability by preventing acts of aggression by one state against another. In order to promote regional stability, it may be necessary to intervene within an internal conflict even though doing so may compromise the recipient state's efforts to build a strong state capable of effective governance.

In this regard, it could be argued that the policy of creating safe havens in northern Iraq was driven not so much by outsiders' humanitarian desire to protect the Kurds from a bloodbath at the hands of the Ba'athist regime as by the logic of a strategic situation in which the goal was to keep the Kurds contained within Iraq. According to this argument, the political instability generated by the flow of Kurdish refugees from Iraq into Turkey, which has its own Kurdish issue, has resulted in repeated Turkish military operations against the Kurdish population located in the northern part of its neighbor Iraq.

From the perspective of maintaining regional stability and preventing acts of aggression by one state across the border with another state, the obvious solution to the cross-border violence between Turkey and Iraq would be to eliminate the reasons for the flow of refugees by intervening so as to provide protection to the Kurds on the Iraqi side of the border against efforts by the Iraqi regime to forcibly remove them. This would reduce the need for this population to cross over into Turkey. In essence, it was just this sort of calculation which was the logic behind the notion of the safe havens and the no-fly zone above the 36th parallel.

At the same time, however, such intervention leaves the Kurdish population effectively stateless in a situation in which they remain *within* Iraq but are not fully *part of* Iraq. Consequently, the issues which have been responsible for repeated uprisings by the Kurds, including that in March and April of 1991 remain unresolved.

A further complication is the fact that the effectiveness of the safe haven as a gathering point for Kurdish refugees requires that a safe haven against Iraq presumably would also have to be a safe haven against Turkey. Otherwise, the threat of Turkish military action would render the area unsafe and thereby undermine efforts to encourage Kurds to remain. Securing the area against Turkish as well as Iraqi forces, however, opens up the possibility that this area will become a base of operations from which members of the Kurdish separatist movement in Turkey (the PKK) can launch attacks inside Turkey (as in fact did occur) with impunity. In fact, this very situation has resulted in repeated Turkish reprisals inside northern Iraq despite Allied efforts to provide a secure environment there for the Kurds.

The situation described in this scenario comes closest to Ayoob's notion of a Third World security predicament. The problem as he outlines it, and as it is described here, is that internal and external security are linked. The potential for acts of aggression across international boundaries designed to stem the flow of refugees to escalate into full-scale war between states, which may also draw in other states both within the region and beyond, provides a competing rationale in favor of intervention even though such intervention may occur at the expense of considerations involving the building of effective states.

At the same time, however, the problem is that failure to build effective states serves to maintain a status quo within the region characterized by continued instability. Thus, one is faced with a "chicken-and-egg" dilemma in which there is no way to reconcile regional stability with either the success or failure of the state-building process. In this paradoxical situation, intervention attempts to preserve stability at the *regional* level by interfering with a process which can create stability at the *state* level. As a result, stability at the regional level is achieved by preserving *in*stability at the state level even though instability at the state level produces continued instability at the regional level.

Somewhat reminiscent of the logic behind the self-defeating notion of the security dilemma under conditions of international anarchy (in which the pursuit of security yields insecurity necessitating the further futile pursuit of security ad infinitum), the result of the incompatibility between the *demands* of the state-building process and the *requirements* for regional stability is external intervention within a state for an indeterminate period of time. This intervention, however, fails to resolve the underlying issues producing instability within the state. *Instead of precipitating a timely withdrawal of outside forces, however, failure, in turn, leads to continued intervention within the state even though, or perhaps because, that intervention is unsuccessful. The result is that outside forces can neither fix the situation nor withdraw.* Indeed, some would argue that this is the current dilemma facing the coalition forces in Iraq following the overthrow of Saddam Hussein in 2003.

A third possible result of violent state-building is that the region might be carved up in such a way that each ethnic group would achieve statehood. Although brought about through diplomacy rather than violence, to a certain extent, this outcome resembles the plan envisioned by the Treaty of Sèvres in 1920, at least as it concerned the situation of the Kurds. The premise of this scenario is that the proliferation of ethnic states/statelets would result in the creation of homogeneous entities capable of developing effective self-government.

The difficulty with this approach is that it ignores the reasons *why* this did not occur within the territory of the defeated/defunct Ottoman

Empire in the many years since the end of the First World War. While the notion that the creation of homogeneous ethnic states as an early stage in the state-building process is consistent with the theory developed in this study, this scenario fails to factor in the role played by the interests and actions of either regional or extra-regional powers. Thus, for example, while the Iranians supported the Kurds in northern Iraq as a way to advance their own interests with regard to Iraq (both during the time of the Shah and also during the Iran-Iraq war), it is clear that Iran, which also has a fairly sizable Kurdish population, has no interest in seeing the emergence of an independent Kurdistan in northern Iraq because of its potential consequences in terms of demands for autonomy or independence on the part of the Kurdish population within Iran. Indeed, in the one instance in which an autonomous Kurdish entity emerged in Iran, the so-called Mahabad Republic in 1946, it was crushed by Iranian forces by the end of that year.

One problem with allowing the creation of such a state to emerge in Iraq is that it would undermine the principle of uti possidetis and would open the door to irredentist claims against Iranian territory. In this regard, Iran and Turkey have been willing to put aside other differences in order to cooperate in pursuit of their shared interest in thwarting the political goals of the Kurds in Iraq. The alternative would be one of regional instability in which all borders would be open to redefinition and, therefore, every state in the region would be less secure.

At the heart of this discussion lies a terrible dilemma for the post-colonial world. On the one hand, the world consists of thousands of ethnic groups. The creation of demographically homogeneous states corresponding to the ideal of the nation-state (understood in ethnic as opposed to civic terms) arguably would result in a potentially unwieldy number of ministates—many of which would not be viable either economically or in terms of their security concerns. On the other hand, the sort of disregard for demographic homogeneity which characterizes the boundaries of many post-colonial states has undermined the governing capacity of elites to exercise control over distinct segments of their own populations because the members of these non-ruling groups tend to view the regime not as fellow members of a single national community but rather as an alien presence. This perception hearkens back to the way that members of various anti-colonial movements once viewed the presence of European administrators, forces, and colonial settlers.

This difficult situation raises the fundamental political question of determining what should be the organizing principle for newer states in the modern world. During the era of decolonization after World War II, members of the international community linked the principle of national self-determination to territory rather than population. Consequently, colonial territories had the right to pursue independence, but demographic groups within former colonies did not have this right. This double standard represents the triumph of practicality over principle. Critics of extending this principle to ethnic groups can point with some justification to the *potential* practical difficulties associated with an infinite regression to smaller and smaller entities in the name of establishing homogeneous units.

There are two basic problems with this argument, however. First, whatever the merits on the grounds of practicality, there is no distinction *as a matter of principle* which explains why the right of self-determination should be applied to territorial units rather than peoples. Second, the notion of an endless regression to smaller and smaller units is a slippery slope argument. To be sure, any argument pushed to its most extreme conclusion can be made to appear logically absurd. Just as there is the *potential* that embracing the idea of homogeneity as an organizing principle would result in smaller and smaller entities, logically, there is an equally great *potential* that rejecting the idea of homogeneity would result in larger and larger entities until eventually the states system itself would be replaced by a world government. If homogeneity is not a legitimate rationale for separate states in the case of the republics of the former Yugoslavia, or in the case of Iraq, how can it be a rationale for separate states for the French and the Germans? Theoretically, if the principle of homogeneity were to be rejected, all Europeans could be part of a single state. If so, what would be the justification for not including the states of North America? Again, if homogeneity is not a legitimate basis upon which to build separate states, why stop at the inclusion of North America? Why not include Latin America, Africa, and Asia? Thus, the same sort of slippery slope argument can be used to posit ever more inclusive units if homogeneity is discarded as an organizing principle.

The beauty of the model developed in this study is that while ethnic homogeneity is presented as the basis upon which effective governance can be established in a world in which ethnic identification is on the rise, governance is also tied to an indigenous (violent) process of state formation as opposed to one in which state boundaries are arbitrarily determined from the outside in such a manner as to lump together groups of people who lack any basis for a sense of shared community and, therefore, any basis for accepting the authority of so-called state leaders.

This model also suggests that the idea of ethnically homogeneous states in place of heterogeneous post-colonial states is part of a *process* of indigenous state-building rather than a terminal point. Consequently, nothing in this theory denies the possibility that at some future point when authority has been consolidated within ethnic (mini)states that such states might opt for membership in a wider political association somewhat akin to membership by European states in the EU. Such membership would be *voluntary*, however, rather than imposed and would reflect the economic and security needs of the members in much the same way that the original thirteen colonies/states joined together to form the United States in 1789. Thus, while not a prediction that such will happen in this case, the theory leaves room for the possibility that larger units may emerge eventually as part of a continuation of the ongoing state-building process involving the consolidation in the number of states in the world. This, however, would be radically different from an imposed solution to the problem of the absence of community within post-colonial states through the insistence upon the preservation of the territorial integrity of post-colonial states. In the case of voluntary association, presumably the governing elites would have the capacity to control this wider territory because the constituent parts (former ethnic states) would have acceded to this arrangement.

The fourth and final possible scenario would be the mirror image of the first alternative. Instead of some states successfully removing ethnic minorities while others are forced to accept these individuals, thereby producing winners and losers in the state-building enterprise, this option would be for all states in the region to establish strong states. Instead of merely removing minorities, they would be eliminated altogether by means of genocide. In the absence of some form of external intervention and the unwillingness of any state to accept the ethnic group in question, the only way to homogenize all states in the region would be through a campaign of mass murder. This is state-building at its most brutal.

Leaving aside for a moment the obvious moral considerations about mass murder and whether a state constructed in such a fashion deserves to exist (the fact that they are put aside in no way is intended to suggest that they are unimportant) because a good case has been made elsewhere that few, if any, states could satisfy the requirement for humane state-building, there are serious practical constraints upon this scenario. One constraint not addressed by this study is the role that public opinion in other parts of the world—the so-called "CNN effect"–plays in determining whether the outside world will allow a program of genocide to unfold without intervention.

The evidence to date would seem to be mixed. In Croatia and Bosnia, the outside world responded—albeit belatedly and perhaps ineffectually. In Iraq, television images of the Kurdish humanitarian crisis on the Turkish border do appear to have contributed to the eventual creation of safe havens whereas the lack of coverage of the crisis occurring on the Iranian border or in the case of the Shi'a in the south meant that there was no similar public pressure to intervene in these cases. On the other hand, in Rwanda, the response was one of seeming indifference combined with the fear of entanglement in a quagmire. Such fears were particularly acute in the aftermath of the attacks on American and Pakistani forces in the case of the humanitarian operation in Somalia in the early 1990s. One possible conclusion from this mixed record is that television coverage drives policy and, therefore, the demand for intervention by public and elite opinion alike largely depends upon which humanitarian crises receive media attention.

Perhaps even more important as a constraint is the possibility that a program of genocide could also pose a threat to regional stability. If, for example, the group in question is a minority in one state but a majority in another state, efforts to harm the members of that community by the host society would likely produce intervention by that ethnic group's compatriots in a neighboring state.

Although the claims were largely manufactured to serve other political ends, arguably the classic example of this was the situation which existed when Hitler demanded that portions of Czechoslovakia containing the so-called "Sudeten" Germans be annexed to Germany because of alleged abuses against these ethnic Germans by the government of Czechoslovakia. The potential that such demands, whether rooted in actual circumstances or utilized as a way to promote other interests, could result in interstate conflict again serves to pit the issue of regional stability against the needs of the state-building process.

One final issue, which was not part of the original theory, but which is worthy of further research, is the question of whether ethnicity is a useful social category for research into the question of state-building. Whereas the theory addressed in this study treated ethnic groups as monolithic social groups competing against other monolithic groups for control of the state, the situation in Iraq suggests that ethnic and sectarian groups were not nearly so monolithic. In the south of Iraq, the Shi'a were divided between those who were more secular in their orientation and those who were more religiously motivated. Sandra Mackey goes further to point out that the Shi'a also are divided by tribal differences. Likewise, the Kurds were clearly divided by faction as well as possessing differing cultural characteristics amongst themselves. If anything, the rivalry between Barzani and Talabani suggests that rival state makers are just as likely to emerge *within* an ethnic group (Kurds) as *between* ethnic (sectarian?) groups (Kurds versus Arabs or Sunnis versus Shi'is).

To sum up, the picture which emerges from this case study is one which is considerably more complex than the rather parsimonious theory of the relationship between ethnic conflict, state-building, and external intervention. Although the theory suggests that intervention interferes with the state-building process, this study has demonstrated a somewhat different result. Intervention has the potential to both create states *and* to interfere with their development along the path to effective governance. The important point is the *type* of intervention one is talking about. Imperialist intervention in the early part of the twentieth century resulted in the creation of what have been referred to here as post-colonial states. For the most part, these have been weak states owing to the arbitrary nature of colonial boundaries. Indeed, the notion of the modern territorial state (as distinct from empires or city-states) is itself a Western creation, which was exported to much of the colonial world. Yet, it is important to note that, while colonial intervention may be responsible for the existence of post-colonial states, more recent examples of external intervention, especially in the post-Cold War era, have had the perhaps unintended effect of interfering with the state-building process by preserving artificial state boundaries and preventing the forcible consolidation of state authority within those boundaries.

Although, as this chapter has made clear, there is certainly room for fine-tuning the theory in response to specific circumstances, it would seem that the negative consequences for the state-building process in Iraq of Operation Provide Comfort have been consistent with the general outlines of the theory regarding interference with ethnic conflict. As will be seen momentarily, these consequences have also had implications for the issue of democratization currently facing that country.

Before turning to this issue, it should be stated that while the broad outlines of the theory may be supported by the evidence in northern Iraq, it is too soon to draw any firm conclusions. Further study is required in order to refine the internal and external *conditions* under which intervention might either facilitate or interfere with the state-building process. Also in need of further study is the possibility that different *types* of UN intervention may have differing effects upon the state-building process. Although there was some brief discussion of this in *Chapter Eight*, a more in-depth examination of these and other cases of intervention in ethnic conflicts in the post-Cold War era would be useful as a way to test and perhaps refine the theory presented here.

At the present time, however, it would seem that the combination of no-fly zones, safe havens, and humanitarian assistance associated with Operation Provide Comfort in northern Iraq and similar operations in the south later on have contributed to the instability in Iraq today. They are responsible for both *preserving* the territorial integrity of this post-colonial state (whose population is deeply divided along ethnic and sectarian lines) and *preventing* efforts by the regime to create a shared sense of Iraqi national identity (nation-building) by homogenizing the society through the forcible removal of ethnic Kurds and the suppression of members of the Shi'a sect. Instead, as a direct result of this outside interference, these disparate elements of Iraqi society are forced into a very uneasy co-existence within the same country. As the experience of Bosnia teaches, this insistence upon the territorial integrity of the state without a corresponding political community is a recipe for civil war and savage acts of brutality.

In this regard, the humanitarian impulses behind the events of the early 1990s have consequences for the post-Saddam era. In the aftermath of the toppling of Saddam Hussein in 2003, a good deal of emphasis has been placed upon the attempt to create a new and democratic government. The implications for democratization in the specific case of Iraq (and more broadly for any post-colonial state attempting to democratize under conditions in which an ethnic conflict has been interrupted through outside intervention) of the theory developed here are that such efforts are likely to fail. Consistent with John Stuart Mill's point regarding the need to resolve the national question *before* democratic elections can take place, the unwillingness on the part of outsiders to allow the regime to create a sense of shared Iraqi national identity within the borders of the state as part of its own violent efforts at consolidation of authority has inadvertently interfered with the creation of the foundations for a stable, democratic political system.

As a result, this premature attempt at democratization, in which elections occurred within a society still deeply polarized between rival ethnic and sectarian groups, produced an electoral outcome whose legitimacy continues to be a matter of controversy. The Shi'a Arabs, which constitute a numerical majority of the population with a long history of grievances against the dominant Sunni Arab community, embraced the prospect of democratic elections as a way to obtain political power. Conversely, many within the Sunni Arab population have rejected the electoral path as well as the results of these elections. This is not difficult to understand. For them, acceptance of the electoral results would mean acquiescence in the loss of the privileged position that they have enjoyed since the beginning of the Iraqi state in 1932 (and even before that under Ottoman rule).

The one surprise appears to have been the Kurds. On the face of it, one would have expected that the Kurds would have rejected any participation in Iraqi elections since participation might be seen as tantamount to a surrender of their dream of independence. It could be argued that electoral participation within the Iraqi political system represents a tacit acknowledgment that Kurdish northern Iraq is an integral part of Iraq. If so, then by extension, they would be members of the Iraqi national community and, as such, not entitled to their own state. Yet, the fact remains that the Kurds did participate in the electoral process. Indeed, the president of Iraq at the time of this writing, Jalal Talabani, is himself a Kurd.

The most plausible explanation for Kurdish participation would seem to be one of pragmatism. It appears that a calculation was made that the time was not right to push for independence. Since the US-led coalition is committed to the territorial integrity of Iraq, the Kurds had more to gain by operating within the Iraqi political system than they could hope to achieve by following the example of the Sunni Arabs and boycotting the elections. In particular, they could work to preserve the autonomy which they have had since 1991. Perhaps at some future point in time, the Kurds may still pursue their dream of independence.

Despite the willingness of the Kurds to participate, there is no denying the escalation of violence which occurred in the run up to the 2005 elections and which has continued ever since. As stated previously, this is symptomatic of the problem described by John Stuart Mill and is perfectly consistent with what can, and should, be expected in a situation in which democratization precedes the development of a national community. It is for this reason that the oft-stated analogies between democratization in Iraq and democratization in postwar West Germany and Japan are deeply flawed. These analogies fail to take into account the fact that both Germany and Japan had already established a sense of national community *prior to democratization*. Due to this crucial difference, it is no surprise that the Iraqi elections did nothing to stem the violence. In fact, a good argument could be made that they actually contributed to both its escalation and continuation into the indefinite future.

Unlike the Kurds, the Sunni Arabs did not perceive any pragmatic advantage to participation in the electoral process. As the previously dominant community, their lack of numerical strength could only result in defeat and minority status. Under the circumstances, they saw no reason to legitimize by their participation elections, which, from their point of view, were imposed from the outside.[4] As a result, the Sunni Arabs have rejected the electoral process and waged an ongoing campaign of violence. This violence is directed against both the outside forces present in Iraq as well as the Shi'a-dominated government. Since it was installed following the ouster of Saddam Hussein and as a direct consequence of President George W. Bush's call for democratic elections in Iraq, this government has been seen as nothing more than a puppet regime, which collaborates with, and depends upon for its survival, the occupation forces.

Of course, the precise nature of the violence in Iraq will depend largely upon the question of whether outside forces remain in the country. If they do, the likelihood is that the Sunni Arabs will continue their insurgency against both these foreign troops and aid workers and probably against the Shi'a-dominated regime as well. Their goal would be to remove the outside presence and to topple the government as a prelude to restoring Sunni Arab rule. If, on the other hand, foreign troops were to withdraw from Iraq (a highly unlikely scenario in the short-term at least), the probability is that the current violence would continue, and perhaps even escalate. The Sunni Arabs would attempt to either bring down the government or, alternatively, to secede and create a separate Sunni Arab enclave in the so-called Sunni Triangle in the middle of the country. For their part, the Shi'a Arabs would most likely fight to preserve an Iraqi regime which reflects their numerical superiority. Likewise, in the absence of outside forces acting as guarantors of their status within Iraq (and faced with the prospect of a possible return to power of the Sunni Arab Ba'athists), the Kurds almost certainly would enter into the fray. The likelihood is that they would resort to violence as a way to push for independence—with all of the implications that would have both for the territorial integrity of Iraq and for the stability of the wider region.

The likely scenarios presented here for the future of Iraq are all unpleasant. They are, however, consistent with the theory developed in this study. The key point is that democratic elections in deeply divided societies are not capable of dealing with fundamental questions about the boundaries of the state or the identity of the society. In order for them to be accepted by the various participants, there must first be a degree of consensus within the society. This consensus requires the prior existence of a political community. For this reason, democratization must be built upon the foundation of a state-building process, which first establishes territorial boundaries viewed as legitimate by the population of the country. While boundaries can be determined through military conquest alone, the establishment of boundaries perceived by the population to be *legitimate* depends not only upon the conquest of territory but also upon the creation of a political community or nation within that territory. In post-colonial states, such as Iraq, which lack a shared sense of national identity, the most likely way that such an identity can come into being is through *violent* conflict between the constituent ethnic and sectarian groups within the state and the removal of all but the militarily successful community.

Outside interference with this violent conflict *of the sort which occurred in Iraq following the 1991 uprisings* prevents this convergence of population and territory from taking place. Of course, this is not to suggest that intervention in an ethnic conflict cannot under any circumstances contribute to the creation of a political community. As stated, there is a potential role for intervention but only if it is used in the service of facilitating military victory by the party most able to win on the battlefield. That party can then consolidate its authority within the state through ethnic/sectarian homogenization. The path of intervention adopted in 1991 in Iraq and in other post-Cold War ethnic conflicts since that time, however, has been predictably counterproductive precisely because the conflict between rival ethnic state makers is merely frozen in place due to the insistence upon both the preservation of the territorial integrity of the post-colonial state and the delivery of humanitarian assistance. The external preservation of territorial integrity offers no opportunity for groups to exit from the state while the delivery of humanitarian assistance interrupts the process of so-called "ethnic cleansing." Taken together, intervention designed to achieve both of these goals also ends up inadvertently preserving the ethnic/sectarian polarization of the population. Since the state has not been able to move beyond these wrenching political conflicts over boundaries and the nature of the political community, democratization of the sort envisioned by President George W. Bush has little hope for success and a much greater likelihood of serving as a catalyst for further violence.

Thus, the evidence to date has not falsified the theory. It would appear that well-intentioned, but short-sighted, attempts to interfere with ethnic conflicts in post-colonial states in the absence of a theory which can relate this type of conflict to the state-building process tends to result in tragic unintended consequences. This type of intervention may very well save lives in the short-term. It would seem, however, that it ends up wreaking havoc upon societies and their political systems for generations to come while quite possibly costing perhaps even more lives in the long-run.

Notes

NOTES TO THE PREFACE

1. According to international law, the borders of post-colonial states should conform to the boundaries established by their colonial masters prior to decolonization.
2. Since the more commonly used term "nation-state" is subject to more than one meaning (some of which include an ethnic component while others do not), the substitution of the term "ethnic state" offers greater precision and, therefore, clarity.

NOTES TO CHAPTER ONE

1. J. Milton Yinger, "Ethnicity," *Annual Review of Sociology*, Volume 11 (1985), 152.
2. Milica Zarkovic Bookman. *The Demographic Struggle for Power: The Political Economy of Demographic Engineering in the Modern World.* (Portland, Oregon: Frank Cass &Co. Ltd., 1997), 6.
3. For a listing of some of the more well-known works in each category, see Milton J. Esman, *Ethnic Politics*, (Ithaca: Cornell University Press, 1994), 10n.8. See also Bookman, 15n.13.
4. Ibid., 10.
5. Ibid., 10–11.
6. Ibid., 11.
7. Ibid., 11.
8. Yinger, 163.
9. Chaim Kaufmannn. "Possible and Impossible Solutions to Ethnic Civil Wars," in Robert J. Art and Robert Jervis (ed.) *International Politics: Enduring Concepts and Contemporary Issues.* Fifth Edition. (New York: Addison-Wesley Educational Publishers, Inc., 2000), 446–447.
10. Ibid., 440.
11. Ibid., 441.
12. Bookman, 1.

13. Kaufmann, 441.
14. Interestingly, a distinction is made between so-called "Israeli Arabs" and "Palestinian Arabs" based not upon any cultural or other difference between them but rather upon residence on one side or the other of the so-called "Green Line" (a line which divides Israel proper from the occupied territories of the West Bank and Gaza).
15. Adam Roberts. "The United Nations and International Security," in Robert J. Art and Robert Jervis (ed.) *International Politics: Enduring Concepts and Contemporary Issues.* Fifth Edition. (New York: Addison-Wesley Educational Publishers, Inc., 2000), 143.
16. Joshua Bernard Forrest, "State Inversion and Nonstate Politics," in Leonardo A. Villalon and Phillip A. Huxtable (ed.) *The African State at a Critical Juncture: Between Disintegration and Reconfiguration.* (Boulder, Colorado: Lynne Rienner Publishers, Inc., 1998), 51–52.
17. Esman, 18–19.
18. Bookman, 1.
19. See Mohammed Ayoob. *The Third World Security Predicament: State Making, Regional Conflict, and the International System.* (Boulder, Colorado: Lynne Rienner Publishers, Inc.), 36–37.
20. Ibid., 37.
21. Karen Barkey; Sunita Parikh. "Comparative Perspectives on the State," *Annual Review of Sociology*, vol. 17. (1991), 544.
22. Ayoob, 35.
23. Forrest, 49.
24. Walker Connor. "Nation-Building or Nation-Destroying?" *World Politics*, 24 no.3, (April 1972), 328.
25. Ibid., 329.
26. Two of the leading exponents of this idea that modernization undermines parochial loyalties and replaces them with a wider sense of nationality are Karl Deutsch and Eugen Weber. For a discussion of their respective views on this subject, see Karl Deutsch, *Nationalism and Social Communication: An Inquiry into the Foundations of Nationality*, (Cambridge, Mass.: MIT Press, 1953) and Eugen Weber, *Peasants into Frenchmen: The Modernization of Rural France 1870–1914*, (Stanford: Stanford University Press, 1976).

    For another interpretation of Deutsch's work which suggests a more ambivalent position on this issue, see Connor, "Nation-Building," 321–327.

    In recent years, the view that modernization undermines traditional loyalties has come under increasing criticism from those who suggest that instead of undermining ethnicity, modernization may actually intensify it. For a discussion of this viewpoint, see Esman, *Ethnic Politics*, 17–18 as well as the works cited by him on page 18n.19.
27. Anthony D. Smith *The Ethnic Revival.* (New York: Cambridge University Press, 1981), 2.
28. Ibid., 26–27.
29. Ibid., 3.

30. Boutros Boutros-Ghali, "Report of the Secretary-General Pursuant to the Statement Adopted by the Summit Meeting of the Security Council on 31 January 1992 A/47/277-S/24111, June 1992," in Boutros Boutros-Ghali, *An Agenda for Peace 1995*, Second Edition, (New York: Department of Public Information, 1995), 41–42 paragraph 11.
31. John Lewis Gaddis, "The Cold War, the Long Peace, and the Future," in Michael J. Hogan (ed.) *The End of the Cold War: Its Meaning and Implications.* (New York: Cambridge University Press, 1992), 32.
32. This concept, which initially served as the title of an article in *Atlantic Monthly* in March 1992, was later turned into a book by the same name.
33. Smith, 4.
34. Yinger, 161.
35. Esman, 14.

NOTES TO CHAPTER TWO

1. John A. Hall. *Coercion and Consent: Studies on the Modern State.* (Cambridge, Massachusetts: Polity Press, 1994), xii.
2. I. William Zartman, "Introduction: Posing the Problem of State Collapse," in I. William Zartman (ed.) *Collapsed States: The Disintegration and Restoration of Legitimate Authority.* (Boulder, Colorado: Lynne Rienner Publishers, Inc., 1994), 8.
3. Barkey and Parikh, "Comparative Perspectives," 528.
4. Brian L. Job, "The Insecurity Dilemma: National, Regime, and State Securities in the Third World," in Brian L. Job (ed.) *The Insecurity Dilemma: National Security of Third World States.* (Boulder, Colorado: Lynne Rienner Publishers, Inc., 1992), 20.
5. Mark Kesselman, "Order or Movement?: The Literature of Political Development as Ideology," World Politics, Volume 26, Issue 1 (October, 1973), 143.
6. See Robert H. Jackson and Carl G. Rosberg. "Why Africa's Weak States Persist: The Empirical and the Juridical in Statehood," *World Politics*, Volume 35, Issue 1 (October, 1982), 1–24.
7. Ibid., 4.
8. Ibid., 23.
9. Ayoob, 80–81.
10. On this last point, see Steven R. Ratner, "Drawing a Better Line: UTI Possidetis and the Borders of New States," *American Journal of International Law*, Volume 90, Issue 4 (October, 1996), 602.
11. Bookman, 142.
12. J. Samuel Barkin and Bruce Cronin, "The State and the Nation: Changing Norms and the Rules of Sovereignty in International Relations," *International Organization*, Volume 48, Issue 1 (Winter, 1994), 108.
13. Ibid., 108.
14. Ibid., 126.

15. Thomas G. Weiss, David P. Forsythe, and Roger A. Coate. *The United Nations and Changing World Politics.* (Boulder, Colorado: Westview Press, Inc., 1994), 89–90.

16. Youssef Cohen, Brian R. Brown, and A.F.K. Organski, "The Paradoxical Nature of Statemaking: The Violent Creation of Order," 1981. *American Political Science Review.* vol.75 no.4, 1981, 901–902.

17. Bruce D. Porter. *War and the Rise of the State.* (New York: The Free Press, 1994), 12–13.

18. Ibid., 2.

19. Ibid., 258.

20. For an interesting and provocative discussion of this very point, see Michael Howard, "Managing Conflict—The Role of Intervention: Lessons from the Past," *Managing Conflict in the Post-Cold War World: The Role of Intervention: Report of the Aspen Institute Conference August 2–6, 1995.* (Washington, D.C.: The Aspen Institute, 1996), 35–43.

21. The precedent for the forcible removal of individuals was the case of the evacuation of the Yamit settlement as part of the final stage of the Israeli withdrawal from the Sinai when that territory returned to Egyptian control in 1982.

22. Charles Tilly, "Reflections on the History of European State-Making" in Charles Tilly (ed.) *The Formation of National States in Western Europe.* (Princeton: Princeton University Press, 1975), 42.

23. Porter does not use the term "states" indicating that at this early stage, it probably would be inappropriate to refer to them as states—at least as that term is understood in the modern sense.

24. Porter, 12.

25. Ibid., 12.

26. Cohen, Brown, and Organski, 902.

27. Barry Buzan. *People, States and Fear.* (Boulder, Colorado: Lynne Rienner Publishers, Inc., 1991), p. 99.

28. Tilly, "Reflections," 81.

29. Ibid., 81. For a more detailed discussion of the differences between the two periods, see pages 81–82.

30. Peter H. Merkl, "The Study of European Political Development," *World Politics.* Volume 29, Issue 3, April, 1977, 465.

31. Ibid., 82.

32. Charles Tilly, "Western State-Making and Theories of Political Transformation" in Charles Tilly (ed.) *The Formation of National States in Western Europe.* (Princeton: Princeton University Press, 1975), 601.

33. Stein Rokkan, "Dimensions of State Formation and Nation-Building: A Possible Paradigm for Research on Variations Within Europe" in Charles Tilly (ed.) *The Formation of National States in Western Europe.* (Princeton: Princeton University Press, 1975), 563.

34. See Ibid., 570–572 for a further elaboration of these four phases.

35. Ibid., 572–573.

36. Ibid., 598.

37. Ibid., 598 and 600.

38. Ayoob, 6–7.

39. Ibid., 21.
40. See pages 42–43n. 49 and 50. See also the discussion in Jackson and Rosberg.
41. Ayoob, 30–31.
42. Ibid., 87–88.
43. Ibid., 178.
44. Porter, 2.
45. Ibid., 10.
46. Ibid., 10.
47. Ibid., 17.
48. Ibid., 18.
49. Ibid., 18–19.
50. Barrington Moore. *The Social Origins of Dictatorship and Democracy.* (Boston: Beacon Press, 1966), 429.
51. Ibid., xv. For a more detailed explanation of Moore's concept of a bourgeois revolution, see Ibid., 429–430.
52. See Ibid., xv-xvi.
53. Ibid., 504–506.

NOTES TO CHAPTER THREE

1. Peter R. Baehr and Leon Gordenker. *The United Nations in the 1990s.* Second Edition. (New York: St. Martin's Press, 1994), 98.
2. Joseph R. Rudolph, "Intervention in Communal Conflicts," *Orbis.* v. 39 (Spring 1995), 9.
3. For a discussion of this concept, see Nathan A. Pelcovits. *The Long Armistice: UN Peacekeeping and the Arab-Israeli Conflict,1948–1960.* (Boulder, Colorado: Westview Press, Inc., 1993).
4. William J. Durch (ed.). *The Evolution of UN Peacekeeping.* (New York: St. Martin's Press, 1993), 12.
5. Sally Morphet, "UN Peacekeeping and Election Monitoring" in Adam Roberts and Benedict Kingsbury (ed.). *United Nations, Divided World.* Second Edition. (New York: Oxford University Press, 1993), 228.
6. Paul F. Diehl. *International Peacekeeping.* (Baltimore: Johns Hopkins, 1993), 40.
7. William J. Durch, "Getting Involved: The Political-Military Context," in William J. Durch (ed.) *The Evolution of UN Peacekeeping.* (New York: St. Martin's Press, 1993), 36.
8. John Mackinlay. *The Peacekeepers: An Assessment of Peacekeeping Operations at the Arab-Israeli Interface.* (Winchester, Massachusetts: Unwin Hyman, Inc., 1989), p. 214.
9. Weiss, Forsythe, and Coate, 87–88.
10. Ibid., 90.
11. Max Boot, "Paving the Road to Hell: the Failure of U.N. Peacekeeping," *Foreign Affairs* v.79 no.2 (March/April 2000), 3.
12. Thomas M. Franck and Nigel S. Rodley, "After Bangladesh: The Law of Humanitarian Intervention by Military Force," *American Journal of International Law.* Volume 67, Issue 2 (April, 1973), 278–279.

13. Ibid., 284.
14. Jerome Slater and Terry Nardin, "Nonintervention and Human Rights," *The Journal of Politics*. Volume 48, Issue 1 (February, 1986), 86.
15. Ibid., 92.
16. Francis M. Deng, Sadikiel Kimaro, Terrence Lyons, Donald Rothchild, and I. William Zartman. *Sovereignty as Responsibility: Conflict Management in Africa*. (Washington, D.C.: The Brookings Institution, 1996), xviii.
17. Ibid., 223.

NOTES TO CHAPTER FOUR

1. See John H. Herz. *Political Realism and Political Idealism: A Study in Theories and Realities*. (Chicago: The University of Chicago Press, 1951), 17.
2. See Chapter One *fn*. 28.
3. Stanley Hoffmann. *World Disorders: Troubled Peace in the Post-Cold War Era*. (Lanham, Maryland: Rowman & Littlefield Publishers, Inc., 1998), 35.
4. Richard Adamiak, "The 'Withering Away' of the State: A Reconsideration," in *The Journal of Politics*, Volume 32, Issue 1 (February, 1970), 5.
5. See John H. Herz, "Rise and Demise of the Territorial State" and "The Territorial State Revisited—Reflections on the Future of the Nation-State" both in John Herz. *The Nation-State and the Crisis of World Politics*. (New York: David McKay Company, Inc., 1976) for a thorough discussion of his understanding of the origins of the territorial state and his uncertainty about its future prospects. The former article appears to suggest a greater degree of ambivalence on the subject of the future of the state while the latter article expresses a greater degree of confidence in the continued survival of the territorial state.
6. Paul Hirst, "Politics: Territorial or Non-Territorial?" http://www.theglobalsite.ac.uk/press/104hirst.htm
7. Gene M. Lyons and Michael Mastanduno (ed.) *Beyond Westphalia? State Sovereignty and International Intervention*. (Baltimore: Johns Hopkins University Press, 1995), 14.
8. James N. Rosenau, "Sovereignty in a Turbulent World," in Gene M. Lyons and Michael Mastanduno (ed.) *Beyond Westphalia? State Sovereignty and International Intervention*. (Baltimore: Johns Hopkins University Press, 1995), 193.
9. Thomas G. Weiss and Jarat Chopra, "Sovereignty Under Siege: From Intervention to Humanitarian Space," in Gene M. Lyons and Michael Mastanduno (ed.) *Beyond Westphalia? State Sovereignty and International Intervention*. (Baltimore: Johns Hopkins University Press, 1995), 88.
10. Ibid., 88.
11. Howard H. Lentner, "Developmental States and Global Pressures: Accumulation, Production, Distribution," 9. http://www.bus.uts.edu.au/apros2000/Papers/Lentner.pdf
12. Kenneth N. Waltz. *Theory of International Politics*. (Reading, Massachusetts: Addison-Wesley Publishing Company, Inc., 1979), 95–96.

13. See Boutros Boutros-Ghali, "An Agenda for Peace, Preventive Diplomacy, Peacemaking Peace-keeping," Paragraph 17. Report of the Secretary-General pursuant to the statement adopted by the Summit Meeting of the Security Council on 31 January 1992, A/47/277-S/24111, 17 June 1992. http://www.un.org/Docs/SG/agpeace.html
14. Boutros-Ghali, "An Agenda for Peace," Paragraph 10.
15. For a similar argument, see Gabriel Ben-Dor. *State and Conflict in the Middle East: Emergence of the Postcolonial State*. (New York: Praeger Publishers, 1983), 10–11.
16. Susan L. Woodward, "Failed States: Warlordism and 'Tribal' Warfare," 1998, 1. http://www.nwc.navy.mil/press/Review/1999/spring/art2-sp9.htm
17. Asbjorn Eide, "Minorities in a Decentralized Environment," Prepared for UNDP international conference on human rights entitled "Human Rights for Human Development," Yalta, Ukraine: September 2–4, 1998, 5. http://www.riga.lv/minelres/publicat/Eide_Yalta98.htm
18. Ibid., 5.

NOTES TO CHAPTER FIVE

1. See Lothar Brock, "State Failure and Global Change: From Violent Modernization to War as a Way of Life?" Paper presented at the Failed States Conference at Purdue University, April 7–11, 1999. http://www.ippu.purdue.edu/info/gsp/FSIS_CONF2/Brock.html; for a similar argument, see Michael Stohl and George Lopez, "Westphalia, the End of the Cold War and the New World Order: Old Roots to a "NEW" Problem," 3. Paper presented at a Conference entitled "Failed States and International Security: Causes, Prospects, and Consequences." Purdue University, February 25–27,1998.
2. For a similar discussion, see Pauletta Otis, "Ethnic Conflict: What Kind of War is This?" Autumn, 1999. http://www.nwc.navy.mil/press/Review/1999/autumn/art1-a99.htm
3. For a good definition of state strength, see Ann C. Mason, "Colombian State Failure: The Global Context of Eroding Domestic Authority," 13. Paper presented at the Conference on Failed States, Florence, Italy, April 10–14, 2001. http://www.ippu.purdue.edu/info/gsp/FSIS_CONF4/Papers/Mason.doc
4. For a discussion of some of these traditional criteria of legitimacy, see Ibid., 5.
5. James N. Rosenau, "Human Rights in a Turbulent and Globalized World." http://hypatia.ss.uci.edu/brysk/Rosenau.html
6. Mason, 10.
7. Ibid., 10–11.
8. David Carment and Patrick James, "Escalation of Ethnic Conflict: A Survey and Assessment." http://www.carleton.ca/~dcarment/papers/escalati.html
9. For a discussion of these concepts as part a wider theory of modernization, see Emile Durkheim. *The Division of Labor in Society*. (New York: Free Press, 1984).

10. For a good discussion of this point about the importance of sufficient time to build strong states, see Mohammed Ayoob. *The Third World Security Predicament: State Making, Regional Conflict, and the International System*. For a response to Ayoob, see Georg Sorensen, "War and State Making—Why Doesn't it Work in the Third World?" 4–5. Paper delivered at the Failed States Conference, Florence, April 10–14, 2001. http://www.ippu.purdue.edu/info/gsp/FSIS_CONF4/Papers/Sorensen.doc

11. Christopher Clapham, "War and State Formation in Ethiopia and Eritrea," 2. Paper presented at the Failed States Conference, Florence, 10–14 April 2001. http://www.ippu.purdue.edu/info/gsp/FSIS_CONF4/Papers/Clapham_Ethiopia.doc

12. For a detailed discussion of this sequence of events, see Gregory H. Fox, "Strengthening the State." http://ijgls.indiana.edu/archive/07/01/fox.shtml

13. Robert H. Jackson, "Surrogate Sovereignty? Great Power Responsibility and 'Failed States'," 16–17. Working Paper No. 25, November, 1998. http://www.ippu.purdue.edu/info/gsp/FSIS_CONF2/Jackson.html

14. Clapham, 1.

15. See Ayoob, *The Third World Security Predicament*; see also Fox, "Strengthening the State"; and Youssef Cohen, B.R. Brown, and A.F.K. Organski, "The Paradoxical Nature of Statemaking: The Violent Creation of Order," *American Political Science Review*. vol.75 no.4, 1981.

16. See Tilly, "Reflections on the History of European State-Making" in Charles Tilly (ed.) *The Formation of National States in Western Europe*; Sorensen, "War and State Making"; and Clapham, "War and State Formation in Ethiopia and Eritrea."

    It is also worth mentioning that while doubting the ability of post-colonial states to develop effective statehood within the constraints imposed by the contemporary international system, Ayoob also has doubts about the effectiveness of the Western European model for Third World states. He characterizes this dilemma as the security predicament for the Third World.

17. For a brief summary of Tilly's argument, see Georg Sorensen "War and State Making," 3.

18. For a good summary of the literature on this point, see Clapham, 1.

19. See, for example, Harold K. Jacobson. *Networks of Interdependence: International Organizations and the Global Political System*. First edition (New York: Knopf, 1979); see also "Concepts of International Politics in Global Perspective," 3. http://www.etext.net/free/Concepts/Intro.htm

20. For a good discussion of some of these phenomena, see Rosenau, "Human Rights in a Turbulent and Globalized World"; for further clarification of the phenomenon of globalization and its effect upon the state, see Martin Van Creveld, "The Fate of the State," from *Parameters*, Spring 1996, 4–18 especially Part III. http://carlisle-www.army.mil/usawc/Parameters/96spring/creveld.htm

21. Hans-Henrik Holm, "The Responsibility That Will Not Go Away: Weak States in the International System," 11. Paper presented at a Conference entitled "Failed States and International Security: Causes, Prospects, and

Consequences." Purdue University, February 25–27, 1998. http://www. ippu.purdue.edu/info/gsp/FSIS_CONF/hholms_paper.html
22. See Mikhail Sergeevich Gorbachev. *Perestroika: New Thinking for Our Country and the World*. First Edition. (New York: Harper & Row Publishers, Inc., 1987).

NOTES TO CHAPTER SIX

1. For a discussion of these issues, see Samuel H. Beer. *Britain Against Itself: The Political Contradictions of Collectivism*. First Edition. (New York: Norton, 1982).
2. The term "collectivism" as used by Beer in this case is not intended to have any of the Marxist connotations sometimes associated with the term.
3. For a discussion of the role of structure in political systems, see Kenneth Waltz. *Theory of International Politics*. (Reading, Massachusetts: Addison-Wesley Publishing Company, Inc., 1979).
4. See Ernest J. Wilson III, "Globalization, Information Technology and Conflict in the Second and Third Worlds: A Critical Review of the Literature," 13. http://www.bsos.umd.edu/cidcm/papers/ewilson/itrevrbf.pdf; for a more general discussion of the erosion of state capacities by globalization following the end of the Cold War, see Holm, 10.
5. For a discussion of the relationship between the Cold War and the juridical norms of the international community regarding territorial integrity, see Sorensen, "War and State Making," 10.
6. Mohammad J. Kuna. "Violence and State Formation in Postcolonial Societies: The Case of Northern Nigeria, 1900–1966," *United Nations University/Institute of Advanced Studies Working Paper No. 67*. Tokyo, Japan, (July 7, 1999), 1. http://www.ias.unu.edu/publications/iaswp.cfm
7. See Wilson, "Globalization, Information Technology and Conflict in the Second and Third Worlds," 33.
8. For an excellent discussion of the relationship between the development of the modern sovereign state and the control of extraterritorial violence, see Janice E. Thomson. *Mercenaries, Pirates, and Sovereigns: State-Building and Extraterritorial Violence in the Early Modern Europe*. (Princeton: Princeton University Press, 1994).
9. For a discussion of the impact of globalization and liberalization upon the capacities of weak and poor states, see Christopher Clapham, "Sierra Leone: The Global-Local Politics of State Collapse and Attempted Reconstruction," 2. Paper presented at the Failed States Conference, Florence, 10–14 April 2001. http://www.ippu.purdue.edu/gsp/FSIS_CONF4/Papers/Clapham_Sierra_Leone.doc.
10. For a discussion of the impact of economic liberalization and specifically structural adjustment programs upon the capacities of African states, see Stephen Ellis, "Democracy in Sub-Saharan Africa: Where did it Come from? Can it be Supported?" (ECDM Working Paper 6). (Maastricht: ECDM September 1995) http://www.oneworld.org/ecdpm/pubs/wp6_

gb.htm; see also John Stremlau and Francisco Sagasti, "Preventing Deadly
Conflict: Does the World Bank Have a Role?" Report prepared for the
Carnegie Commission on Preventing Deadly Conflict. http://www.ccpdc.
org/pubs/world/world.htm; and Michael Parenti. *Democracy for the Few.*
Seventh Edition. (New York: Bedford/St. Martin's, 2002), 87.

11. See Stohl and Lopez, 1.

12. Ravi L. Kapil, "On the Conflict Potential of Inherited Boundaries in
Africa," *World Politics*, Volume 18, Issue 4 (July, 1966), 659.

13. Another similarity between Yugoslavia and the Soviet Union was the
attempt to utilize federal boundaries as a way to dissect ethnic communities in an effort to dilute their influence. For a discussion of the problems
such *internal* boundaries create when they become *international* boundaries, see Steven R. Ratner, "Drawing a Better Line: UTI Possidetis and
the Borders of New States," *American Journal of International Law*, Volume 90, Issue 4 October, 1996.

14. See Jennifer Jackson Preece, "Ethnic Cleansing as an Instrument of
Nation-State Creation: Ethnic Cleansing and the Normative Transforma-
tion of International Society," 1. http://www.ippu.purdue.edu/info/gsp/
FSIS_CONF3/papers/JacksonPreece.html; for a similar argument, see
Milica Zarkovic Bookman. *The Demographic Struggle for Power: The
Political Economy of Demographic Engineering in the Modern World.*
(Portland, Oregon: Frank Cass &Co. Ltd., 1997).

15. Jackson Preece, 3–4.

16. Ibid., 2–3.

17. Susan L. Woodward. *Balkan Tragedy: Chaos and Dissolution After the
Cold War.* (Washington, D.C.: The Brookings Institution, 1995), 242.

18. Ibid., 242.

19. Ibid., 242.

20. Jackson Preece, 2.

21. Susan L. Woodward, "Failed States: Warlordism and 'Tribal' Warfare," 3,
1998. http://www.nwc.navy.mil/press/Review/1999/spring/art2-sp9.htm.
For a similar argument, see Michael Stohl and George Lopez, "Westpha-
lia, the End of the Cold War and the New World Order: Old Roots to a
"NEW" Problem," 11. Paper presented at a Conference entitled "Failed
States and International Security: Causes, Prospects, and Consequences."
(Purdue University, February 25–27,1998). See also Hans-Henrik Holm,
"The Responsibility That Will Not Go Away (sic.) Weak States in the
International System," 2. Paper presented at a Conference entitled "Failed
States and International Security: Causes, Prospects, and Consequences."
(Purdue University, February 25–27, 1998).

22. For a good summary of the Realist view of the relationship between
power and international institutions, see Beth Simmons and Lisa Martin, "International Organisations and Institutions," 8–10, in Walter
Carlsnaes, Thomas Risse, and Beth Simmons (ed.) *Handbook of International Relations.* (London et al.: Sage, 2002). http://www.polisci.
berkeley.edu/Faculty/bio/permanent/Simmons.B/Intl_Organizations_
Institutions.pdf

23. See Robert Gilpin. *War and Change in World Politics*. (New York: Cambridge University Press, 1981); see also "Concepts of International Politics," 8.
24. Holm, 3.
25. Ibid., 13–14.
26. In order to see the relatively recent nature of these norms and their linkage to the bipolar system which existed during the Cold War, one need only consider the willingness of the major powers to acquiesce in the dismemberment of Czechoslovakia following the big power discussions at Munich in 1938.
27. The UN operation in the Congo in the early 1960s (ONUC) designed to preserve the territorial integrity of the new state against efforts by rebels in Katanga province to secede attests to the importance of this norm as a way to prevent possible superpower confrontation.
28. Hans-Herik Holm, "The Disaggregated World Order: Foreign Policy Towards Failed States," Section 2.2. http://www.ippu.purdue.edu/info/gsp/FSIS_CONF2/Holm.html
29. The decision of the NATO countries to reject Serbian arguments that the Kosovo crisis represented an internal matter and their willingness to support intervention on behalf of the ethnic Albanians living there, ostensibly for humanitarian purposes although the claim is dubious given the effects of intervention upon the Albanians, is evidence of this post-Cold War relaxation of certain norms associated with juridical statehood.
30. See Jendayi E. Frazer, "Transnational Political Development or State-Making in a Global Era," 6. Paper delivered at the ODC-Kennedy School Conference on America's National Interests in Multilateral Engagement: A Bipartisan Dialogue. http://www.odc.org/conference/confpapers/poldev.doc
31. Ibid., 5.
32. Holm, "The Disaggregated World Order," Section 2.1.
33. See Stohl and Lopez, 5.
34. For a discussion of this issue of dependence upon foreign forces and the failure to develop internal capabilities by state elites, see Clapham, "Sierra Leone," 13.
35. Frazer, 8.
36. James Hughes and Gwendolyn Sasse, "Comparing Regional and Ethnic Conflicts in Post-Soviet Transition States: An Institutional Approach," (Paper Prepared for ECPR Joint Sessions, Grenoble, 7–11 April, 2001, Workshop #2), 10–11. http://www.essex.ac.uk/ecpr/jointsessions/grenoble/papers/ws2/hughes_sasse.pdf
37. For a succinct discussion of the many challenges to state sovereignty at the present time, see Weiss and Chopra, "Sovereignty Under Siege: From Intervention to Humanitarian Space," 97 cited previously in Chapter Five.

NOTES TO CHAPTER SEVEN

1. For a discussion of this concept, see Boutros-Ghali, "An Agenda for Peace," paragraph 20. For some additional reading on this subject, see

Olara A. Otunnu, "The Peace-and Security Agenda of the United Nations: From a Crossroads into the Next Century." Paper prepared for The Commission on Global Governance. http://www.cgg.ch/olara.htm; Report of the Somalia Commission of Inquiry, "Peacekeeping: Concepts, Evolution, and Canada's Role." http://www.dnd.ca/somalia/vol1/v1c10e.htm; and J. David Whaley and Barbara Piazza-Georgi, "The Linkage Between Peacekeeping and Peacebuilding." Published in Monograph No. 10, *Conflict Management, Peacekeeping and Peacebuilding*, April 1997. http://www.iss.co.za/Pubs/Monographs/No10/Whaley.html

2. For a brief discussion of this issue, see Boutros-Ghali, "Supplement to an Agenda for Peace," paragraph 18.

3. For a discussion of this concept, see Boutros-Ghali, "An Agenda for Peace," paragraphs 42–44; for further discussion of this concept and its application in the post-Cold War era, see Boutros-Ghali, "Supplement to an Agenda for Peace," paragraphs 77–80.

4. See Boutros-Ghali, "An Agenda for Peace," paragraphs 55–59; see also Boutros-Ghali, "Supplement to An Agenda for Peace," paragraphs 47–56.

5. For a discussion of a similar point regarding the idea of allowing the violence to continue until one party achieves military victory, see Thomas G. Weiss, "Elusive Peace: Negotiating an End to Civil Wars" (review article), *The American Political Science Review*, Volume 90, Issue 3, (Sep., 1996), 711.

6. See Edward N. Luttwak, "Give War a Chance," *Foreign Affairs*, Volume 78, Number 4, (July/August 1999), 36–44.

7. The question of whether, in fact, nonintervention constitutes a distinct policy option raises interesting philosophical and political issues: Is there any such thing as doing nothing or is doing nothing actually a form of doing something? Since choosing either engagement or disengagement undoubtedly will affect both the trajectory and the outcome of a conflict, is there really any such thing as nonintervention? These questions are beyond the scope of this particular study and are raised here merely to point out the inherent complexity of this seemingly clear-cut notion of nonintervention. For purposes of clarity, the use of the term "nonintervention" in this study refers to the absence of external *military* involvement—although clearly there are other forms which intervention may take.

8. See Chapter Two *fn*.20.

9. For a discussion of the expulsion of Native Americans peoples as an early form of "ethnic cleansing," see Andrew Bell-Fialkoff, "A Brief History of Ethnic Cleansing," *Foreign Affairs*, Volume 72, Number 3, (Summer 1993), 113.

10. Speech delivered on December 29, 1940. For text of the speech, see "The Arsenal of Democracy." http://www.usembassy.de/usa/etexts/speeches/rhetoric/fdrarsen.htm

11. See Benny Morris. *Righteous Victims: A History of the Zionist-Arab Conflict, 1881–2001.* (New York: Vintage Books, 2001), 191–214.

12. Ibid., 235.

13. See Ibid., 252–253.
14. See Rex Brynen, "Palestinian Refugees and the Middle East Peace Process." Paper prepared for the New Hampshire International Seminar/Yale-Maria Lecture in Middle East Studies, University of New Hampshire, 3 April 1998. http://www.arts.mcgill.ca/MEPP/PRRN/papers/UNH.html

    For further reading on this controversial subject from a pro-Israeli perspective, see Dan Kurzman. *Ben-Gurion: Prophet of Fire.* (New York: Simon and Schuster, 1983), 281; Chaim Herzog. *The Arab-Israeli Wars: War and Peace in the Middle East.* (New York: Random House, Inc., 1982), 37–8; Martin Gilbert. *Israel: A History.* (New York: William Morrow and Company, Inc., 1998), 172–173.

    For a view more sympathetic to the Arab position, see Simha Flapan. *The Birth of Israel: Myths and Realities.* (New York: Pantheon Books, 1987), 83–118.

    For a view incorporating the many nuances of this issue, see Morris, *Righteous Victims,* 252–258.
15. At the time, a small number of Jews led by Judah Magnes of Hebrew University formed an organization known as Ihud, which favored the creation of a binational state in Palestine. As there was no support within the Arab community and only minimal support within the Jewish community for the idea, binationalism was effectively discredited as an option.
16. Prior to 1967, Israel was only about eight miles wide at its narrowest point.
17. Nils A. Butenschon. "Politics of Ethnocracies: Strategies and Dilemmas of Ethnic Domination." An extended version of a paper presented at the National Conference of Political Science, Geilo, Norway, 11–12 January 1993. http://www.statsvitsenkap.uio.no/ansatte/serie/notat/fulltekst/0193/Ethnocr-5.html
18. See Paul F. Diehl, "Peacekeeping Operations and the Quest for Peace," *Political Science Quarterly,* Volume 103, Issue 3, (Autumn, 1988), 491 and 506; see also James A. Stegenga, "Peacekeeping: Post-Mortems or Previews?" *International Organization,* (Volume 27, Issue 3, Summer, 1973), 381.
19. See Boutros-Ghali, "Supplement to An Agenda for Peace," paragraph 34.
20. Richard K.Betts, "The Delusion of Impartial Intervention," in Richard K. Betts. *Conflict After the Cold War: Arguments on Causes of War and Peace.* Second edition. (New York: Longman, 2002), 598.
21. See Roy Licklider, "The Consequences of Negotiated Settlements in Civil Wars, 1945–1993," *The American Political Science Review,* (Volume 89, Issue 3, Sep., 1995), 686.
22. For a discussion of the distinction between state-building and nation-building, see Harold Karan Jacobson, "Onuc's Civilian Operations: State-Preserving and State-Building," *World Politics,* Volume 17, (Oct., 1964), 76.
23. See Michael J. Matheson, "United Nations Governance of Postconflict Societies," *American Journal of International Law,* (Volume 95, Issue 1, Jan., 2001), 79–80.
24. See Ibid., 81–83.

25. See the discussion in *Chapter Two* on this very point.

26. For a discussion of falsification as a scientific concept, see Karl Popper, "Science as Falsification." 1963. http://www.freethought-web.org/ctrl/popper_falsification.html; for a more detailed discussion, see Karl R. Popper. The Logic of Scientific Discovery. (New York: Routledge, 1992).

27. By "significant contradiction," I mean to suggest one which is not amenable to minor adjustments in the theory in accordance with specific fact situations. Thus, for example, if one were to identify a case in which external intervention brought an ethnic conflict to a conclusion and resulted in the creation of stable state structures, this would represent a "significant contradiction" to the findings expected from the theory.

NOTES TO CHAPTER EIGHT

1. For a discussion of some of the ambiguities involved in attempting to define this term, see Ian R. Manners and Barbara McKean Parmenter, "The Middle East: A Geographic Preface," in Deborah J. Gerner (ed.) *Understanding the Contemporary Middle East.* (Boulder, Colorado: Lynne Rienner Publishers, Inc., 2000), 9; see also David E. Long and Bernard Reich, "Introduction," in David E. Long and Bernard Reich (ed.) *The Government and Politics of the Middle East and North Africa.* Fourth Edition. (Boulder, Colorado: Westview Press, 2002), 2; and Naji Abi-Aad and Michel Grenon. *Instability and Conflict in the Middle East: People, Petroleum and Security Threats.* (New York: St. Martin's Press, Inc., 1997), 1; and Leonard Binder, "Prolegomena to the Comparative Study of Middle East Governments," *The American Political Science Review,* Vol. 51, No. 3, (September 1957), 652 *fn.* 3.

2. Deborah J. Gerner and Philip A. Schrodt, "Middle Eastern Politics," in Deborah J. Gerner (ed.) *Understanding the Contemporary Middle East.* (Boulder, Colorado: Lynne Rienner Publishers, Inc., 2000), 97.

3. James A. Bill and Robert Springborg. *Politics in the Middle East.* Fifth Edition. (New York: Addison Wesley Longman, Inc., 2000), 30; see also Gabriel Ben-Dor. *State and Conflict in the Middle East: Emergence of the Postcolonial State.* (New York: Praeger Publishers, 1983), 231–236.

4. For a good discussion of the differences between the Western European and Middle Eastern experiences with state-building, see Ian S. Lustick, "The Absence of Middle Eastern Great Powers: Political 'Backwardness' in Historical Perspective," *International Organization,* Vol. 51, No. 4 (Autumn, 1997), 653–683. Unlike the present study, however, Lustick is not primarily concerned with the role of intervention in obstructing governing capacity or empirical sovereignty per se but specifically with its negative impact upon the efforts of Middle Eastern state makers to establish regional hegemony. See, for example, pages 663–675.

5. For a fuller discussion of this point, see Ibid., 656–660.

6. Ben-Dor, 234

7. For more on this point about Iraqi national identity, see Sandra Mackey. *The Reckoning: Iraq and the Legacy of Saddam Hussein.* (New York: W. W. Norton & Company, Inc., 2002), 83.

8. An exception to this general trend would be the case of war making and state making in Saudi Arabia. Ibn Saud, ruler of the Najd region in the Arabian Peninsula, militarily defeated Husayn Ibn Ali (the Sharif Husayn), who was the ruler of the Hejaz region, in order to forcibly consolidate control in the new state of Saudi Arabia. For a similar point regarding Saudi Arabia, see Gerner and Schrodt, 94. One might also point to the case of Israel, whose borders and population distribution between Arabs and Jews is largely the result of military conflict.

9. Arthur Goldschmidt, Jr., "The Historical Context," in Deborah J. Gerner (ed.) *Understanding the Contemporary Middle East.* (Boulder, Colorado: Lynne Rienner Publishers, Inc., 2000), 51.

10. Goldschmidt, 56.

11. For a concise discussion of the history and politics of modern Turkey, see George S. Harris, "Republic of Turkey," in David E. Long and Bernard Reich (ed.) *The Government and Politics of the Middle East and North Africa.* Fourth Edition. (Boulder, Colorado: Westview Press, 2002), 9–46.

12. For the terms of the agreement, see "MidEast Web Historical Documents: The Sykes-Picot Agreement: 1916." http://www.mideastweb.org/mesykespicot.htm

13. Following the Bolshevik Revolution in 1917, Russia, which had been a party to the original negotiations under the tsar, revealed the contents of this agreement to the Sharif Husayn.

14. For a discussion of these commitments, see Goldschmidt, 57.

15. Ibid., 57–58.

16. For a discussion of this point with specific reference to Iraq, see Nelida Fuccaro, "Ethnicity, State Formation, and Conscription in Postcolonial Iraq: The Case of the Yazidi Kurds of Jabal Sinjar," *International Journal of Middle East Studies*, Vol. 29, No. 4 (November, 1997), 560.

17. See Abbas Kelidar, "States without Foundations: The Political Evolution of State and Society in the Arab East," *Journal of Contemporary History*, Vol. 28, No.2, (April, 1993), 321; see also Mary Ann Tetreault, "International Relations," in Deborah J. Gerner (ed.) *Understanding the Contemporary Middle East.* (Boulder, Colorado: Lynne Rienner Publishers, Inc., 2000), 131–134; see also Bill and Springborg, 27.

18. Roy Andersen, Robert F. Seibert, and Jon G. Wagner. *Politics and Change in the Middle East: Sources of Conflict and Accomodation.* Seventh edition. (Upper Saddle River, New Jersey: Pearson Prentice Hall, 2004), 60–62.

19. For a discussion of the difference between formal independence and the achievement of self-determination, see Ibid., 72.

20. Lisa Anderson, "The State in the Middle East and North Africa," *Comparative Politics*, (Vol. 20, No. 1, October 1987), 13.

21. Kelidar, 316.

22. Gerner and Schrodt, 97.
23. From the time of the death of Muhammad in 632 C.E., there had been a divergence between the ideal of unity and the reality of internal division over the issue of succession. Although honored more in the breach than in the observance, the ideal in Islamic political thought had always included the notion of the unity of the Islamic community (ummah) under the heading of the Dar al-Islam (House of Islam) as opposed to the Dar al-Harb (literally House of War). Since it contradicted this ideal, the division of this community into separate communities corresponding to distinct territorial entities was regarded as illegitimate.
24. This Islamic term refers to "Protected Peoples" or "Peoples of the Book." Included within this category are such groups as: Jews, Christians, and Zoroastrians—each of whom is said to possess a revelation from God. As such, they are to be free to worship their own religion and to enjoy a protected, albeit inferior, status in return for the payment of a special tax (jizya) and a willingness to submit to Islamic rule.
25. Both pan-Arabism and pan-Islamism.
26. Rooted in either ethnic or confessional identities.
27. For a similar argument, see Lisa Anderson, 4–5.
28. Ibid., 75.
29. Ian Lustick suggests that in the post-Cold War era, these systemic conditions may be returning to something closely resembling that which existed in Western Europe due to the increasing reluctance of external powers to intervene in certain situations. See Lustick, "The Absence of Middle Eastern Great Powers," 678.
30. For a discussion of this issue, see Abi-Aad and Grenon, 91–116; see also Mahmoud, 74.
31. See Ibid., 107; Bill and Springborg, 296; Andersen, Seibert, and Wagner, 283; and Rodney Wilson, "The Middle East after the Gulf War: The Regional Economic Impact," in Haifaa A. Jawad (ed.) *The Middle East in the New World Order.* (New York: St. Martin's Press, Inc., 1994), 135.
32. Abi-Aad and Grenon, 103–104.
33. For a discussion of the role of identity in the ideologies and politics of the region, see Bill and Springborg, 21–24.
34. Ibid., 27–28.
35. Kelidar, 328.
36. See Curtis R. Ryan, "Syrian Arab Republic" in David E. Long and Bernard Reich (ed.) *The Government and Politics of the Middle East and North Africa.* Fourth Edition. (Boulder, Colorado: Westview Press, 2002), 230.
37. See Abi-Aad and Grenon, 106; Goldschmidt, 77.
38. Abi-Aad and Grenon, 83–86.
39. Sandra Mackey. *The Reckoning: Iraq and the Legacy of Saddam Hussein.* (New York: W. W. Norton & Company, Inc., 2002.), 115.
40. For a detailed discussion of this issue, see the report entitled "Iraq: Continuous and Silent Ethnic Cleansing: Displaced Persons in Iraqi Kurdistan and Iraqi Refugees in Iran," *International Federation for Human Rights,* January 2003. http://www.i-a-j.org/pdf/irak3501fin_ENG.pdf

41. See Carole A. O'Leary, "The Kurds of Iraq: Recent History, Future Prospects," *Middle East Review of International Affairs*, Vol. 6, No. 4, (December 2002), 25.
42. See Deborah J. Gerner, "Trends and Prospects," in Deborah J. Gerner (ed.) *Understanding the Contemporary Middle East.* (Boulder, Colorado: Lynne Rienner Publishers, Inc., 2000), 388–389.
43. Bill and Springborg, 27–31.
44. For a similar argument, see Kelidar, 321; see also Lisa Anderson, 13.
45. Gerner, 389–390.
46. Gerner and Schrodt, 93–97; Bill and Springborg, 180.
47. This argument resembles Louis Hartz' claim concerning the difference between European and American societies. Just as he argues that liberalism, itself an outgrowth of the feudal tradition in Europe, came to America as a founding principle in the absence of the struggle to overcome the feudal experience, the argument here is that similarly the state came to the Middle East without the struggles associated with the state-building process. See Louis Hartz. *The Liberal Tradition in America: An Interpretation of American Political Thought Since the Revolution.* (New York: Harcourt, Brace, 1955).
48. For an interesting discussion of the twin issues of state-building and regime security, see Mohammad-Mahmoud Mohamedou. *Iraq and the Second Gulf War: State Building and Regime Security.* (Bethesda, Maryland: Austin & Winfield, Publishers, 1998), 56–68.

     Unlike Mohamedou, this study views the two issues as inextricably connected *during the early stages of the state-building process.* Efforts designed to further regime security, particularly internal security, inevitably, even if inadvertently, contribute to the state-building process through the consolidation or centralization of power within the boundaries of the state.
49. Mohamedou, 73.

NOTES TO CHAPTER NINE

1. For more on this issue, see Andreas Wimmer. *Nationalist Exclusion and Ethnic Conflict: Shadows of Modernity.* (New York: Cambridge University Press, 2002), 85–113.
2. For a good discussion of British war aims with regard to Mesopotamia (Iraq), including the issue of Mosul, during the First World War, see V. H. Rothwell, "Mesopotamia in British War Aims, 1914–1918," The Historical Journal, Vol. 13, No. 2 (June 1970), 273–294.
3. Mohamedou, 79–80.
4. For the complete text of the treaty, see "The Treaty of Peace Between the Allied and Associated Powers and Turkey Signed at Sèvres, August 10, 1920." http://www.lib.byu.edu/~rdh/wwi/versa/sevres1.html
5. For the text of this treaty, see "Treaty of Peace with Turkey Signed at Lausanne, July 24, 1923." http://www.lib.byu.edu/~rdh/wwi/1918p/lausanne.html

6. Dilip Hiro. *Desert Shield to Desert Storm: The Second Gulf War*. (New York: Routledge, Chapman and Hall, Inc., 1992), 14; see also Rothwell, 292.

7. The issue of control of oil-rich Kirkuk would play an important part in the relationship between the Iraqi government in Baghdad and the Kurds including various campaigns to "Arabize" the region. For more on this, see the report entitled "Iraq: Forcible Expulsion of Ethnic Minorities" in *Human Rights Watch* Vol.15, No. 3 (E), March 2003.

8. Sandra Mackey. *The Reckoning: Iraq and the Legacy of Saddam Hussein*. (New York: W. W. Norton & Company, Inc., 2002), 115.

9. Rothwell, 287.

10. Faisal was the son of Hussein ibn Ali, the Sharif of Mecca, who had entered into wartime agreements with the British to fight against the Ottoman Empire. After the war, Faisal attempted to assume the throne in Damascus but was expelled by the French, who had set up a mandate over Syria and Lebanon. The expulsion of Faisal by the French put the British in an awkward position as they had promised his father an independent Arab state in return for a revolt by the Arabs against the Ottomans. Consequently, the creation of the Iraqi mandate provided the British with a way to honor their commitment by placing Faisal on the throne of the new country while at the same time guaranteeing a pro-British regime.

11. This recognition by the British indicates that they were not, as is sometimes suggested with regard to the actions of colonial powers when it came to the process by which colonial boundaries were determined, completely oblivious to the concerns of the local population. It would seem that a more appropriate conclusion would be that they understood at least some of these concerns but chose to act in ways which furthered their own interests as they understood them rather than the interests of the people in the area.

12. Mackey, 112.

13. Hiro, 14.

14. In the year of Iraqi independence, the Kurds constituted fourteen percent of the total population. See Wimmer, 173.

15. About fifteen percent of Kurds are Shi'a Muslims. See Michael Rubin, "Are Kurds a Pariah Minority?" Reprinted from *Social Research*, Vol. 70 No. 1 Spring 2003. http://www.findarticles.com/cf_0/m2267/1_70/102140955/print.jhtml

16. Ibid.

17. Carole A. O'Leary, "The Kurds of Iraq: Recent History, Future Prospects," *Middle East Review of International Affairs*, Vol. 6, No. 4, December 2002, 17; see also Mackey, 63–64.

18. See Wimmer, 174; see also Mohamedou, 80.

19. For more on the role of national consensus and domestic cohesion as elements of state-building, see Mohamedou, 59–60.

20. Mackey, 83.

21. Mohamedou, 84.

22. Mackey, 214.

23. Mohamedou, 92.
24. O'Leary, 25.
25. Mohamedou, 92; see also Mackey, 219.
26. O'Leary, 25. O'Leary identifies three separate Arabization campaigns or phases by Iraqi regimes against the Kurds occurring in 1963, 1974, and 1984. For more on this, see O'Leary, 25–26. For more on the 1963 campaign, see Mackey, 193.
27. Mohamedou, 99.
28. Ibid., 104; for a more detailed discussion of the issues involved in the border dispute between Iran and Iraq, see Joseph J. Cusimano, "An Analysis of Iran-Iraq Bilateral Border Treaties." http://web.macam.ac.il/~arnon/Int-ME/extra/AN%20ANALYSIS%20OF%20IRAN
29. It is worth noting that, while Saddam Hussein had little sympathy for the Iraqi Kurdish desire for autonomy or independence, his regime would later offer support for Kurdish separatists in northern Iran following the Islamic revolution in that country. See Lawrence Freedman and Efraim Karsh. The Gulf Conflict, 1990–1991: Diplomacy and War in the New World Order. (Princeton: Princeton University Press, 1993), 20.
30. For more on this issue, see Mackey, 212–213; see also Con Coughlin. *Saddam: King of Terror.* (New York: HarperCollins Publishers Inc., 2002), 118–119.
31. Coughlin, 118.
32. For a copy of the text, see "Algiers Accord—1975," March 6, 1975. http://www.mideastweb.org/algiersaccord.htm
33. Mohamedou, 103.
34. The issue of support for the Iraqi Kurds provides an opportunity to observe the interface between regional and global political systems. In this regard, the Iranians, who at the time were backing the Iraqi Kurds, were themselves receiving assistance from the United States, which viewed the Shah's regime as a bulwark against Soviet penetration into the Persian Gulf. In a sense, therefore, the Kurdish rebellion was being underwritten at the regional level by the Iranians and at the global level by the United States. The Algiers Agreement ended Iranian support for the Kurds and, consequently, also the support of the United States for the Kurds.
35. For more on the reasons for this effort to align Iraq with the Soviet Union in the early 1970s, see Coughlin,105–109.
36. Ibid., 104.
37. Lustick, "The Absence of Middle Eastern Great Powers," 674.
38. For the text of Bush's speech, see *The Middle East.* Ninth edition. (Washington, D.C.: Congressional Quarterly, Inc., 2000), 533–534.
39. Freedman and Karsh, 407.
40. Mackey, 285.
41. Freedman and Karsh, 407; see also Coughlin, 274.
42. See Weiss (1999), 49–50.
43. Although occurring simultaneously, the fighting inside Iraq actually consisted of two distinct and uncoordinated insurrections by the Kurds in the north and the Shi'a in the south.

44. Thomas Hobbes, "Of the Natural Condition of Mankind as Concerning Their Felicity and Misery." http://oregonstate.edu/instruct/phl302/texts/hobbes/leviathan-c.html

45. Thomas G. Weiss. Military-Civilian Interactions in Humanitarian Crises. (New York: Rowman & Littlefield Publishers, Inc., 1999), 49; see also Malanczuk, 117.

46. For the text of the resolution, see "Resolution 688 (1991)." S/RES/0688 (1991). 5 April 1991. http://www.fas.org/news/un/iraq/sres/sres0688.htm

47. For a brief description of these operations, see "Operation Southern Watch." www.fas.org/man/dod-101/ops/southern_watch.htm

48. Mohamedou, 184.

49. Hiro, 400.

50. Faleh Abd al-Jabbar, "Why the Uprisings Failed," *Middle East Report*, No. 176, Iraq in the Aftermath, (May-June, 1992), 8.

51. Mackey, 287. It should be mentioned that Hiro acknowledges this incident as well. See Hiro, 400.

52. See, for example, Peter W. Galbraith, "Refugees from War in Iraq: What Happened in 1991 and What May Happen in 2003," Migration Policy Institute Policy Brief. No. 2, (February 2003), 3. http://www.migration policy.org/pubs/MPIPolicyBriefIraq.pdf; see also Freedman and Karsh, 410.

53. Coughlin, 276.

54. Al-Jabbar, 8.

55. Mackey, 24–25; see also Galbraith, 4.

56. Mackey, 112.

57. Ibid.,117.

58. Galbraith, 4.

59. Weiss (1999), 47.

60. For more on these costs, see Mackey, 269; see also al-Jabbar, 5.

61. Coughlin, 274.

62. Gailbraith, 4.

63. The issue of President Bush's role in encouraging the uprising will be discussed further in the context of the Kurdish revolt in the north.

64. Hiro, 400.

65. Ibid., 401. For more on this, see Mackey, 288.

66. Hiro, 401; see also Mackey 287.

67. Al-Jabbar, 10.

68. Mackey, 288.

69. Pierre-Jean Luizard and Joe Stork, "The Iraqi Question from the Inside," *Middle East Report*, No. 193, The Iraqi Sanctions Dilemma, March–April, 1995, 19.

70. Mackey, 288.

71. It should be noted, however, that a democratic Iraq with a Shi'a majority presumably would translate into a situation in which they would predominate. It should also be noted that such a situation contains the seeds for further civil conflict and is precisely the situation confronting Iraq following the toppling of Hussein in 2003 and the attempt to establish a government for the country.

72. Mackey, 285–286.
73. Ibid., 291.
74. Ibid., 25, 295.
75. Ibid., 289.
76. For more on the history of involvement by the Republican Guards in both the Gulf War and the subsequent uprisings, see Ibrahim al-Marashi, "The Republican Guard [Al-Haris Al-Jamhuri]." http://cns.miis.edu/research/iraq/rguard.htm
77. Ibid., 285.
78. Coughlin, 280.
79. Ibid., 290.
80. The Soviet Union officially came to an end on December 25, 1991.
81. Mackey, 339–341.
82. Malanczuk, 117.
83. Mackey, 348–349.
84. Coughlin, 287.
85. For a brief description of these challenges, see "Operation Southern Watch." http://www.fas.org/man/dod-101/ops/southern_watch.htm
86. Coughlin, 289.
87. Al-Jabbar, 13.
88. Mackey, 287.
89. Hiro, 401.
90. Mackey, 25.
91. Galbraith, 4.
92. See the discussion of the belated efforts by the Allies to challenge Hussein's control over that territory beginning in 1992.
93. Mackey, 291–292.
94. Ibid., 289.
95. Ibid., 296.
96. Ibid., 288.
97. Galbraith, 4.
98. Ibid., 4.
99. Robert G. Rabil, "Operation 'Termination of Traitors': The Iraqi Regime Through its Documents," *Middle East Review of International Affairs*, Vol. 6, No. 3 (September, 2002), 16.
100. Mackey, 292.
101. Ibid., 292.
102. Ibid., 293.
103. Hiro, 407.
104. Weiss (1999), 50.
105. Hiro, 407.
106. Weiss (1999), 50; Mackey, 293–294.
107. For a more detailed description of this campaign, see Rabil, 18–23.
108. For a description of this campaign in Iraq as "ethnic cleansing, see O'Leary, 18.
109. Mackey, 262.
110. Ibid., 262.

111. Ibid., 262.
112. Weiss (1999), 47.
113. Malanczuk, 118.
114. Hiro, 407.
115. Malanczuk, 119; Mackey, 351.
116. For the text of the resolution, see "Resolution 660 (1991)." S/RES/0660 (1990). 2 August 1990. http://www.fas.org/news/un/iraq/sres/sres0660.htm
117. Barry Rubin, "The United States in the Middle East, 1991." http://www.biu.ac.il/SOC/besa/meria/us-policy/data1991.html
118. Malanczuk, 119.
119. Mackey, 28.
120. Freedman and Karsh, 413.
121. Ibid., 424.
122. Weiss (1999), 49.
123. Coughlin, 278–279.
124. Sarah Graham-Brown, "Intervention, Sovereignty and Responsibility," *Middle East Report*, No. 193, The Iraq Sanctions Dilemma (March-April, 1995), 4.
125. Coughlin, 277.
126. Malanczuk, 117 *fn.* 12.
127. Coughlin, 276.
128. Ibid., 117; Freedman and Karsh, 415; and Mackey, 348.
129. Freedman and Karsh, 414.
130. Malanczuk, 117.
131. A similar concern for the possibility of hostile control of the region's oil had resulted in Western, particularly American, efforts to expel the Soviet Union from Afghanistan during the 1980s. Likewise, it led to the Gulf War coalition against the 1990 Iraqi invasion of Kuwait.
132. Opposition to Sadat's peace initiative towards Israel was one of the reasons for his assassination by Islamic militants on October 6, 1981. The date is significant because it was the anniversary of the launching of the surprise Yom Kippur/Ramadan War in 1973 against Israel.
133. While counterfactuals are always risky, it seems plausible to suggest that since the peace treaty between Jordan and Israel was not signed until 1994 by King Hussein and Prime Minister Rabin, it is likely that this agreement would never have taken place had a pro-Iranian regime overthrown the Jordanian monarchy in the aftermath of the breakup of neighboring Iraq in 1991.
134. Malanczuk, 117. For a more detailed discussion of the Kurdish issue in Turkey, see Philip Robins, "The Overlord State: Turkish Policy and the Kurdish Issue," *International Affairs*. Vol. 69, No. 4 (October, 1993), 657–676.
135. Hiro, 406.
136. As an indication of the sensitivity with which Turkey views the issue of Kurdish assimilation into Turkish society as a way of preserving the territorial integrity of the state, officially these Kurds are referred to as "mountain Turks." See Robins, 661.

137. For more on this issue, see Sabri Sayari, "Turkey and the Middle East in the 1990s," in *Journal of Palestine Studies*, Vol. 26, No. 3 (Spring 1997), 46–47.
138. Hiro, 406.
139. For a more detailed discussion of this issue, see William Hale, "Turkey, the Middle East and the Gulf Crisis," *International Affairs (Royal Institute of International Affairs 1944-)*, Vol. 68, No. 4 (October 1992), 687–692; see also Robins, 673–675.
140. For the text of the resolution, see "Resolution 688 (1991)." S/RES/0688 (1991). 5 April 1991. http://www.fas.org/news/un/iraq/sres/sres0688.htm
141. Malanczuk, 119.
142. Ibid., 119–120.
143. Weiss (1999), 50.
144. Ibid., 50.
145. Despite an even more severe humanitarian crisis along the Iraq-Iran border, the absence of media coverage meant that there was no comparable pressure to respond and, consequently, no action was taken by the coalition in this situation.
146. Weiss (1999), 53.
147. Ibid., 53.
148. Ibid., 55.
149. Freedman and Karsh, 422.
150. Weiss (1999), 60.
151. Ibid., 60. Weiss does note, however, that repatriation does not necessarily mean that the Kurds were able to return to their places of origin. Instead, repatriation is used to refer to the return to the protected areas within northern Iraq.
152. Ibid., 60.
153. Ibid., 54.
154. Graham-Brown, 4.
155. Ronald Ofteringer and Ralf Backer, "The Republic of Statelessness: Three Years of Humanitarian Intervention in Iraqi Kurdistan," *Middle East Report*, No. 187/188, Intervention and North-South Politics in the 90's (March-June, 1994), 42. Mackey places the vote total at 44.6 percent for the KDP's Barzani and 44.3 percent for the PUK's Talabani. See Mackey, 308.
156. O'Leary, 19.
157. Ofteringer and Backer, 42.
158. Mackey, 308.
159. Ofteringer and Backer, 44.
160. Graham-Brown, 8.
161. For a more detailed discussion of the sanctions imposed upon Iraqi Kurdistan, see Ofteringer and Backer, 43.
162. It should be pointed out that this is a dubious claim given the willingness of NATO to act on behalf of the Kosovar Albanians while not prejudging the status of Kosovo during the 1999 war.

163. Graham-Brown, 7.
164. Ibid.,7.
165. Mackey, 310; Graham-Brown, 7.
166. Isam al-Khafaji, "The Destruction of Iraqi Kurdistan," *Middle East Report*, No. 201, Israel and Palestine: Two States, Bantustans or Binationalism? (October-December, 1996), 36.
167. Mackey, 311–312.

NOTES TO CHAPTER TEN

1.   Without going into all of the differences, suffice it to say that, as with all analogies, the differing circumstances in each case make comparisons imprecise. Nevertheless, it is possible to reason analogically so as to identify a pattern from which certain generalizations can be made.
2.   Woodward, *Balkan Tragedy*, 213–214.
3.   Although it had nothing to do with the population transfer between Muslims and Hindus at the founding of Pakistan and India, this statement needs to be qualified somewhat given the fact that the eastern part of Pakistan eventually seceded and became Bangladesh.
4.   In terms of this issue of imposed democracy, perhaps a more apt analogy to Iraq would be the advent of democracy in Germany following World War I, which resulted in instability and, ultimately, the failure of the Weimar Republic.

Bibliography

BOOKS AND ARTICLES

Abd al-Jabbar, Faleh, "Why the Uprisings Failed," *Middle East Report*, No. 176, Iraq in the Aftermath, May-June, 1992, 2–14.

Abi-Aad, Naji and Grenon, Michel. *Instability and Conflict in the Middle East: People, Petroleum and Security Threats.* New York: St. Martin's Press, Inc., 1997.

Abi-Saab, Georges. *The United Nations Operation in the Congo 1960–1964.* New York: Oxford University Press, 1978.

Adamiak, Richard "The 'Withering Away' of the State: A Reconsideration," in *The Journal of Politics,* Volume 32, Issue 1 (February, 1970), 3–18.

"Address Before a Joint Session of the Congress on the State of the Union," January 29, 1991. http://bushlibrary.tamu.edu/papers/1991/91012902.html

Ajami, Fouad. *The Arab Predicament: Arab Political Thought and Practice since 1967.* New York: Cambridge University Press, 1981.

Al-Khafaji, Isam, "The Destruction of Iraqi Kurdistan," *Middle East Report,* No. 201, Israel and Palestine: Two States, Bantustans or Binationalism? October-December, 1996, 35–38, 42.

Al-Marashi, Ibrahim, "The Republican Guard [Al-Haris Al-Jamhuri]." http://cns.miis.edu/research/iraq/rguard.htm

Andersen, Roy R., Seibert, Robert F., and Wagner, Jon G. *Politics and Change in the Middle East: Sources of Conflict and Accomodation.* Seventh edition. Upper Saddle River, New Jersey: Pearson Prentice Hall, 2004.

Anderson, Lisa, "The State in the Middle East and North Africa," *Comparative Politics,* Vol. 20, No. 1, October 1987, 1–18.

Ayoob, Mohammed. *The Third World Security Predicament: State Making, Regional Conflict, and the International System.* Boulder: L. Rienner Publishers, 1995.

Baker, Pauline H. and Ausink, John A., "State Collapse and Ethnic Violence: Toward a Predictive Model," from *Parameters,* Spring 1996. http://carlisle-www.army.mil/usawc/Parameters/96spring/baker.htm

Baehr, Peter R. and Gordenker, Leon. *The United Nations in the 1990s* Second Edition. New York: St. Martin's Press, 1994.

Bannerman, M. Graeme, "Republic of Lebanon," in David E. Long and Bernard Reich (ed.) *The Government and Politics of the Middle East and North Africa*. Fourth Edition. Boulder, Colorado: Westview Press, 2002.

Barkey, Karen; Parikh, Sunita. "Comparative Perspectives on the State," *Annual Review of Sociology*, vol. 17. (1991), 523–549.

Barkin, J. Samuel and Cronin, Bruce, "The State and the Nation: Changing Norms and the Rules of Sovereignty in International Relations," *International Organization*, Volume 48, Issue 1 (Winter, 1994), 107–130.

Ben-Dor, Gabriel. *State and Conflict in the Middle East: Emergence of the Post-colonial State*. New York: Praeger Publishers, 1983.

Bereciartu, Gurutz Jauregui (translated by William A. Douglass). *Decline of the Nation-State*. Reno, Nevada: University of Nevada Press, 1994.

Beer, Samuel H. *Britain Against Itself: The Political Contradictions of Collectivism*. First Edition. New York: Norton, 1982.

Bell-Fialkoff, Andrew, "A Brief History of Ethnic Cleansing," *Foreign Affairs*, Volume 72, Number 3, Summer 1993, 110–121.

Betts, Richard K., "The Delusion of Impartial Intervention," in Richard K. Betts. *Conflict After the Cold War: Arguments on Causes of War and Peace*. Second edition. New York: Longman, 2002.

Bill, James A. and Springborg, Robert. *Politics in the Middle East*. Fifth Edition. New York: Addison Wesley Longman, Inc., 2000.

Binder, Leonard, "Prolegomena to the Comparative Study of Middle East Governments," *The American Political Science Review*, Vol. 51, No. 3, September 1957, 651–668.

Bookman, Milica Zarkovic. *The Demographic Struggle for Power: The Political Economy of Demographic Engineering in the Modern World*. Portland, Oregon: Frank Cass &Co. Ltd., 1997.

Boot, Max, "Paving the Road to Hell: the Failure of U.N. Peacekeeping," *Foreign Affairs* v.79 no.2 March/April 2000, 143–148.

Boyd, James M. *United Nations Peace-Keeping Operations: A Military and Political Appraisal*. New York: Praeger Publishers, 1971.

Bratton, Michael "Beyond the State: Civil Society and Associational Life in Africa," *World Politics*, Volume 41, Issue 3, April, 1989, 407–430.

Bright, Charles and Harding, Susan (ed.) *Statemaking and Social Movements*. Ann Arbor, Michigan: The University of Michigan Press, 1984.

Brock, Lothar, "Nation-building—Prelude or Belated Solution to the Failing of States?" http://www.ippu.purdue.edu/info/gsp/FSIS_CONF4/Papers/Brock. doc

———. "State Failure and Global Change: From Violent Modernization to War as a Way of Life?" Paper presented at the Failed States Conference at Purdue University, April 7–11, 1999. http://www.ippu.purdue.edu/info/gsp/FSIS_CONF2/Brock.html

Brown, Seyom. *International Relations in a Changing Global System: Toward a Theory of the World Polity*. Boulder, Colorado: Westview Press, Inc., 1992.

Brynen, Rex, "Palestinian Refugees and the Middle East Peace Process." Paper prepared for the New Hampshire International Seminar/Yale-Maria Lecture in Middle East Studies, University of New Hampshire, 3 April 1998. http://www.arts.mcgill.ca/MEPP/PRRN/papers/UNH.html

Bull, Hedley. *The Anarchical Society: A Study of Order in World Politics.* New York: Columbia University Press, 1977.

Butenschon, Nils A., "Politics of Ethnocracies: Strategies and Dilemmas of Ethnic Domination." An extended version of a paper presented at the National Conference of Political Science, Geilo, Norway, 11–12 January 1993. http://www.statsvitsenkap.uio.no/ansatte/serie/notat/fulltekst/0193/Ethnocr-5.html

Buzan, Barry. *People, States and Fear.* 2nd edition. Boulder, Colorado: Lynne Rienner Publishers, Inc., 1991.

Camp, Glen D., "Greek-Turkish Conflict over Cyprus," *Political Science Quarterly,* Volume 95, Issue 1, Spring, 1980, 43–70.

Carment, David and James, Patrick, "Escalation of Ethnic Conflict: A Survey and Assessment." http://www.carleton.ca/~dcarment/papers/escalati.html

Childers, Erskine (ed.) *Challenges to the United Nations.* Phyllis Bennis, "Blue Helmets—For What? Under Whom?" New York: St. Martin's Press, 1994.

Clapham, Christopher. "War and State Formation in Ethiopia and Eritrea." Paper presented at the Failed States Conference, Florence, 10–14 April 2001. http://www.ippu.purdue.edu/info/gsp/FSIS_CONF4/Papers/Clapham_Ethiopia.doc

———. "Sierra Leone: The Global-Local Politics of State Collapse and Attempted Reconstruction," Paper presented at the Failed States Conference, Florence, 10–14 April 2001. http://www.ippu.purdue.edu/gsp/FSIS_CONF4/Papers/Clapham_Sierra_Leone.doc

Cohen, Ronald and Service, Elman R. *Origins of the State.* Philadelphia: The Institute for the Study of Human Issues, 1978.

Cohen, Youssef, Brown, B.R., and Organski, A.F.K. "The Paradoxical Nature of Statemaking: The Violent Creation of Order," 1981. *American Political Science Review.* vol.75 no.4, 1981, 901–910.

Connor, Walker. *The National Question in Marxist-Leninist Theory and Practice.* Princeton: Princeton University Press, 1984.

———. "Nation-Building or Nation-Destroying?" *World Politics,* 24 no. 3, April 1972, 319–355.

Coughlin, Con. *Saddam: King of Terror.* New York: HarperCollins Publishers Inc., 2002.

Cox, Robert W. "Social Forces, States and World Orders: Beyond International Relations Theory," in Robert Keohane (ed.) *Neorealism and its Critics.* New York: Columbia University Press, 1986.

Cusimano, Joseph J., "An Analysis of Iran-Iraq Bilateral Border Treaties." http://web.macam.ac.il/~arnon/Int-ME/extra/AN%20ANALYSIS%20OF%20IRAN

Dahrendorf, Ralf. *Society and Democracy in Germany.* Garden City, New York: Doubleday & Company, Inc., 1967.

Daniel, Donald C.F. and Hayes, Bradd C. (ed.) *Beyond Traditional Peacekeeping.* New York: St. Martin's Press, 1995.

Deegan, Heather, "Democratization in the Middle East," in in Haifaa A. Jawad (ed.) *The Middle East in the New World Order.* New York: St. Martin's Press, Inc., 1994.

Deng, Francis M.; Kimaro, Sadikiel; Lyons, Terrence; Rothchild, Donald; and Zartman, I. William. *Sovereignty as Responsibility: Conflict Management in Africa.* Washington, D.C.: The Brookings Institution, 1996.

Diamond, Larry and Plattner, Marc F. (ed.) *Nationalism, Ethnic Conflict, and Democracy.* Baltimore: The Johns Hopkins University Press, 1994.

Diehl, Paul F. *International Peacekeeping.* Baltimore: Johns Hopkins, 1993.

———. "Peacekeeping Operations and the Quest for Peace," *Political Science Quarterly,* Volume 103, Issue 3, Autumn, 1988, 485–507.

Dobbie, Colonel Charles. "A Concept for Post-Cold War Peacekeeping," *Survival* vol. 36, no.3 Fall 1994, 121–148.

Dorff, Robert H., "Democratization and Failed States: The Challenge of Ungovernability," from *Parameters,* Summer 1996. http://carlisle-www.army.mil/usawc/Parameters/96summer/dorff.htm

Durch, William J. (ed.) *The Evolution of UN Peacekeeping.* New York: St. Martin's Press, 1993.

———. *UN Peacekeeping, American Politics, and The Uncivil Wars of the 1990s.* New York: St. Martin's Press, 1996.

Durch, William J. and Blechman, Barry M. *Keeping the Peace: The United Nations in the Emerging World Order.* Washington, D.C.: The Henry L. Stimson Center, March 1992.

Durkheim, Emile. *The Division of Labor in Society.* New York: Free Press, 1984.

Eide, Asbjorn, "Minorities in a Decentralized Environment," Prepared for UNDP international conference on human rights entitled "Human Rights for Human Development," Yalta, Ukraine: September 2–4, 1998. http://www.riga.lv/minelres/publicat/Eide_Yalta98.htm

Ellis, Stephen, "Democracy in Sub-Saharan Africa: Where did it Come from? Can it be Supported?" (ECDM Working Paper 6). Maastricht: ECDM September 1995. http://www.oneworld.org/ecdpm/pubs/wp6_gb.htm

Ertman, Thomas. *Birth of the Leviathan: Building States and Regimes in Medieval and Early Modern Europe.* New York: Cambridge University Press, 1997.

Esposito, John L. and Khan, Mohammed A. Muqtedar, "Religion and Politics in the Middle East," in Deborah J. Gerner (ed.) *Understanding the Contemporary Middle East.* Boulder, Colorado: Lynne Rienner Publishers, Inc., 2000.

Esman, Milton J. *Ethnic Politics.* Ithaca: Cornell University Press, 1994.

Evans, Peter; Rueschemeyer, Dietrich; and Skocpol, Theda (ed.) *Bringing the State Back In.* New York: Cambridge University Press, 1985.

Flapan, Simha. *The Birth of Israel: Myths and Realities.* New York: Pantheon Books, 1987.

Fox, Gregory H., "Strengthening the State." http://ijgls.indiana.edu/archive/07/01/fox.shtml

Franck, Thomas M. and Ridley, Nigel S. "After Bangladesh: The Law of Humanitarian Intervention by Military Force," *American Journal of International Law*, Volume 67 Issue 2 April, 1973, 275–305.

Frazer, Jendayi E., "Transnational Political Development or State-Making in a Global Era." Paper delivered at the ODC-Kennedy School Conference on America's National Interests in Multilateral Engagement: A Bipartisan Dialogue. http://www.odc.org/conference/confpapers/poldev.doc

Freedman, Lawrence and Karsh, Efraim. *The Gulf Conflict, 1990–1991: Diplomacy and War in the New World Order*. Princeton: Princeton University Press, 1993.

Fuccaro, Nelida, "Ethnicity, State Formation, and Conscription in Postcolonial Iraq: The Case of the Yazidi Kurds of Jabal Sinjar," *International Journal of Middle East Studies*, Vol. 29, No. 4, November, 1997, 559–580.

Gaddis, John Lewis,"The Cold War, the Long Peace, and the Future," in Michael J. Hogan (ed.) *The End of the Cold War: Its Meaning and Implications*. New York: Cambridge University Press, 1992.

Galbraith, Peter W., "Refugees from War in Iraq: What Happened in 1991 and What May Happen in 2003," *Migration Policy Institute*. Policy Brief. No. 2, February 2003. http://www.migrationpolicy.org/pubs/MPIPolicyBriefIraq.pdf

Gerner, Deborah J., "Trends and Prospects," in Deborah J. Gerner (ed.) *Understanding the Contemporary Middle East*. Boulder, Colorado: Lynne Rienner Publishers, Inc., 2000.

Gerner, Deborah J. and Schrodt, Philip A. "Middle Eastern Politics," in Deborah J. Gerner (ed.) *Understanding the Contemporary Middle East*. Boulder, Colorado: Lynne Rienner Publishers, Inc., 2000.

Gilbert, Martin. *Israel: A History*. New York: William Morrow and Company, Inc., 1998.

———. "'The Final Solution'—An Essay by Martin Gilbert." http://www.english.uiuc.edu/maps/holocaust/finalsolution.htm

Gilpin, Robert, "No One Loves a Political Realist," in Robert J. Art and Robert Jervis (ed.) *International Politics: Enduring Concepts and Contemporary Issues*. Fifth edition. New York: Addison-Wesley Educational Publications Inc., 2000.

———. *War and Change in World Politics*. New York: Cambridge University Press, 1981.

Goldschmidt, Arthur Jr., "The Historical Context," in Deborah J. Gerner (ed.) *Understanding the Contemporary Middle East*. Boulder, Colorado: Lynne Rienner Publishers, Inc., 2000.

Gorbachev, Mikhail Sergeevich. *Perestroika: New Thinking for Our Country and the World*. First Edition. NewYork: Harper & Row Publishers, Inc., 1987.

Graham-Brown, Sarah, "Intervention, Sovereignty and Responsibility," *Middle East Report*, No. 193, The Iraq Sanctions Dilemma, March-April, 1995, 2–12, 32.

Gunter, Michael M. *The Kurds of Iraq: Tragedy and Hope*. New York: St. Martin's Press, 1992.

Hale, William, "Turkey, the Middle East and the Gulf Crisis," *International Affairs (Royal Institute of International Affairs 1944–)*, Vol. 68, No. 4, October 1992, 679–692.

Hall, John A. *Coercion and Consent: Studies on the Modern State.* Cambridge, Massachusetts: Polity Press, 1994.

Harris, George S. "Republic of Turkey," in David E. Long and Bernard Reich (ed.) *The Government and Politics of the Middle East and North Africa.* Fourth Edition. Boulder, Colorado: Westview Press, 2002.

Hartz, Louis. *The Liberal Tradition in America: An Interpretation of American Political Thought Since the Revolution.* New York: Harcourt, Brace, 1955.

Herz, John H. *Political Realism and Political Idealism: A Study in Theories and Realities.* Chicago: The University of Chicago Press, 1951.

———. "Rise and Demise of the Territorial State"in John Herz. *The Nation-State and the Crisis of World Politics.* New York: David McKay Company, Inc., 1976.

———. "The Territorial State Revisited—Reflections on the Future of the Nation-State" in John Herz. *The Nation-State and the Crisis of World Politics.* New York: David McKay Company, Inc., 1976.

Herzog, Chaim. *The Arab-Israeli Wars: War and Peace in the Middle East.* New York: Random House, Inc., 1982.

Hinnebusch, Raymond A., "Egypt, Syria and the Arab State System in the New World Order," in Haifaa A. Jawad (ed.) *The Middle East in the New World Order.* New York: St. Martin's Press, Inc., 1994.

Hiro, Dilip. *Desert Shield to Desert Storm: The Second Gulf War.* New York: Routledge, Chapman and Hall, Inc., 1992.

Hirst, Paul, "Politics: Territorial or Non-Territorial?" http://www.theglobalsite. ac.uk/press/104hirst.htm

Hoffmann, Stanley. *World Disorders: Troubled Peace in the Post-Cold War Era.* Lanham, Maryland: Rowman & Littlefield Publishers, Inc., 1998.

Holm, Hans-Henrik, "The Responsibility That Will Not Go Away: Weak States in the International System." Paper presented at a Conference entitled "Failed States and International Security: Causes, Prospects, and Consequences." Purdue University, February 25–27, 1998. http://www.ippu.purdue.edu/info/ gsp/FSIS_CONF/hholms_paper.html

———. "The Disaggregated World Order: Foreign Policy Towards Failed States." http://www.ippu.purdue.edu/info/gsp/FSIS_CONF2/Holm.html

Horowitz, Donald. *Ethnic Groups in Conflict.* Berkeley: University of California Press, 1985.

Howard, Michael, "Managing Conflict—The Role of Intervention: Lessons from the Past," *Managing Conflict in the Post-Cold War World: The Role of Intervention: Report of the Aspen Institute Conference August 2–6, 1995.* Washington, D.C.: The Aspen Institute, 1996.

Hughes, James and Sasse, Gwendolyn, "Comparing Regional and Ethnic Conflicts in Post-Soviet Transition States: An Institutional Approach," Paper Prepared for ECPR Joint Sessions, Grenoble, 7–11 April, 2001, Workshop #2. http://www.essex.ac.uk/ecpr/jointsessions/grenoble/papers/ws2/ hughes_sasse.pdf

Hume, Cameron. *The United Nations, Iran, and Iraq: How Peacemaking Changed.* Indianapolis: Indiana University Press, 1994.

Huntington, Samuel P., "The Clash of Civilizations?" *Foreign Affairs*, Volume 72, Number 3, Summer 1993, 22–49.

"Iraq: Continuous and Silent Ethnic Cleansing: Displaced Persons in Iraqi Kurdistan and Iraqi Refugees in Iran," *International Federation for Human Rights*, January 2003. http://www.i-a-j.org/pdf/irak3501fin_ENG.pdf

"Iraq: Forcible Expulsion of Ethnic Minorities," *Human Rights Watch*, Vol. 15, No.3 (E), March 2003. http://hrw.org/reports/2003/iraq0303/

Ismael, Tareq. *Iraq and Iran: Roots of Conflict*. Syracuse: Syracuse University Press, 1982.

Jackson, Robert H., "Surrogate Sovereignty? Great Power Responsibility and 'Failed States'," Working Paper No. 25, November, 1998. http://www.ippu.purdue.edu/info/gsp/FSIS_CONF2/Jackson.html

Jackson, Robert H. and Rosberg, Carl G. "Why Africa's Weak States Persist: The Empirical and the Juridical in Statehood," *World Politics*, Volume 35, Issue 1, October, 1982, 1–24.

Jacobson, Harold K. . *Networks of Interdependence: International Organizations and the Global Political System*. First edition. New York: Knopf, 1979.

———. "Onuc's Civilian Operations: State-Preserving and State-Building," *World Politics*, Volume 17, Oct., 1964, 75–107.

Jansen, G. H. . *Militant Islam*. New York : Harper & Row Publishers, Inc., 1979.

Jawad, Haifaa A., "Pan-Islamism and Pan-Arabism: Solution or Obstacle to Political Reconstruction in the Middle East?" in Haifaa A. Jawad (ed.) *The Middle East in the New World Order*. New York: St. Martin's Press, Inc., 1994.

Job, Brian L. "The Insecurity Dilemma: National, Regime, and State Securities in the Third World," in Brian L. Job (ed.) *The Insecurity Dilemma: National Security of Third World States*. Boulder, Colorado: Lynne Rienner Publishers, Inc., 1992.

Joffe, George, "Democracy in the Maghreb," in Haifaa A. Jawad (ed.) *The Middle East in the New World Order*. New York: St. Martin's Press, Inc., 1994.

Kapil, Ravi L., "On the Conflict Potential of Inherited Boundaries in Africa," *World Politics*, Volume 18, Issue 4, July, 1966, 656–673.

Kaufman, Stuart, "Peacebuilding and Conflict Resolution." Paper prepared for conference entitled "Living Together After Ethnic Killing: Debating the Kaufmann Hypothesis," Rutgers University, New Brunswick, New Jersey, October 14, 2000. http://cgsd.rutgers.edu/skaufman.pdf

Kaufmann, Chaim, "Possible and Impossible Solutions to Ethnic Civil Wars," in Robert J. Art and Robert Jervis (ed.) *International Politics: Enduring Concepts and Contemporary Issues*. Fifth Edition. New York: Addison-Wesley Educational Publishers, Inc., 2000.

Kelidar, Abbas, "States without Foundations: The Political Evolution of State and Society in the Arab East," *Journal of Contemporary History*, Vol. 28, No.2, April, 1993, 315–339.

Keller, Edmond J. and Rothchild, Donald (ed.) *Africa in the New International Order*. Boulder, Colorado: Lynne Rienner Publishers, Inc., 1996.

Kesselman, Mark. "Order or Movement?: The Literature of Political Development as Ideology," *World Politics*, Volume 26, Issue 1, October, 1973, 139–154.

Klare, Michael T. and Thomas, Daniel C. *World Security: Challenges for a New Century*. Second Edition. New York: St. Martin's Press, 1994.

Kuna, Mohammad J. . "Violence and State Formation in Postcolonial Societies: The Case of Northern Nigeria, 1900–1966," *United Nations University/ Institute of Advanced Studies Working Paper No. 67*. Tokyo, Japan, July 7, 1999. http://www.ias.unu.edu/publications/iaswp.cfm

Kurzman, Dan. *Ben-Gurion: Prophet of Fire*. New York: Simon and Schuster, 1983.

Kuzio, Taras, "'Nationalising States' or Nation-building? A Critical Review of the Theoretical Literature and Empirical Evidence." http://www.taraskuzio.net/ lectures/national.pdf

Lentner, Howard H., "Developmental States and Global Pressures: Accumulation, Production, Distribution." http://www.bus.uts.edu.au/apros2000/Papers/ Lentner.pdf

Licklider, Roy, "The Consequences of Negotiated Settlements in Civil Wars, 1945–1993," *The American Political Science Review*, Volume 89, Issue 3, Sep., 1995, 681–690.

Limbert, John W. and Gasiorowski, Mark J., "Islamic Republic of Iran," in David E. Long and Bernard Reich (ed.) *The Government and Politics of the Middle East and North Africa*. Fourth Edition. Boulder, Colorado: Westview Press, 2002.

Lipschutz, Ronnie D., "Seeking a State of One's Own: An Analytical Framework for Assessing Ethnic and Sectarian Conflicts." http://www.ceu.hu/cps/blue-bird/eve/statebuilding/lipschutz.pdf

Long, David E. and Reich, Bernard, "Introduction," in David E. Long and Bernard Reich (ed.) *The Government and Politics of the Middle East and North Africa*. Fourth Edition. Boulder, Colorado: Westview Press, 2002.

Luizard, Pierre-Jean and Stork, Joe, "The Iraqi Question from the Inside," *Middle East Report*, No. 193, The Iraqi Sanctions Dilemma, March-April, 1995, 18–22.

Lustick, Ian S. "The Absence of Middle Eastern Great Powers: Political 'Backwardness' in Historical Perspective," *International Organization*, Vol. 51, No. 4, Autumn, 1997, 653–683.

———. *Unsettled States, Disputed Lands*. Ithaca: Cornell University Press, 1993.

Luttwak, Edward N., "Give War a Chance," *Foreign Affairs*, Volume 78, Number 4, July/August 1999, 36–44.

Lyons, Gene M. and Mastanduno, Michael (ed.) *Beyond Westphalia? State Sovereignty and International Intervention*. Baltimore: Johns Hopkins University Press, 1995.

Mackey, Sandra. *The Reckoning: Iraq and the Legacy of Saddam Hussein*. New York: W. W. Norton & Company, Inc., 2002.

Mackinlay, John. *The Peacekeepers: An Assessment of Peacekeeping Operations at the Arab-Israeli Interface*. Winchester, Massachusetts: Unwin Hyman, Inc., 1989.

Malanczuk, Peter, "The Kurdish Crisis and Allied Intervention in the Aftermath of the Second Gulf War," *European Journal of International Law* Vol. 2 No. 2 (1991), 114–132.

Manners, Ian R. and Parmenter, Barbara McKean, "The Middle East: A Geographic Preface," in Deborah J. Gerner (ed.) *Understanding the Contemporary Middle East.* Boulder, Colorado: Lynne Rienner Publishers, Inc., 2000.

Mansfield, Edward D. and Snyder, Jack "Democratization and War," in Richard K. Betts. *Conflict After the Cold War: Arguments on Causes of War and Peace.* Second edition. New York: Longman, 2002.

Marr, Phebe, "Republic of Iraq," in David E. Long and Bernard Reich (ed.) *The Government and Politics of the Middle East and North Africa.* Fourth Edition. Boulder, Colorado: Westview Press, 2002.

Mason, Ann C., "Colombian State Failure: The Global Context of Eroding Domestic Authority," Paper presented at the Conference on Failed States, Florence, Italy, April 10–14, 2001. http://www.ippu.purdue.edu/info/gsp/FSIS_CONF4/Papers/Mason.doc

Matheson, Michael J., "United Nations Governance of Postconflict Societies," *American Journal of International Law,* Volume 95, Issue 1, Jan., 2001, 76–85.

Mayall, James, "Non-Intervention, Self-Determination and the 'New World Order," *International Affairs (Royal Institute of International Affairs 1944-),* Vol. 67, No. 3, July 1991, 421–429.

Merkl, Peter H., "The Study of European Political Development," *World Politics.* Volume 29, Issue 3, April, 1977, 462–475.

"MidEast Web Historical Documents: The Sykes-Picot Agreement: 1916." http://www.mideastweb.org/mesykespicot.htm

The Middle East. Ninth edition. Washington, D.C.: Congressional Quarterly, Inc., 2000.

Mill, John Stuart, "Of Nationality as Connected with Representative Government," in *Considerations on Representative Government.* Edited and with an Introduction by Currin V. Shields. Indianapolis: The Bobbs-Merrill Company, Inc., 1975.

Mohamedou, Mohammad-Mahmoud. *Iraq and the Second Gulf War: State Building and Regime Security.* Bethesda, Maryland: Austin & Winfield, Publishers, 1998.

Moore, Barrington Jr. *Social Origins of Dictatorship and Democracy.* Boston: Beacon Press, 1966.

Morgenthau, Hans J. *Politics Among Nations: The Struggle for Power and Peace.* Brief Edition. Revised by Kenneth W. Thompson. New York: McGraw-Hill, Inc., 1993.

Morphet, Sally, "UN Peacekeeping and Election Monitoring" in Adam Roberts and Benedict Kingsbury (ed.) *United Nations, Divided World* Second Edition. New York: Oxford University Press, 1993.

Morris, Benny. *Righteous Victims: A History of the Zionist-Arab Conflict, 1881–2001.* New York: Vintage Books, 2001.

"New World Order: George Bush's Speech, 6 Mar 1991." http://www.al-bab.com/arab/docs/pal/pal10htm

Ofteringer, Ronald and Backer, Ralf, "The Republic of Statelessness: Three Years of Humanitarian Intervention in Iraqi Kurdistan," *Middle East Report,* No.

187/188, Intervention and North-South Politics in the 90's, March-June, 1994, 40–45.

O'Leary, Carole A., "The Kurds of Iraq: Recent History, Future Prospects," *Middle East Review of International Affairs*, Vol. 6, No. 4, December 2002, 17–29.

"Operation Southern Watch." http://www.fas.org/man/dod-101/ops/southern_ watch.htm

Otis, Pauletta, "Ethnic Conflict: What Kind of War is This?" Autumn, 1999. http://www.nwc.navy.mil/press/Review/1999/autumn/art1-a99.htm

Otunnu, Olara A., "The Peace-and Security Agenda of the United Nations: From a Crossroads into the Next Century." Paper prepared for The Commission on Global Governance. http://www.cgg.ch/olara.htm;

"Palestine Information Project." http://members.aol.com/edwardmast/history.html

Pappe, Ilan. *The Making of the Arab-Israeli Conflict: 1947–51.* New York: St. Martin's Press, 1992.

Parenti, Michael. *Democracy for the Few.* Seventh Edition. New York: Bedford/ St. Martin's, 2002.

Pelcovits, Nathan A. *The Long Armistice: UN Peacekeeping and the Arab-Israeli Conflict, 1948–1960.* Boulder, Colorado: Westview Press, Inc., 1993.

Popper,Karl R. *The Logic of Scientific Discovery.* New York: Routledge, 1992.

———. "Science as Falsification." 1963. http://www.freethought-web.org/ctrl/ popper_falsification.html

Porter, Bruce D. *War and the Rise of the State.* New York: The Free Press, 1994.

Preece, Jennifer Jackson, "Ethnic Cleansing as an Instrument of Nation-State Creation: Ethnic Cleansing and the Normative Transformation of International Society." http://www.ippu.purdue.edu/info/gsp/FSIS_CONF3/papers/Jackson Preece.html

Rabil, Robert G., "Operation 'Termination of Traitors': The Iraqi Regime Through its Documents," *Middle East Review of International Affairs*, Vol. 6, No. 3 (September, 2002), 14–24.

Ratner, Steven R. "Drawing a Better Line: UTI Possidetis and the Borders of New States," *American Journal of International Law*, Volume 90, Issue 4 (October, 1996), 590–624.

———. *The New UN Peacekeeping: Building Peace in Lands of Conflict After the Cold War.* New York: St. Martin's Press, 1995.

Reinhard, Wolfgang (ed.) *Power Elites and State Building.* New York: Oxford University Press, 1996.

Renan, Ernest, "What is a Nation?" in Geoff Ely and Ronald Grigor Suny (ed.) *Becoming National: A Reader.* New York: Oxford University Press, Inc., 1996.

Righter, Rosemary. *Utopia Lost: The United Nations and World Order.* New York: The Twentieth Century Fund Press, 1995.

Roberts, Adam. "The United Nations and International Security," in Robert J. Art and Robert Jervis (ed.) *International Politics: Enduring Concepts and Contemporary Issues.* Fifth Edition. New York: Addison-Wesley Educational Publishers, Inc., 2000.

Robins, Philip, "The Overlord State: Turkish Policy and the Kurdish Issue," *International Affairs.* Vol. 69, No. 4, October, 1993, 657–676.

Rokkan, Stein. "Dimensions of State Formation and Nation-Building: A Possible Paradigm for Research on Variations Within Europe" in Charles Tilly (ed.) *The Formation of National States in Western Europe*. Princeton: Princeton University Press, 1975.

Rosenau, James N., "Human Rights in a Turbulent and Globalized World." http:// hypatia.ss.uci.edu/brysk/Rosenau.html

———. "Sovereignty in a Turbulent World," in Gene M. Lyons and Michael Mastanduno (ed.) *Beyond Westphalia? State Sovereignty and International Intervention*. Baltimore: Johns Hopkins University Press, 1995.

Rothwell, V. H., "Mesopotamia in British War Aims, 1914–1918," in *The Historical Journal*, Vol. 13, No. 2., June 1970, 273–294.

Rubin, Michael, "Are Kurds a Pariah Minority?" from *Social Research*, Vol. 70 No. 1 Spring 2003, 295–331.

Rudolph, Joseph R., "Intervention in Communal Conflicts," *Orbis*. v. 39 (Spring 1995), 259–273.

Ryan, Curtis R., "Hashimite Kingdom of Jordan," in David E. Long and Bernard Reich (ed.) *The Government and Politics of the Middle East and North Africa*. Fourth Edition. Boulder, Colorado: Westview Press, 2002.

———. "Syrian Arab Republic" in David E. Long and Bernard Reich (ed.) *The Government and Politics of the Middle East and North Africa*. Fourth Edition. Boulder, Colorado: Westview Press, 2002.

Sayari, Sabri, "Turkey and the Middle East in the 1990s," in *Journal of Palestine Studies*, Vol. 26, No. 3, Spring 1997, 44–55.

Semb, Anne Julie, "The New Practice of UN-Authorized Intervention: A Slippery Slope of Forcible Interference?" *Journal of Peace Research*, Vol. 37, No. 4, Special Issue on Ethics of War and Peace, July, 2000, 469–488.

Simmons, Beth and Martin, Lisa, "International Organisations and Institutions," in Walter Carlsnaes, Thomas Risse, and Beth Simmons (ed.) *Handbook of International Relations*(forthcoming). London et al.: Sage, 2002. http:// www.polisci.berkeley.edu/Faculty/bio/permanent/Simmons.B/Intl_Organizations_Institutions.pdf

Singer, J. David, "The Levels-of-Analysis Problem in International Relations," *World Politics*, Volume 14, Issue 1, The International System: Theoretical Essays, Oct., 1961, 77–92.

Skocpol, Theda. *Social Revolutions in the Modern World*. New York: Cambridge University Press, 1994.

———. *States and Social Revolutions*. New York: Cambridge University Press, 1979.

Slater, Jerome and Nardin, Terry, "Nonintervention and Human Rights," *The Journal of Politics*. Volume 48, Issue 1 (February, 1986), 86–96.

Smith, Anthony D. *The Ethnic Revival*. New York: Cambridge University Press, 1981.

———. "The Ethnic Sources of Nationalism," *Survival* vol. 35, no.1. Spring 1993, 48–62.

Smock, David R. and Crocker, Chester A. (ed.) *African Conflict Resolution: The U.S. Role in Peacemaking*. Washington, D.C.: United States Institute of Peace Press, 1995.

Smooha, Sammy, "Control of Minorities in Israel and Northern Ireland," *Comparative Studies in Society and History*, Vol. 22, No. 2, April, 1980, 256–280.

Sorensen, Georg, "Development in Fragile/Failed States," Paper delivered at the Failed States Conference at Purdue University, April 7–11, 1999. http://www.ippu.purdue.edu/info/gsp/FSIS_CONF2/Sorensen.html

———. "War and State Making—Why Doesn't it Work in the Third World?" Paper delivered at the Failed States Conference, Florence, April 10–14, 2001. http://www.ippu.purdue.edu/info/gsp/FSIS_CONF4/Papers/Sorensen.doc

Stegenga, James A., "Peacekeeping: Post-Mortems or Previews?" *International Organization*, Volume 27, Issue 3, Summer, 1973, 373–385.

Stohl, Michael and Lopez, George, "Westphalia, the End of the Cold War and the New World Order: Old Roots to a "NEW" Problem." Paper presented at a Conference entitled "Failed States and International Security: Causes, Prospects, and Consequences." Purdue University, February 25–27,1998.

Stremlau, John and Sagasti, Francisco, "Preventing Deadly Conflict: Does the World Bank Have a Role?" Report prepared for the Carnegie Commission on Preventing Deadly Conflict. http://www.ccpdc.org/pubs/world/world.htm

Taras, Raymond C. and Ganguly, Rajat. *Understanding Ethnic Conflict: The International Dimension*. Second Edition. New York: Longman Publishers, 2002.

Tetreault, Mary Ann, "International Relations," in Deborah J. Gerner (ed.) *Understanding the Contemporary Middle East*. Boulder, Colorado: Lynne Rienner Publishers, Inc., 2000.

Thomson, Janice E. *Mercenaries, Pirates, and Sovereigns: State-Building and Extraterritorial Violence in Early Modern Europe*. Princeton: Princeton University Press, 1994.

Tilly, Charles. "Reflections on the History of European State-Making" in Charles Tilly (ed.) *The Formation of National States in Western Europe*. Princeton: Princeton University Press, 1975.

———. "Western State-Making and Theories of Political Transformation" in Charles Tilly (ed.) *The Formation of National States in Western Europe*. Princeton: Princeton University Press, 1975.

UNA-UK. *UN & Conflict Resolution: Generating Support for the UN's Role in Conflict Resolution*. Briefing Paper. "United Nations Peacekeeping." http://www.una-uk.org/UN&C/Peacekeeping.html

Van Creveld, Martin, "The Fate of the State," from *Parameters*, Spring 1996, 4–18. http://carlisle-www.army.mil/usawc/Parameters/96spring/creveld.htm

Wallensteen, Peter, "State Failure, Ethnocracy and Democracy: New Conceptions of Governance," Paper presented at a Conference entitled "Failed States and International Security: Causes, Prospects, and Consequences," Purdue University, February 25–27, 1998. http://www.ippu.purdue.edu/info/gsp/FSIS_CONF/wall_paper.html

Waltz, Kenneth N. *Theory of International Politics*. Reading, Massachusetts: Addison-Wesley Publishing Company, Inc., 1979.

Weber, Eugen. *Peasants into Frenchmen: The Modernization of Rural France, 1870–1914*. Stanford, California: Stanford University Press, 1976.

Weber, Max. "Science as a Vocation," http://www.ne.jp/asahi/moriyuki/abukuma/weber/lecture/science_vocation.html

Weiss, Thomas G. (ed.) *Collective Security in a Changing World*. Boulder, Colorado: Lynne Rienner Publishers, Inc., 1993.

———. "Elusive Peace: Negotiating an End to Civil Wars" (review article), *The American Political Science Review*, Volume 90, Issue 3, Sep., 1996.

———. *Military-Civilian Interactions: Intervening in Humanitarian Crises*. New York: Rowman and Littlefield Publishers, Inc., 1999.

Weiss, Thomas G. and Chopra, Jarat, "Sovereignty Under Siege: From Intervention to Humanitarian Space" in Gene M. Lyons and Michael Mastanduno (ed.) *Beyond Westphalia? State Sovereignty and International Intervention*. (Baltimore: Johns Hopkins University Press, 1995

Weiss, Thomas G.; Forsythe, David P.; and Coate, Roger A. *The United Nations and Changing World Politics*. Boulder, Colorado: Westview Press, Inc., 1994.

Whaley, J. David and Piazza-Georgi, Barbara, "The Linkage Between Peacekeeping and Peacebuilding." Published in Monograph No. 10, *Conflict Management, Peacekeeping and Peacebuilding*, April 1997. http://www.iss.co.za/Pubs/Monographs/No10/Whaley.html

Wilson, Ernest J. III, "Globalization, Information Technology and Conflict in the Second and Third Worlds: A Critical Review of the Literature." http://www.bsos.umd.edu/cidcm/papers/ewilson/itrevrbf.pdf

Wilson, Rodney, "The Middle East after the Gulf War: The Regional Economic Impact," in Haifaa A. Jawad (ed.) *The Middle East in the New World Order*. New York: St. Martin's Press, Inc., 1994.

Wimmer, Andreas. *Nationalist Exclusion and Ethnic Conflict: Shadows of Modernity*. New York: Cambridge University Press, 2002.

Woodward, Susan L. *Balkan Tragedy: Chaos and Dissolution After the Cold War*. Washington, D.C.: The Brookings Institution, 1995.

———. "Failed States: Warlordism and 'Tribal' Warfare," 1998. http://www.nwc.navy.mil/press/Review/1999/spring/art2-sp9.htm

Yetiv, Steve A. *The Persian Gulf Crisis*. Westport, Connecticut: Greenwood Press, 1997.

Yinger, J. Milton, "Ethnicity," *Annual Review of Sociology*, Volume 11 (1985), 151–180.

Zartman, I. William, "Introduction: Posing the Problem of State Collapse," in I. William Zartman (ed.) *Collapsed States: The Disintegration and Restoration of Legitimate Authority*. Boulder, Colorado: Lynne Rienner Publishers, Inc., 1994.

———. *Elusive Peace*. Washington, D.C.: The Brookings Institution, 1995.

DOCUMENTS

Boutros-Ghali, Boutros. "An Agenda for Peace, Preventive Diplomacy, Peacemaking Peace-keeping," Report of the Secretary-General pursuant to the statement adopted by the Summit Meeting of the Security Council on 31 January 1992, A/47/277-S/24111, 17 June 1992. http://www.un.org/Docs/SG/agpeace.html

———. "Supplement to An Agenda for Peace: Position Paper of the Secretary-General on the Occasion of the Fiftieth Anniversary of the United Nations," Report of the Secretary-General on the Work of the Organization, 3 January 1995, A/50/60-S/1995/1. http://www.un.org/Docs/SG/agsupp.html

"Resolution 660 (1991)." S/RES/0660 (1990). 2 August 1990. http://www.fas.org/news/un/iraq/sres/sres0660.htm

"Resolution 688 (1991)." S/RES/0688 (1991). 5 April 1991.

Index